THE GUARDIAN GREEN TRAVEL GUIDE

Edited by Liane Katz

guardianbooks

Dedication

To my family: past, present and future

Contributors

David Adam
David is the *Guardian's* environment correspondent and previously worked as the paper's science correspondent and at the science journal *Nature*.

Rhiannon Batton
Rhiannon is the author of *High Ground: How To Travel Responsibly Without Roughing It*.

Gemma Bowes
Gemma is acting deputy editor of *Guardian Travel*, having previously worked on *Observer Escape*, and is a specialist on winter sports.

Hilary Bradt
Hilary co-founded Bradt Travel Guides in 1974 and made a name for publishing ground-breaking guides to pioneering destinations. In 2008 she was awarded an MBE for services to the tourist industry and charity.

Kate Carter
Kate is the life and style editor of guardian.co.uk, which is committed to ethical living and fashion coverage.

Isabel Choat
Isabel is acting editor of *Guardian Travel*, which has a strong emphasis on environmentally and socially responsible trips.

Melissa Corkhill
Melissa is editor of *The Green Parent* magazine (thegreenparent.co.uk).

Julian Fitter
Julian is co-author of the Collins *Traveller's Guide to the Wildlife of the Galapágos*.

Gwladys Fouché
Gwladys writes about the Nordic countries for the *Guardian* and other media.

Louise France
Louise is a freelance journalist and contributing editor to *Observer Food* and *Observer Woman*.

Carolyn Fry
Carolyn writes regularly for the *Guardian* on travel and environmental issues. She is the author of *The Impact of Climate Change: The World's Greatest Challenge in the 21st Century* and a freelance writer and editor.

Ed Gillespie
Ed is co-founder and creative director of Futerra Sustainable Communications. He completed an epic, 13-month flight-free trip around the world in 2007-8, writing a weekly column for the *Observer* and a blog at lowcarbontravel.com.

Susan Greenwood
In 2006, Susan Greenwood was the *Guardian's* 'green netjetter', cycling solo across America using the Transamerica cycle path. Aided by her solar-powered laptop she blogged on her journey and local efforts at eco-friendly tourism. Read her blog diary at: guardian.co.uk/travel/netjetters.

Tom Hall
Tom Hall is travel editor at Lonely Planet. He writes a regular column answering readers' questions for the *Observer's* Escape travel section as well as talking about travel on television and radio.

Richard Hammond
Richard writes on eco-travel issues for the *Guardian* and edited Alastair Sawday's *Green Places to Stay*. He is the founder of online green travel forum greentraveller.co.uk.

Leo Hickman
Leo is the *Guardian's* ethical living columnist and author of *A Life Stripped Bare: My Year Trying to Live Ethically*; *A Good Life: The Guide to Ethical Living* and *Final Call: Investigating Who Really Pays for Our Holidays*.

Alok Jha
Alok is the *Guardian's* green technology correspondent and presents guardian.co.uk's Science Weekly podcast.

Mel Kinder
Mel is operational assistant at Wildlife Worldwide (wildlifeworldwide.com) which won a Responsible Tourism Award in 2006.

Benji Lanyado
Benji Lanyado is the *Guardian's* budget travel columnist and resident travel blogaholic. He spends his spare time running YounginEurope.com.

Catherine Mack
Catherine is a regular contributor to the *Observer* and guardian.co.uk and writes the column, Ethical Traveller, in the *Irish Times*. She is the author of *Ecoescape Ireland*, the country's first green travel guide. She has an Msc in responsible tourism management.

Chris Moss
Chris edited Time Out's guide to Flight-Free Europe, published in July 2008.

Gavin McOwan
Gavin is a subeditor for and regular contributor to *Guardian Travel*.

Polly Pattullo
Polly is a journalist and editor specialising in ethical travel. She is the author of *The Ethical Travel Guide: Your Passport to Exciting Alternative Holidays* and *Last Resorts: The Cost of Tourism in the Caribbean*.

Andy Pietrasik
Andy is acting editor of guardian.co.uk/travel having previously edited the *Guardian's* print travel section.

Kevin Rushby
Kevin is *Guardian Travel's* Grumpy Green columnist and the author of four travel books, and a history book, *Paradise*, an account of utopian ideas over the past 3,000 years.

Alastair Sawday
Alastair is the founder of Alastair Sawday Publishing, best known for its *Special Places to Stay* series and more recently *Go Slow England*. He has long promoted environmental awareness, standing as a Green party candidate in 1992.

Sarah Siese
Sarah writes on bespoke luxury travel and is the creator of the *Heaven on Earth* series, including *Heaven on Earth – Kids*, and *Heaven on Earth – Green*.

Mark Smith
Mark is better known as "The Man in Seat 61" and for his comprehensive and ground-breaking website on rail travel: seat61.com. He recently published his first handbook on rail travel from the UK to Europe, *The Man in Seat 61: A Guide to Taking the Train Through Europe*.

Louise Tickle
Louise is a regular freelance contributor to the *Guardian* and specialises in travel, the environment and ethical business.

Veronica Tonge
Veronica is the author of several reports analysing the impacts of skiing.

Gwyn Topham
Gwyn is deputy comment editor of the *Guardian* and a former travel editor of guardian.co.uk. He is the author of *Overboard: The Stories Cruise Lines Don't Want Told*.

Martin Wainwright
Martin is northern editor of the *Guardian*. He is the author of *The Man Who Loved The Lakes*, *The Coast to Coast Walk* and the co-author of the *Which? Guide to Yorkshire & The Peak District*.

Steps leading to Man O' War Bay, Dorset

CONTENTS

FOREWORD

We have, apparently, an inalienable right to travel – under the UN Universal Declaration of Human Rights. In 2001, The UN even declared that "obstacles should not be placed in the way of …participation in international tourism." So, there you have it. Travel and tourism are a Good Thing. Aren't they?

But have we gone a bit mad about travel? Is it now a way of adding meaning to our frenzied lives? Many of us are distraught if wer are not hatching plans to go abroad. We gaily whiz off to another country and just don't want to know about the consequences. The discussions I have about travel tend to be animated and combative, for there is much more at stake than our holidays and the UN's optimism: economies, businesses, cultural change, employment patterns, the jobs of millions of people all over the world. But there is something else lurking behind the debate, something more problematic: our confusion when faced with moral issues after a decade of unprecedented material comfort. In other words, we are part of the problem.

Environmental campaigners are used to pitting themselves against vested interests, such as oil companies. The challenge in the case of travel is that most of us have become part of the vested interest. We may argue passionately against waste and plastic bags, for renewable energy and conservation, but squirm at the mention of flying, or of mass tourism – for we have just booked our flight to New Zealand. And nobody is going to stop us, for it is our "right". We know, too, that hotels in distant places employ people, that money pours into the national economies and that millions depend on tourism. So off we fly, perhaps offsetting the carbon emissions to feel better. We have successfully "parked" the demanding and complex issues involved.

It doesn't help those who are morally confused that some of the best-known green campaigners and world reformers are also globetrotters. It doesn't help that millions of us fly about as tourists and that gap-year students and other young people jet off to exotic places as soon as they have the money. We love them for their free-spirited take on life. Then there are, of course, the corporate executives for whom globetrotting is part of the job. It is very hard to see any wood for all the trees. The trees are "us"; we are all at it.

Travel and tourism do not, of course, operate in a vacuum; they are part of the real world. Leo Hickman's book, *The Final Call*, explores their impacts. He ends with a clarion call to us to "approach our holidays with fresh imagination … to encourage tourism to be a positive force", for many of our favourite destinations are facing tourism-induced disaster. He recommends that we plan our holidays over a three-year span, gradually weaning ourselves off long-haul and exploitative travel. It would be easy, painless and sensible.

Tourism Concern has for years exposed the truth behind much of the pleasure we derive from our foreign travel: exploited workers, ruined ecosystems, income diverted to overseas parent companies. It is deeply uncomfortable to be told that your holiday, costing so little, may cost a great deal at the other end. So we tend to avert our eyes and block our ears. We won't listen to George Monbiot telling us to stop flying, or to Rough

Guides' Mark Ellingham's warning that we are binge-flying.

This denial is a pandemic. It is not just the real cost of travel that we are deaf and blind to, it is much of what we do. World grain stocks are at their lowest level ever, and nearly 20 million are starving in Africa; China is bent on providing enough cars to its people by 2030 to consume, alone, more oil than the world now produces. Still we think that we can consume without penalty. The world-respected Earth Policy Institute's latest analysis has changed its subtitle from "Rescuing a Planet under Stress and a Civilisation in Trouble" to "Mobilising to Save Civilisation". Madness and denial are everywhere, so what on earth can we do about it?

Read on, for there are solutions aplenty within these pages. They are a reminder that the joys of travel can coexist with awareness. We should not avert our eyes to the real moral difficulties that travel involves but we can turn negative behaviour into positive behaviour. We can share a car and ride a bike, eat organic food and take the train. In all cases we may have more fun and stay healthier in the process. Green travel is usually, in my view, simply a better – and more intelligent – way to go.

Alastair Sawday

Setting up camp in Padjelanta National Park, Sweden

photo: shutterstock/RJR

INTRODUCTION

Mention "green travel" to most people and they are, at first, wildly enthusiastic. The concept combines many of their favourite ingredients – adventure, escapism, wildlife and fun – and all of it apparently possible with a clear conscience. Then a shadow of doubt appears; they begin to look puzzled. What does the term actually mean? Can we still take the odd flight? Will we all have to holiday at home from now on? Britons made 14.4m trips outside Europe in 2006 compared to just 2.9m 20 years earlier. So, for a nation in the throes of a love affair with long-haul travel, could this be a recipe for heartbreak?

More and more of us want to "do the right thing" abroad as well as at home, but it's easy to be overwhelmed by the complex ethical issues surrounding our holiday choices and put our heads in the sand. We worry that the remote habitats we trek around the world to see will not survive if the travel boom continues, but wonder if we are ready to give up flying, or whether our individual actions can make the necessary impact as developing nations join the tourism party. There is a scarcity of realistic, practical advice that recognises both our love of travel and the need to lessen tourism's impact on the environment. We are either told that flying is evil, full stop, or we are directed to choose "eco-lodges", no matter how far-flung. We are advised to ditch the plane for the train, while also being told to worry about the impact on developing countries if our tourist dollars cease to flow.

This book aims to redress the balance. It has been designed to demystify the key issues around responsible travel and to guide and inspire you through the planning of your next holiday. Its chapters will help you make informed choices about where to go, how to get there, where to stay and how to target your spending power. Alongside practical advice on how to tell the genuine green from the rising tide of "greenwash", you will find hundreds of ideas for ethical trips and simple steps we can all take to travel more responsibly. We can take more breaks closer to home, bring our good environmental habits on holiday with us and use our tourist dollars wisely when we choose to travel longhaul.

The truth is that green travel amounts to more than just the decision: to fly or not to fly. It is about far more than hotels and travel companies ticking a set of boxes on a questionnaire – or fitting solar panels and serving organic breakfasts. It is a whole philosophy that is as much about common sense as sparkling new technology and which the responsible traveller must adopt alongside the tourism industry. It boils down to travelling mindfully and in moderation: respecting natural resources – be they rainforests or hotel water supplies – involving and benefiting local communities, staying for longer and reopening our eyes to the adventures on our doorstep as well as those across the globe. It is about taking a holistic look at our annual carbon emissions and coming to informed decisions about the share our travels represent.

Ethical travellers need to lead by example and prove there is a market for responsible holidays. We need to audit our existing travel habits and enjoy similar holiday experiences less carbon-intensively. We need to discover new destinations with our eyes open to the impact on local people and environments.

It may not happen overnight, but small steps this year can lead to larger strides in future. So challenge yourself and challenge the travel industry to embrace truly responsible travel: the benefits to all are priceless.

WHERE SHOULD WE GO?

The choice of destination is at once the most exciting, most hotly debated and most stressful part of planning a holiday. The investment of so much time, money and hope in an experience that must relax, interest, challenge and recharge means we are less willing to take risks or make compromises, and expectations are high.

For the responsibly minded traveller, the question becomes even more complex. Are some destinations "greener" or more "responsible" than others? Perhaps it depends on how you approach the question. Certainly the marketing brains at tourist boards the world over are beginning to work overtime to convince you of their superiority when it comes to sustainable tourism.

The carbon crunch

From a purely low-carbon perspective taking holidays closer to home or in a destination reached without flying is certainly the best option. The UN World Tourism Organisation (UNWTO) estimates that air travel contributes 40% of the tourism industry's global CO_2 emissions, compared to 13% from rail and coach travel and 20% from the accommodation sector. It is also the case that many mountainous and coastal regions much beloved of travellers (and relied upon by travel companies) are the areas most at risk from the consequences of global warming. An OECD report in 2006 found that a two-degree rise in temperature in the Alps, which could occur by 2050, would reduce the number of viable ski slopes from 666 to 400.

Where the grass is greener

For their part, an increasing number of countries, regions and cities are promoting themselves as eco-destinations in their own right, citing efforts at energy efficiency and low carbon living. Iceland, for example, generates 80% of its electricity from hydropower and the remainder from geothermal energy, meaning a low carbon footprint for its hotels and attractions. But while destinations can and should do much to reduce their local tourism industry's footprint – for example through hotel certification schemes, conservation programmes and the promotion of public transport and low-carbon activities – the greatest proportion of your holiday footprint will usually stem from the transport used to reach your destination.

We want to show you how to discover the exotic and the adventurous, the heritage and the wilderness on our doorsteps, both in the UK and Europe – all of which are easily reached without setting foot in an airport. We will also recognise certain global destinations' innovative attempts at fostering greener tourism and explore the impact a sudden drop in air-based, longhaul tourism could have on developing destinations and conservation projects.

Long-haul with a conscience

There is no escaping this conundrum. The vast majority of long-haul leisure travellers do not have the time or money to take the overland route so a trip out of Europe almost always means a flight. And with aviation contributing 40% of the tourism industry's greenhouse gas emissions – and growing at 6.4% a year in the UK – guilt about flying is on the rise. A YouGov poll in 2006 found 56% of people were concerned about the environmental impact of air travel although only 13% had changed their habits as a result.

Yet responsible tourism businesses in the developing world see these concerns as Euro-centric naval gazing. They take a different view of sustainability, and urge a holistic view, incorporating the importance of tourist revenue to the development of local communities and the preservation of rare (and carbon-absorbing) habitats. "If you look at contributions to carbon emissions across the planet, travel takes a lot of flak because it's seen as a luxury and nonessential," says Chris Roche of Wilderness Safaris. "We are not being similarly critical of industry creating non-essential and non-beneficial goods."

Responsible tourism professor Harold Goodwin agrees that aviation has been unfairly – and conveniently – singled out as a source of greenhouse gas emissions. "Flying has been used as a scapegoat by the government," he says. "It's a soft target – it enables you to say you're doing something but you're not doing anything about housing, production, car commuting and meat-eating. We're denying all the carbon embedded in the Chinese goods we buy."

It is not an easy circle to square. Certainly, based on current trends, we are not going to stop flying overnight. But assuming that we do cut down, many in the travel industry argue that it will become even more important to use your presence and spending power to greatest effect when you do choose to travel long-haul. Many developing countries have invested heavily in tourism over the last decade, often urged on by international bodies such as the World Bank. Cambodia, for example, has seen tourist arrivals shoot up from 220,000 in 1995 to 1,700,000 in 2006 while tourist spending now represents 21.6% of the country's exports. Consider the impact if those visitors stopped arriving overnight. "Green tourism has often neglected and sometimes denied the importance of development for communities," argues Goodwin. "We have a long history of expecting others to forgo development – we need to work with communities to balance economic development and the conservation of their environment."

Vital income for development

If you take a broader view of responsible tourism, you might also consider the potential impact of your visit (or the withdrawal of it) on developing countries and threatened habitats. Of the $735bn generated globally by tourism receipts in 2006, almost a third

($221bn) went to developing countries, and tourism is now a major source of foreign exchange in 46 of the 49 Least Developed Countries, according to the UNWTO. Tourist businesses are also large providers of direct employment, are free of protectionist tariffs, create further jobs through suppliers and can prompt a country to develop its infrastructure. Mauritius and Morocco rely on tourism for more than 30% of their GDP, while in Jamaica the figure is more than 40%, according to the World Bank.

Of course there is much debate about how many of these tourist dollars actually end up in the hands of local communities, but by looking into the community policies of tour operators and accommodation providers, ethical travellers can choose to spend their time and money supporting a growing number of socially and environmentally beneficial enterprises. And it is more than likely that by choosing a holiday with high levels of community involvement, you, the visitor, will have a far more rewarding time too.

A catalyst for conservation

From the point of view of conservation, there are many examples of where the value of wildlife habitats to the tourist market has helped to preserve and protect natural resources. A study by Martha Honey of the Centre on Ecotourism and Sustainable Development, found that in South Africa, income from wildlife tourism was nearly 11 times greater – and job creation was 15 times greater – than from cattle ranching. Meanwhile in Kenya, a single lion is estimated to be worth $7,000 and an elephant herd $610,000 in annual tourist income.

Unfortunately, there are also instances, particularly in east Africa, where indigenous people have been displaced in order to develop wildlife experiences for tourists, so it is particularly important to check that local people are getting some benefit from your safari spending. After all, seasonal visitors should not be dictating how local people should and shouldn't be using their natural resources, and local communities need to share the benefits of tourism for the conservation to be sustainable.

"For me, it's about creating opportunities for people and communities to make a living as an alternative to stripping nature in order to survive," says Roger Diski, founder of Rainbow Tours. "There is often no other way for rural communities to survive … Through tourism, wildlife has a value – all you can do is try to mitigate the bad effects and maximise the good effects."

The credit crunch

As the economic downturn bites, it is natural to reassess our travel spending alongside all other expenditure. As cost-saving becomes the priority, the danger is that cheaper holidays and greener breaks are seen as mutually exclusive, when in fact the two can go hand in hand.

As with organic or fair trade food, there is a common perception that to travel ethically will involve paying over the odds. Certainly, a green hotel makeover requires considerable up-front investment, for instance installing ground heat pumps or solar panels. But these technologies immediately start to reap savings in an era of rising energy costs. "I definitely don't think it should cost [a hotel] more," says Jan Peter Bergqvist, vice president of sustainable business at Scandic Hotels, which has saved $29m through resource efficiency since 1996. Rainbow Tours founder Roger Diski agrees: "I don't see any difference in price to do things right."

Another common assumption about greener travel is that weaning ourselves off budget flights and on to alternative forms of transport is going to be more expensive. Trains, especially in the UK, can appear prohibitively pricey at first, but once you consider the hidden extra costs of flying and realise that overnight trains provide accommodation as well as transport, costs can be comparable. The key is often in booking ahead.

Throughout these pages you will find hundreds of ideas for low-impact holidays at little or no extra cost, longer expeditions involving work or volunteering, insider's tips on taking famous rail journeys on the cheap and discovering the wilder corners of the UK using the minimum outlay of carbon or cash. After all, the cheapest holidays are often those closest to home.

WHERE SHOULD WE STAY?

Shifting sands

Booking a hotel used to be as simple as dropping into a travel agent, flicking through the brochures and comparing prices, proximity of nightlife and the colour of the sand. It's unlikely that carbon footprints and sustainability topped your checklist. And even if they were on your radar, until the late 90s, pre-departure information was limited and vulnerable to marketing gloss.

With the rise of the internet, we have wrested control over our accommodation choices away from the "experts"; the information at the end of a Google search is now boundless. We can trawl TripAdvisor for "warts and all" hotel reviews and unearth a wealth of smaller, privately owned properties that would previously have remained the preserve of specialist guidebooks or locals in the know.

For the traveller with a conscience, this is a great opportunity to check the environmental and social credentials of your accommodation before you book a stay. Smaller outfits can often make changes more quickly than large hotel chains, and any property that is reducing its carbon footprint and resource usage will usually shout about it online.

Conscious choices

Tourists can use around 10 times more water than a local. So choosing a low-impact hotel and using resources responsibly while travelling can mean the difference between blindly taking precious water and energy supplies away from local residents and actively helping to safeguard the landscapes, wildlife and cultures of the places you love to visit.

It is not all about altruism either; a responsible holiday – be it in Cornwall or Colombia – will be more rewarding, genuinely carefree and offer a better chance to engage with your destination and its culture. Not to mention the potential for supporting local development and conservation projects. And the evidence also suggests that many of us are keen to get it right when it comes to checking in. Some 24% of British travellers (and 45% of those who read the *Guardian*) "would prefer to stay in a hotel that employs local people", according to a January 2008 report from Mintel, while only 36% percent (15% among *Guardian* readers) would rather simply relax on holiday and not worry about ethical concerns.

Greenwash

But the waters are still muddy. Hotels are becoming increasingly aware of the marketing advantages of being seen to "go green". During research for this book we were bombarded by green claims – from a London hotel, which offered discounts on valet parking if your car engine was below a certain size, to jungle lodges with no eco credentials other than the operation of local wildlife tours.

In some cases, pale green initiatives are the precursor to more substantial efforts. In others, they are simply "talking the talk". Greenwash in all sectors is on the rise, and in the absence of a comprehensive international eco-labelling scheme (see pages 54–57) you may well need to evaluate a hotel's claims to be green or responsible for yourself.

However, industry campaigners are optimistic that the situation will only prove temporarily difficult for well-intentioned travellers. "At the moment, there is this window of marketing opportunity for companies to be seen to be ahead of the game. But things will catch up," explains Sue Hurdle, founder of the Travel Foundation, a charity promoting sustainable tourism. Being sustainable "will just be a mark of quality" in five years' time. For now, even if you are not ready to make environmental standards the deciding factor in your choice of hotel, simply by inquiring about a hotel's sustainability policy before or during your stay, you can influence the future direction a manager will take.

Ethical travellers need to lead by example and prove there is a market for responsible holidays. We need to audit our existing travel habits and enjoy similar holiday experiences less carbon-intensively. We need to discover new destinations with our eyes open to the impact on local people and environments.

It may not happen overnight, but small steps this year can lead to larger strides in future. So challenge yourself and challenge the travel industry to embrace truly responsible travel: the benefits to all are priceless.

Liane Katz

HOW TO USE THIS GUIDE

We have split your journey into three main elements.

In section one, What is green travel?, we give you advice and information on how to get to your destination as it is the mode of transport that so often informs green choices.

In section two, Way to go, we give you literally hundreds of ideas of what kind of holiday you can have, with top tips from a huge range of green travel experts – from boat trips to wild camping.

Finally, in association with greentraveller.co.uk we give you a directory of over a hundred hand-picked and visited accommodation ideas.

A note on pricing:

The prices quoted in this guide are correct at the time of going to press. However, markets fluctuate and prices will change over time. Where we suggest that you book your holiday, accommodation or travel from the UK, prices have been quoted in sterling. Otherwise, the currency you will be charged locally has been used.

The Snowdon Mountain Railway,
North Wales
photo: shutterstock/Willem Dijkstra

Hadrian's Wall, Northumberland
photo: britainonview/Rod Edwards

SECTION ONE

WHAT IS GREEN TRAVEL?

What is Responsible Tourism?

Tom Hall, travel editor, Lonely Planet
At its best, travel is good for everyone involved. It's not perfect, but it beats alternative ways to develop the world's special places. I'm excited to see where we get to in five years, as the past five have been tremendous for green travel.

Sue Hurdle, chief executive of the Travel Foundation
Whether it's called eco- or ethical or sustainable tourism, they all mean roughly the same thing: travel that benefits the people and the environment of the destination. Purists would say that tourism can never be sustainable as long as people fly. But it's important to remember the other benefits tourism can bring to destinations, such as an incentive for communities to conserve their natural resources.

Hilary Bradt, travel writer and founder of *Bradt Travel Guides*
I prefer the term "positive travel". It feels more accurate than "green" and covers all sorts of different aspects of travelling in a way that benefits the host country as well as the traveller.

Martin Dunford, co-founder *Rough Guides*
Like most activities, I think it's possible to travel responsibly, with care and respect for the places we visit, making as small an impact as possible. Whether sustainable in the long-term or not, I have no idea, but we have to reconsider some of our habits if it is to have a chance.

 Professor Harold Goodwin, director of the International Centre for Responsible Tourism at Leeds Metropolitan University
There is no point being environmentally concerned all year and then bingeing on holiday. Responsible tourism contributes to making better places for people to live and better places for people to visit. It is about relishing and respecting social and cultural diversity, spending in ways which benefit local producers, reducing our negative environmental impacts and putting something back into the places and communities we visit.

 Justin Francis, founder of responsibletravel.com
If we were truly sustainable, we wouldn't have kids and we wouldn't use any form of energy, heat our homes or drive our cars because everything uses natural resources. Travel and tourism have some very beneficial impacts and some inherently negative impacts as well. It's that three-legged stool of considering the economic impacts, the environmental impacts and the cultural impacts of any trip.

Bird Island, Seychelles
photo: Gregor Kervina

WHY RESPONSIBLE TOURISM MATTERS

The words "travel" and "responsible" don't sit comfortably together. We travel for our own reasons: to do something we love, recharge our batteries or do something silly. Ultimately, we travel because the world's a great place to explore. That it may be, but there's a desperate need for some balance. When hundreds of millions of people go tramping all over the world every year, wear and tear is inevitable. Beaches have litter dropped on them. Resort workers don't always get a fair deal. Great hiking trails have to be closed to stop damage being done to the things that brought people there in the first place.

The good news is that it's never been easier to do the right thing. That's where responsible travel comes in, and why it's grown from a well-intentioned buzzword in the travel industry to become something that affects pretty much every detail of how we holiday.

So what is responsible travel exactly? Ask Mr Google and you'll find experts getting tied up in knots over definitions and terminology. There's no need. As the Travel Foundation suggests, responsible, sustainable, green, eco- and ethical tourism all mean "pretty much the same thing – holidays that benefit the people and environment in destinations".

I'd add to this that responsible travel – and this is why it really matters – equals better travel. Mostly, it's common sense. A local guide, someone who's lived in a special place all their life, is going to do their job with pride and enthusiasm and make your trip richer. Locally sourced specialities will just taste better. And if you're somewhere beautiful, make sure you leave it beautiful for the next person who's lucky enough to come after you. It's that simple.

There are some great trips out there that will immerse you in local communities or take you away from places tourists normally venture. But some of the best responsible holidays rarely shuffle far from a paradise beach or rouse you from your comfy boutique hotel bed. You just take your stressed-out self away and have a great trip. Not only are you more likely to escape the crowds, you'll have a more authentic experience, which is surely what travelling is all about.

It's easy to get it right. Britain leads the world in green-thinking travel companies, many of which are independent, and specialists in their field. They've done the homework for you. Responsible travel isn't a niche, either. Check out how Thomson, Virgin Atlantic and Eurostar or almost any big travel firms are now working hard to be as sustainable as possible.

Responsible travel also matters because it's made us look at our own island in a new light. Scan the travel section of the *Guardian* and many other newspapers and you'd be forgiven for thinking that Britain was a paradise of natural wonders, delicious locally sourced food and sustainably run businesses. This is often true. There's never been a better time to be a flying refusenik.

Travelling more responsibly matters because it helps the places and people you're visiting. Ultimately though, you get a better holiday, which is why this type of travel has grown so quickly. And if someone wants to tell me I'm acting responsibly by cycling through a Cumbrian thunderstorm when I really should be at work, then so much the better.

Tom Hall

WHY TOURISM IS A HUMAN RIGHTS ISSUE

There's no stopping us now. We are no longer content with a modest holiday in our own back yards; we want to explore every nook and cranny of the world. At the same time we have become aware of the damage we can do to the planet when millions of us from the rich north take our holidays in the poor south.

Tourism has become a human rights issue – it impacts on the environment, the survival of indigenous people and the wellbeing of other cultures; it also means that our dollars often never reach those who most deserve them in host countries. The inequalities and exploitation of the poor by the rich is intrinsic to the worst sort of tourism practices.

We are aware that tourism can have these negative impacts, though it's sometimes hard to know what to do about them. But now consumers are on the warpath: we're buying more fair trade produce than ever before and we're beginning to recognise that we can extend this to tourism. Fairly traded ethical tourism means an end to the manufactured smile of the weary waiter or the desperate flirtation of the prostitute on the tropical beach. The result is an economic exchange that benefits our hosts as well as us holidaymakers.

However, with tourism it seems it's hard to act ethically; our intentions may be good but perhaps daydreaming in a hammock is preferable.

One of the problems about ethical tourism is that we're not sure how to do it. We are still left largely in the dark when it comes to making ethical decisions about holidays. The reason is that, until recently, the very powerful tourism industry has been happy to leave us ignorant and powerless. So how would we know that our carefully chosen hotel was built over a sacred site or that local communities were displaced to build it, or that the chambermaids work for a pittance and never get a holiday? We can't know this unless we can trust the tour operators to care about these things. In the past, they did not. Sustainable tourism was, to a great extent, seen as a niche issue, something that only mattered to a hardcore minority; it was argued that it was not the industry's responsibility to review their own behaviour.

But globalisation has bought about a new mindset – and not just among the radical few. More and more consumers are looking to take responsible holidays and the industry is just beginning to respond.

However, there is still only a patchwork of accreditation schemes (see pages 54–57) and the less impressive ones are more concerned with a nod to environmental good practice, often at the expense of social and economic relationships. That's the sort of greenwashing that gives ecotourism, in particular, a bad name.

So it is up to us punters to search out our own ethical holidays. There are pockets of good practice, initiatives linked mainly to the small specialist operators. Look for prominent mission statements that talk of partnership. Go for holidays that are controlled by local people. In this way, you will put your money into the pockets of local people and ensure sustainable development.

Tourism is a tricky business to get right – to satisfy the needs of guests and hosts. Grassroots partnerships can guarantee more equitable tourism that will lead to fair trade tourism becoming a cool way to holiday. It may be glib, but ethical tourism means happy hosts as well as happy tourists. And the smile of the waiter, perhaps no longer so weary, may just be genuine.

Polly Pattullo

The Cape Town Declaration of 2002 recognised responsible tourism to have the following characteristics:

- minimises negative economic, environmental and social impacts
- generates greater economic benefits for local people and enhances the well-being of host communities, improves working conditions and access to the industry
- involves local people in decisions that affect their lives and life chances
- makes positive contributions to the conservation of natural and cultural heritage and to the maintenance of the world's diversity
- provides more enjoyable experiences for tourists through more meaningful connections with local people, and a greater understanding of local cultural, social and environmental issues
- provides access for physically challenged people
- is culturally sensitive, engenders respect between tourists and hosts, and builds local pride and confidence

FIVE SUPER-GREEN CITIES

Freiburg, Germany

A small medieval city in the Black Forest is an unlikely setting for a revolution, but Freiburg is the eco-capital of Germany, and arguably the world, thanks to a long-term sustainable urban development policy. Higher profile projects such as the Paris Vélib' bike rental scheme may have garnered more publicity, but Freiburg's green transport system has been in place for decades (initially approved in 1969), and today its 200,000 or so inhabitants benefit from an impressive network of tramlines and cycle paths. That's not to say it's a dull, worthy place. Far from it.

A university town since 1457, it has a laid back, easy-going atmosphere with lively bars and more vineyards within its municipal area than any other city in the country. The sunshine that ripens the vines also generates much of the city's power – there are three major institutes dedicated to the study of solar energy. Visitors should make time to swing by the Heliotrope, an house with a series of very large, light and airy rooms wrapped around a central spiral staircase, that gently rotates to follow the sun. Stay at the Hotel Victoria (victoria.bestwestern.de), which claims to be the most environmentally friendly private hotel in the world, and utilises an impressive array of energy-saving devices from eco-friendly air-con to low flow showers, insulated windows and use of local produce. (germany-tourism.co.uk)

Curitiba, Brazil

Another unlikely pioneer in green urban living is Curitiba in south-east Brazil. A "master transport plan" was developed back in the mid-60s and today its efficient public bus network carries around 1.5m people daily and is the envy of the world. But its commitment to the environment goes beyond buses, with recycling programmes, including a "trash for food" scheme, one of the highest green space per inhabitant ratios in the world, and a commitment to reducing poverty with job-training and small business schemes for lower-income Curitibanos.

And while its population of nearly two million is putting the original urban plan under strain, Curitiba is still held up as a model of progressive urban planning. An industrialised inland metropolis, it cannot compete with the wow factor setting of Rio or the sultry exoticism of Salvador, but it's not without its charms. Leafy pedestrianised streets, a botanical garden with a greenhouse inspired by Crystal Palace, Oscar Niemeyer's museum and a historic centre are among the attractions. (curitiba-brazil.com)

Copenhagen, Denmark

The crowning of Copenhagen as best city in the world by too-cool-for-school magazine Monocle in June 2008 simply confirmed what Copenhageners have known for years – their quality of life is unrivalled. The city has long been a haven for cyclists – with one of the highest percentages of locals cycling to work and school in the world (36%) – but concern for the environment and improving the lives of its residents permeates every aspect of city life. Organic delis and restaurants are commonplace

(Copenhageners consume more organic produce than any other city in the world): from Emmerys, whose 14 shops sell speciality teas, coffees, chocolates, wines, oils and pasta, to Michelin-starred Geranium, but there are also shops dedicated to selling organic lifestyle products and fashion, like Commonzenz which sells a variety of eco brands and organic perfumery Pureshop.

The city's hotels are also blazing a green trail; Guldsmeden's three hotels in the trendy Vesterbro neighbourhood offer 100% organic breakfasts; at the Alexandra, a "Green Key" hotel, furniture is second hand; and the Scandic hotel chain has committed to radically reducing its CO_2 emissions and uses environmentally friendly materials in its rooms. Even hostels are getting in on the act with Sleep-in-Green using solar energy and eco-friendly cleaning products. (visitcopenhagen.com)

Portland, Oregon

Acres of green space, more than 74 miles of hiking, running and biking trails, an exemplary public transport system, and easy access to the great outdoors, Portland's residents are living the "green American dream". And it's easy for visitors to tap into the dream too. Downtown bistros, diners, delis and coffee shops offer locally sourced organic produce. Check out the Farm Cafe, which serves all-local, all-organic fare and Oregon wines, in a restored wooden building – a good place to line your stomach before tackling some of the city's 28 micrbreweries.

The influence of Portland's artistic and musical community extends beyond its galleries and gig spaces to almost every public space and building. At the hip Ace

Isabel Choat

hotel the emphasis is on locality and community; furniture is largely reclaimed and rooms and hallways are decorated by local artists. An impressive number of vintage thrift stores means you can get more for your dollars. (travelportland.com)

Bristol, UK

Home to both transport charity Sustrans, and the Soil Association, Bristol is at the forefront of Britain's green movement. Both organisations have exerted their influence. Locals have easy access to organic food suppliers with weekly farmers' markets, a regular slow food market and the annual Soil Association organic food festival – the largest celebration of organic food and farming in Europe.

In June 2008, Bristol became the UK's first official cycling city, as part of a £100m government scheme, announcing plans to double the number of cyclists in the city over the next three years. Various initiatives designed to encourage more people to get on their bikes are in the pipeline, including a Paris-style bike rental scheme, cycle lanes and better facilities. The city already has the much-loved Mud Dock and Cycleworks Cafe where cyclists can secure their bike, take a shower and grab a coffee. Other green attractions include the Create Centre, a showcase for sustainable living, and Bordeaux Quay, the harbour-side development housing a restaurant, deli, brasserie, bar, bakery and cookery school in an eco-friendly former warehouse. Local hoteliers are recognising their green responsibilities too, with seven hotels, B&Bs and a campsite boasting Green Tourism Business Scheme awards. (visitbristol.co.uk)

THE SLOW WAY TO GO

When horses pulled carriages and charabancs, when bicycles were considered dangerous beasts, when flags were waved from rooftops to pass on news, there were always people who were nevertheless considered "fast". Young men galloped insanely quickly on their horses, gambled their money away and drank too much. Cities have always encouraged fast living, whatever the century.

However, our western societies have slowly and almost imperceptibly learned to live at a pace that would have alarmed even those insanely galloping young men. We need, it seems, to be elsewhere; anywhere but here. Holidays have to be far away, the further the better. Food has to come from distant countries; friends are cultivated beyond our immediate reach; we work hard in order to have time not to work. So it goes on. But there is hope. The "slow" movement is also, as it were, gathering speed, and it will affect the way we holiday and possibly everything else too. It is more serious than it sounds.

It began in Italy in 1986, when the founding members of the Slow Food organisation resolved to fight the invasion of fast food into their country. "Slow" means local, grown with respect and integrity, and with thought to the consequences. McDonald's is a natural enemy. The idea was such a good one that it had to spread, and this it has done with the "Cittaslow" – Slow Cities are urban reflections of the Slow Food concept: thoughtful places that value peace and quiet, local production, people over cars, a dark night sky, high-quality artisan production, low-energy consumption and, importantly, time to enjoy all these things within a community.

To the oldest among us, these ideas are, well, old. There is nothing new about taking it easy, keeping your own chickens, holidaying at home, enjoying your friends. But for others, these ideas need to be re-articulated and spread, for we are so caught up in the modern world of speed that we have lost our perspective. For some of us, life only seems to have much meaning if we are planning to fly off on holiday. What else is there?

One can, it must be admitted, holiday in a Slow Country. The Kingdom of Bhutan, in the Himalayas, has had the genius to adopt gross national happiness as official policy. Anything that undermines the people's health will be discouraged, as will anything that fruitlessly gobbles up their time. Their old people are valued. All major decisions are tested against their effect on the environment and on society. The United Nations says that Bhutan is one of the world's 10 least-developed countries, yet according to the New Economics Foundation's Happy Planet Index, it is 13th. There are 178 countries: the US comes 150th and the UK 108th.

At a profound level, living slowly is to grasp that happiness comes from the small, simple things: a smile from another, a random act of kindness, the togetherness of families, the burbling of a brook, being with someone you love. Holidaying slowly involves the same sort of sensitivity to one's own deeper needs. The wise among us have never lost the knack of doing it slowly. They set out to read a pile of books in a hammock at the bottom of the garden. They take long, slow picnics by the river, explore the local churches, lie in the long grass and dream, pedal idly from village to village, rejoice in the detail of where they are. They probably stay at home more than most, too. They know that haste, as the Brazilian proverb says, is the mother of imperfection.

Can we call flying a rare and special form of haste? If so, then the imperfections it brings in its wake are grist to that Brazilian mill. As our government juts its jaw and plans airport expansion whatever the economic and ecological cost, it is hard not to wish a grim fate on all airlines and their protagonists. A good way, however, of making a statement is to Go Slow. How about, if you are a binge flyer, a personal travel plan? You could thus plan, say, a long-haul holiday this year, a short-haul one next year and a non-flight one the next. Painless and productive – go on! Or, rather, go slow.

Alastair Sawday

Readers of the *Guardian Green Travel Guide* can buy *Go Slow England*, by Alastair Sawday with Gail McKenzie, for £10.99 (normal price £19.99) plus £2.99 p&p in the UK. Use the special offer code "Guardian Green Travel Guide" when phoning 01275 395431 during office hours. Offer ends June 30 2009.

photo: britainonview

Cycling at Eilean Donan, Scotland

Going slow in Ireland

"You must be afraid of flying" is what every taxi driver says taking me to Dublin port en route to London. I explain that I prefer to travel slowly by train or ferry, when possible, because I've had it with airports and air travel. It is hard to get Dublin taxi drivers to stop talking, but this one usually gets them every time. They look at me in the rear-view mirror like I have two heads.

Slow travel is a huge issue in Ireland because, of course, it is an island. Ireland needs and welcomes tourists, and most of them want to fly there. Budget flights may be helping tourist boards hit their targets, but they are creating a different type of tourism. In Ireland, this is mainly urban, giving the cities a chance to show that they can keep up with the cosmopolitan competition around the globe.

Meanwhile, visitors to Ireland, and Irish people themselves, are ignoring the vast majority of the country, Rural Ireland. They are forgetting to slow down and just get out of town. Jetting around is currently in the Celtic zeitgeist. According to a recent National Irish Bank survey, entitled The Emerald Isle – The Wealth of Modern Ireland, the Irish are buying more luxury private jets than anywhere else in Europe. They are not letting the green grass grow under their feet anymore. Out with the cliched images of men smoking pipes on donkeys. And good riddance, because Ireland's recent economic growth has brought it roaring into the 21st century. Consequently, car ownership is at an all-time high. The cars are newer and faster – according to the report, there are more Mercedes per head in Ireland than in Germany – and so are the roads, which may explain why the state still has one of the highest rates of road accidents in Europe.

The American author Louis L'Amour said in Ride the Dark Trail, "The trail is the thing, not the end of the trail. Travel too fast and you miss all you are travelling for." The best way to do this in Ireland is, of course, to walk. There is a superb network of walking trails, all of which have taken me into an Ireland which I thought was disappearing. So, get your boots on and your map out. The mountains, lakes, rivers and islands are all there for visiting, and there are many people who have set up extraordinary sustainable tourism businesses just waiting to open their doors to you.

DELPHI MOUNTAIN RESORT, COUNTY GALWAY

This resort is an "eco-escape" extraordinaire, nestled between two contrasting stretches of water, Killary harbour and the Bundorragha river, which is fed by numerous mountain streams. Take part in motor-free sports in the forests, rivers and beaches, or just lie back in a bath full of organic seaweed.

From €40 a night (+353 95 42208, delphimountainresort.com).

TRINITY ISLAND LODGE, COUNTY CAVAN

Overlooking nothing but the ruins of a 13th-century abbey, Lough Oughter, swans in flight, and a canoe with your name on it, this lakeland retreat is on its own forested island, in the highly underrated landscape of County Cavan. It is a few seconds' walk from the water, and after a day's swimming, fishing or just bobbing about, you can come back to the wood-burning sauna. No wonder the monks loved it.

From €700 for a weekend, €1,100 for a week (+353 49 43 34314, trinityisland.com).

CNOC SUAIN, COUNTY GALWAY

Stay in one of the refurbished stone cottages on this Connemara farm in the Irish-speaking region of the country. Drink in their own shebeen, and watch performances of Irish music and poetry twice a week by a roaring fire. "We wanted visitors to just stop and absorb the Connemara culture, rather than glimpsing it through a coach window." But this is no theme park, just a family oozing with pride and determination to protect and share some of the joys of its Gaelic heritage.

From €450 for a residential weekend (+353 91 555 703, cnocsuain.com).

THE OLD MILKING PARLOUR, COUNTY WICKLOW

The Old Milking Parlour is only an hour from Dublin, minutes from the Wicklow Mountains, and a six-mile cycle to one of Ireland's finest beaches, Brittas Bay. Architect couple, Delphine and Philip, have converted a milking parlour in what was an old Quaker homestead, and is now their own. They have done so to the highest sustainable standards, combining old and new with flare.

From €400 a weekend in the low season (+353 404 48206, ballymurrin.ie).

THE BENWISKIN CENTRE, COUNTY SLIGO

From this community-run hostel, you can take on some of the finest walking and cycling in Ireland in the Gleniff Horseshoe valley, where Irish myth tells us, lovers Gráinne and Diarmuid spent their last night together before dying, watched on and unaided by jilted lover Fionn. A dramatic landscape in every sense.

From €15 a night (+353 71 91 76721, benwiskincentre.com).

WINEPORT LODGE, COUNTY WESTMEATH

Don't even think about coming here by car. Take a train to Athlone, and you will be picked up at the station. And you won't need a car when you get there, because you won't want to leave. The hot tub, as well as the serene and luscious rooms, overlooks the reeds and waters of Lough Ree.

From €195 a night (wineport.ie, +353 64 39010).

TORY BUSH COTTAGES, COUNTY DOWN

It is worth arriving in darkness, just to be able to watch the sun rise over the heather, moss and bog-covered Mourne Mountains the next morning. The name given to this mountain range, suggests a sad desolate place. Nothing could be further from the truth. My heart literally skipped a beat as I opened the curtains and looked out from this eco-loft into the surrounding hills.

From €130 for a two-night stay (028 4372 4348, torybush.com).

CLARE ISLAND YOGA RETREAT, COUNTY MAYO

People like to escape in different ways – some to the mountains, others to a remote beach. I have a thing about islands, and a particular thing about this one. It draws me back, again and again, and one of these days I will just miss the boat and stay – like Ciara Cullen, who moved there 20 years ago. If it is a real retreat you are after, her timber yoga studio, house and cottage in the hills of Clare Island, overlooking the Atlantic, is about as far from the world, as you can get.

From €250 for a weekend retreat (+353 98 25412, yogaretreats.ie).

SOUTH REEN FARM, COUNTY CORK

The website calls it a retreat. I call it a rural idyll. Hidden in a corner of West Cork, it is surrounded by water, with Lough Cluhir overlooking the farm, the depths of South Reen harbour at the end of the road, and the roaring waves of the Atlantic over the hill. Take a morning dip in the tiny bay, go whale-watching in the afternoon, and kayaking off the pier at midnight.

From €650 a week (+353 28 33258, southreenfarm.com). See also whalewatchwestcork.com and atlanticseakayaking.com.

GREGAN'S CASTLE HOTEL, COUNTY CLARE

Simon and Frederieke, the owners of this family-run hotel, are more than aware of their privileged position, high up in a valley of the extraordinary limestone landscape of The Burren. Instead of playing Lord and Lady of this exquisite manor, they are leaders in the community, taking a strong stance on sustaining The Burren, as well as the livelihoods of those who live there. As a member of the Burren Beef and Lamb Producers Group, the hotel sources all such meat from local farmers, while all smoked fish, salads, eggs and cheeses are sourced from small local producers. From €152 a night (+353 65 7077005, gregans.ie).

Getting there

Travelling to Ireland slowly from the UK: irishferries.com; norfolkline.com; eurolines.com; stenaline.co.uk; sailrail.co.uk; seat61.com.

The reviews above are excerpts from *ecoescape Ireland* by Catherine Mack, published by GreenGuide (ecoescape.org).

Catherine Mack

HOW ECO IS ECOTOURISM?

"Ecotourism" suggests a level of responsibility and hints at efforts to ensure a minimal impact on, for example, a wildlife spectacle. Here lies the paradox: ecotourism is often cited as being the answer to conservation problems, but to be successful, the numbers need to add up. You need lots of visitors to generate a profit – and then you can end up losing sight of your original intention.

Take Kenya's Maasai Mara. Years ago, you could have driven around in your Land Rover, seen your big five and returned to your tented camp having had a real adventure. Today, you are more likely to have to jostle for position with other tourists jammed into other Land Rovers. Is this what the tourists want? Is this what the animals need?

This scenario is becoming all too familiar. The manager of a Bali dive business told me a similar tale. A few years ago, he found a unique dive site where you can dive with sunfish, an odd disc of a fish up to 4m in diameter and usually a beast of open water. It turned out to be one of only a few sites in the world where this experience is guaranteed. Or rather, was.

The fish are still there: I have seen them, hovering like giant Frisbees around "cleaning stations" where reef fish nip off parasites. But the creatures were very skittish and behaved differently to the way they used to. On the surface, it became apparent why: 20 other dive boats were fidgeting around for moorings. The sunfish had become victims of their own accessibility. Now, that first dive operator is wishing he had kept his mouth shut and feels that not only has he helped ruin an experience but also had a negative impact on the wildlife.

So should we all back off, limit time and apply guidelines? Does controlling the experience for the benefit of the animal or the environment alter the "magic" of the moment? To an extent it does, but it is the only way.

It can work; just look at the mountain gorillas of Rwanda famously filmed by David Attenborough in 1978 for the series Life on Earth. Everybody who visits central Africa wants to see gorillas but watching time is restricted to an hour and you are not allowed to get closer than five metres. Despite the restricted access, it seems to work for all involved. Similarly, simple codes of conduct for viewing killer whales in Norway means a much better experience than the one I encountered in Vancouver with the same species being chased by several competing whale-watching companies.

In the end, it boils down to one simple fact: the act of observing something happening causes a change in the thing being observed. There are both good and bad operators out there, but with eco-tourists becoming more aware of the issues, the power of change lies in the wallets of consumers. This, combined with proper guidelines and licensing, in most cases seems to strike a happy balance.

Nick Baker

UK holidays with an international flavour

THAI SPA, NEW FOREST

Getting to Brockenhurst in the New Forest by train is a doddle. There's also an impressive range of accommodation within walking distance of the station, including Careys Manor (01590 623551, careysmanor.com) from £74pp B&B, a smart hotel whose trump card is its Asian-inspired SenSpa where Thai masseurs give cracking (not literally) massages. A taster day at SenSpa costs £119 at weekends and includes use of spa, Thai lunch and a class.

More intimate is Cottage Lodge, an AA five-star 17th-century forester's cottage and B&B and joint winner in the sustainable tourism category of 2008's Enjoy England Awards for Excellence.

From £120 per room B&B at weekend (01590 622 296, cottagehotel.org).

EPIC RIDE, WALES

The Cwmfforest Riding Centre is home to Trans Wales Trails, whose horse-riding adventures include an epic six-day journey from the English border to the Irish sea, passing through the Black Mountains, Mynydd Eppynt, the Elan Valley and over Plynlimon – the highest point in the Cambrian mountains – before a final gallop on the beach near Aberystwyth. The route follows bridleways, open moorland and several trails over private land.

From £920pp, including accommodation in pubs and inns, riding and meals. Experienced riders only, but the company has trips suitable for novices too (01874 711 398, transwales.demon.co.uk).

ISLAND ESCAPE, SARK

Sark's car-free status has helped keep La Grande Greve beach one of the most unspoilt in the Channel Islands. It's in a secluded bay below the isthmus that connects the main island to Little Sark, with sheltered swimming, and rock pools for kids to potter in.

La Sablonnerie is the only hotel on Little Sark (01481 832061, sark.info), from £38pp half-board. Ferry Weymouth-Guernsey £39.50 one way (condorferries.co.uk), then boat to Sark £22 return (sarkshipping.info).

YURT LIFE, HEREFORDSHIRE

Why go to Mongolia to experience nomadic life when you can stay in a yurt in Herefordshire? They are located in 17 acres of woodland in an area of outstanding Natural Beauty, and come with eco-sensitive fixtures. The site is child-friendly, and you can bike or canoe in Monmouth, zipline in the Forest of Dean or trek with llamas, camels, mules or donkeys in Severn Vale.

Four nights midweek from £195 (Woodland Tipis and Yurts, 01432 840 488, woodlandtipis.co.uk).

IN THE SWIM, DEVON

Join a "splash mob" with the Outdoor Swimming Society. Founded by Kate Rew, author of Wild Swim, the society holds regular free communal swims around the country and encourages members to organise their own meets. In 2008 "splash mobs" were held at Burgh Island, Devon, the Thames and the Lake District. Participation is free and swims are peer-led, not lifeguarded (outdoorswimmingsociety.com or the Facebook OSS group for details).

PORTOFINO IN NORTH WALES

This extraordinary Italianate village, famously the setting for the surreal 60s TV drama The Prisoner, was begun in 1925 by the architect Sir Clough Williams-Ellis. It took him half a century, but today the domes and spires that spill down to Cardigan Bay do so with just the Mediterranean charm he was seeking. Far from being a village, however, Portmeirion (pormeirion-village.com) has always been a holiday complex. The Hotel Portmeirion, with 42 rooms and suites, boasts an art deco dining room and seashore location, while Castell Deudraeth, a converted Victorian folly 10 minutes walk away, has a further 11 rooms. Then there are 17 self-catering cottages, built by Williams-Ellis.

Portmeirion is signposted from the A487 at Minffordd, Gwyned, a half-mile walk away, and Cambrian Coast (thecambrianline.co.uk) and Ffestiniog Railway (festrail.co.uk) both have stations at Minffordd.

photo: shutterstock/Gail Johnson

Portmeirion village

WHITE BEACHES, SCILLY ISLES

Ignore the choppers and go to the Isles of Scilly slowly on the Scillonian III ferry service from Penzance to St Mary's (islesofscilly-travel.co.uk), £76/£38 return for adults/kids. Catch a small boat to Tresco, the second largest island, where there is great walking along the granite outcrops and heathland of the north coast. St Martin's has a flattish campsite (stmartinscampsite.co.uk) and a lovely little vineyard (stmartinsvineyard.co.uk).

Accommodation options include the smart New Inn pub (0845 710 5555, tresco.co.uk), doubles from £75.

COOLER CAMPERS, ALL UK

The young and tanned and Californian do not have a monopoly on VW campervans. New for this year is Derby-based Cool Camper Vans, which hires out classic 1970s VW vehicles, all with a "pop top" roof, fridge, two-ring gas cooker and grill, as well as entertainment for rainy days in the form of a TV, a DVD and a PlayStation.

One week's hire from £295 (two-berth) and £395 (four-berth). No extra charge for mileage if you stay below 100 miles per day (01332 661342, coolcampervans.com).

THE ORIENT, MANCHESTER

Forgo the slow boat to China for the UK's largest Chinatown. Among the karaoke bars and noodle joints, Yang Sing, the upmarket Cantonese restaurant, has an adjoining oriental-themed boutique hotel, with rooms styled like 1930s Shanghai: lots of pale green, painted silk screens and bespoke Chinese-made furniture and silk duvets. While the restaurant is strictly Cantonese, the hotel will have a broader oriental theme: Oku, its champagne bar, is named after the homes of Japanese geishas; Chinese karaoke bars and restaurants are right on the doorstep and there are the saki bars and shops of Chinatown just outside the door.

Call the Yang Sing restaurant on 0161 236 2200, or the Yang Sing Oriental hotel (0161 880 0188, yangsingoriental.com) with rooms from £179.

A TASTE OF FLORIDA IN CORNWALL

The St Moritz, a newly built 48-bedroom hotel and apartment complex, looks as if it's been plucked from the palm-fringed avenues of Miami's South Beach and set down near the most fashionable bit of Cornwall. It's art deco with a sense of the paint having just dried. Inside, an acre of wooden flooring lies beneath a glass and concrete atrium strung with lights. Beyond reception, the Cowshed Spa shimmers through a long fringed curtain.

Doubles from £95 low season, B&B (01208 862242, stmoritzhotel.co.uk).

Old town beach in St. Mary's,
Isles of Scilly

NO NEED TO LOSE YOUR SENSE OF HUMOUR

I grew up with parents who said: "Switch lights off when you are not in the room." It drove me almost crazy. How can you switch a light off when you are not in the room? But my mother and father knew what they meant. They had grown up in post-war austerity Britain, with rationing and make-do. They knew how to take holidays within 30 miles of home, how to recycle useful rubbish like paper bags and how to switch lights off when they were not in the room. They were green, although they did not know it. Oft-repeated phrases like, "You're not getting down from the table until you've finished your dinner," may have been early attempts at sustainable food management, but they left me with a propensity, a readiness, a primed and ready-to-go instinct that when the green movement arrived, I would run screaming in the other direction.

Kevin Rushby in Denmark, with partner Sophie and daughter Maddy

photo: Kevin Rushby

I hated it. I hated those childhood holidays in Mablethorpe and Skegness – we lived up the road in Nottingham. I hated the good sense and the lack of waste. Sustainability? Sod that. In the words, approximately, of the song: "Hope I die before I get an allotment." But then all these years later, Sophie, my partner, decided we had to do our bit. I faced the prospect of bus and train journeys with dread. The thought of camping in the English rain instead of jumping on a plane to sunshine and happiness was horrible. She even put me down for an allotment, sugaring the pill with the comforting words: "There's a two-year waiting list."

In the early days, when I reflected on my circumstances, I worried that I would lose my sense of humour. After all, the role model reversal from high-flying, "me generation" hedonist to plodding stop-at-home is harder to stomach than home-grown beans. Would this appalling transition mean a commensurate decline in laughs? Can greens have a sense of humour?

It is not promising territory, I'll admit. For a start, green thrives on guilt and there is precious little amusement in that. Green guilt is the new gilt-edged certainty in life, next to death and taxes. And my speciality, green travel, is pure self-flagellation. On every flight there is someone leaning across you to point out the window at the drowning polar bears. No car journey can be complete without the sickening realisation that you just took five minutes off earth's life expectancy because you could not be arsed to walk a hundred metres to school with the kids. Green guilt is Calvinistic in that you are born a damned sinner with no prospect of salvation because you are not going to do what is right and save the planet. In former ages, saving the world was very much the job for prophets and Bob Geldof, but now we are all responsible. Every felled rainforest, every poisoned sea and every single carbon dioxide molecule is our fault.

But the truth was not so bad. I learned that children don't mind the rain if they grow up with the idea that getting wet can be fun. On a cycling trip through the New Forest, I turned to look at our five-year-old, Maddy. She was on the tag-along bike and had been catching the muddy spray from my back wheel for several miles of dirt road. Her face was covered in mud, but she was grinning, full of glee at this opportunity to get filthy.

When I went on a canoe trip through the Norfolk Broads, camping rough under a tarp, the rain came down relentlessly but I had a wonderful time. Mark Wilkinson, who leads these expeditions, gave up a steady job as a financial adviser, earning big money and taking holidays in Thailand. Yet he says he has never regretted the change and I believe him. We paddled through the squalls, spotting otters and listening for the boom of the bitterns. We built fires and took nips of whisky to warm up. It was every bit as good as the best African safaris I'd done.

Green people are happy people. You don't have to work hard to keep your sense of humour. You won't miss the supermarkets or the flights. Every minute that I am not parked outside Tesco or sitting in a departure lounge gives me pleasure. It is not a penance or a guilt trip. It's fun.

Kevin Rushby

Sailing on the Norfolk Broads

photo: shutterstock/Laurence Gough

JOLLY GREEN JAUNTS

Experts reveal their holiday secrets

Sea kayaking around the coast of Lewis – there's a series of stacks, arches and enormous caves where you can go 200m into the cliffs and there are otters, seals, dolphins and, from time to time, even orcas. It's one of the most exotic holidays I've ever had, and it's not very far away. One of the islands, in particular, is like something out of a Greek myth – we kayaked between very high cliffs and a little passage opened out into a wide lagoon with sand dunes all around it. Wildernessscotland.com can organise kayaking trips around the Scottish isles.
George Monbiot, environmental campaigner and author

Camping on St Agnes in the Scilly Isles is best in May or June when there's hardly anyone there. I love the walk from the quay to the island's campsite across the camomile meadow – I take off my shoes and walk barefoot and it feels like I'm returning to somewhere that's really special. At high tide, the campsite is just 10m from the sea and you really feel that you're at the edge of Britain and that the next stop is America. There's so much wildlife to see. One of the best wildlife experiences is swimming with grey seals.
Jonathan Keeling, Producer, BBC Planet Earth

When you take the train to southern Spain there's something very special about getting off in sight of the north African coast. It takes about 24 hours from Waterloo to Malaga with an overnighter between Paris and Madrid. I was able to do a lot of writing and reading and thinking, and see how the countryside changes from deciduous forest in the UK to olive groves and vineyards in the south of Spain. In Andalucía, we saw a flock of wild flamingos – something you wouldn't see on the two-hour journey by plane.
Tony Juniper, director, Friends of the Earth

I've sat on my favourite rock many times over the years. It's high above Paradise Harbour, a popular stopping-off point on the Antarctic peninsula, and has one of the most spectacular views in the world. A circle of snowy mountains reflected in the water, aptly named Paradise, is home to a huge blue and white glacier and dozens of little clusters of crabeater seals, lounging on pieces of floating ice. Humpback whales cruise by in the open water and minke whales appear among icebergs. It's quite a trek up to "my" rock, but don't worry – you can slide back down the snowy slope on your bottom.
Mark Carwadine, zoologist and photographer

I went to a South African shebeen with an excellent guide, Victor, an unemployed teacher who lives with his family of nine. It was in the middle of a township of more than half a million, mostly very poor people living in tiny tin shacks. To

some, this won't sound like much fun but the evening will stay with me always. It was packed with people talking, singing and dancing to the superb live music. The food was great and the beers flowed. I was miles away from home and should have been feeling well out of my comfort zone, but I had a whale of a time.
Amanda Marks, co-founder,
Tribes Travel

. . . .

My favourite place for a barbecue is on the beach at Sand Point, just north of Weston-super-Mare, of all places. The National Trust owns it and keeps it as a rare oasis of beauty against the south shore of the Bristol Channel. Wales is across the muddy water, the grass rolls away behind and there is no sign of the urban banalities of Clevedon or Weston nearby. Another, close to Bristol, is my favourite circular walk – from Barrow Court across open fields and down to the beginning of a beech-wooded combe to a point above Barrow.
Alastair Sawday, publisher

. . . .

One place from my travels stands out – the Boat Landing guesthouse in Luang Namtha, an economically poor, but ethnically rich area of northern Laos. It serves simple but delicious organic food and the rooms are charming and use local textiles and fabrics. They have solar power and prioritise jobs for locals.
Safia Minney, founder, fairtrade clothing company People Tree

. . . .

Last year, my husband, Duncan, sailed Fairtrade, the boat he built in our back garden, all the way to the Caribbean. Then we drifted lazily in and out of the beautiful bays around St Lucia, St Vincent and Bequia. We discovered Jambe de Bois, the most fantastic cafe run by lovely ladies who served local specialities and great cocktails. It's perched on a beach at Pigeon Island on the north-west coast of St Lucia, and you can moor your dinghy to their jetty and sit with your pina colada looking out into the bay. It's magic.
Sophi Tranchell, managing director, Fairtrade company Divine Chocolate

. . . .

Camp as rough and remote as you can, but stay in the UK. I don't understand why people go to camp sites as the whole purpose of camping is to get away from people. My favourite place to camp is Barbondale in the Yorkshire Dales. Remote, but easy to get to by train from London, it's in a classic v-shaped valley, in an area of open moorland where you can swim in an ice-cold river, get your eggs and bacon from a local farmer and cook them over an open fire. It's also five miles to the Cross Keys Temperance Inn for homemade rabbit pie.
Richard Reed, co-founder, Innocent Drinks

. . . .

I like to tick off the classic hill walks and mountain bike trails around Snowdonia national park. My favourite place is a mountain biking centre called Llandegla, which has built a sustainable structure made with local wood and carried out an environmental assessment to set up the mountain bike trails. It's a really well thought-out place where you can do a 21km circuit and come back for a jumbo cappuccino to finish.
Steve Leonard, Vet and wildlife presenter

Interviews by Richard Hammond

How to tread lightly
EXPLAINER

Water

"Water is an absolutely colossal issue in most tourist destinations," says Sue Hurdle of the Travel Foundation. Of course, this means more than just your baths and showers. It also takes into account your share of the hotel infrastructure and amenities such as golf courses, gardens, swimming pools, and cleaning and washing practices, but some small changes can help reduce your drain on limited local resources.

What can I do?

Take quick showers rather than baths and stick to one a day
Ask that your towels and linens be changed less than daily
Alert management if this does not happen
Turn off the tap while brushing your teeth or shaving
Switch off the shower while you use soap or shampoo
Use half-flush settings on toilets or flush less often

Energy

Aside from the towering challenge of climate change, many tourism operations are situated in developing or remote regions where a reliable energy supply is an expensive luxury. By choosing to stay in energy-efficient, low-impact accommodation, you can reduce your contribution to greenhouse gases as well as lessening the competition for valuable local power supplies. In some cases, energy-saving (and therefore money-saving) technologies used in hotels are also taken up in the local area.

What can I do?

Keep use of air-conditioning and heating to a minimum
Turn off lights and air-conditioning whenever you leave your room
Take a solar-powered charger to recharge your phone
Leave unnecessary, power-thirsty gadgets at home
Lobby your hotel about saving energy – it's in their financial interest too
Think about which hotel amenities you really require
Use public transport, cycle or walk to get around

Richard Hammond and Leo Hickman

Waste

Waste disposal can be a particular problem in island destinations and remote areas such as mountain ranges. Many developing countries have limited recycling facilities and landfill is often the only option. Bottled drinking water, batteries and sanitary waste are particularly challenging to dispose of safely, while water-based pollutants from travellers' toiletries and hotel washing facilities can harm local ecosystems and waterways.

What can I do?
Remove packaging on new toiletries and clothes before departure
Pack biodegradable toiletries such as sunscreens
Don't use hotel toiletries if they are not biodegradable
Use rechargeable batteries or take used disposable batteries home
Recycle or pass on your holiday brochures
Use any recycling facilities at the destination
Where possible use your own bottle and a water filter or purification tablets rather than buying plastic bottled water

Working conditions

Tourism employs one in 11 people across the planet and provides the chief export industry for a third of developing countries. But while ethical tourism companies bring incalculable benefits to local communities, many tourism practices all too often exclude local people from a share of your tourist dollars. "Tourism is a shockingly exploitative industry," says Tricia Barnett, director of Tourism Concern. Low pay, seasonal work and child exploitation are all issues.

What can I do?
Stay in accommodation which is owned by or employs a high proportion of local people
Read up on local issues in guidebooks and online
Ask about staff training programmes and staff accommodation
Ask if staff are employed seasonally or year round
Learn some of the local language and engage with the staff
Leave cash tips

photo: shutterstock/Brian A Jackson

Sourcing

Too many hotels and resorts source food and other supplies from outside their local area, depriving local farmers, craftsmen and business of much-needed income and clocking up the food miles. Often, hotels claim that this is due to the tastes of visiting guests who don't want to try local produce. Programmes such as Adopt a Farmer, run in association with organisations such as the Travel Foundation and Oxfam are tackling this problem in Africa and the Caribbean, while, in the Gambia, 80% of the hotels used by First Choice now source some food from local producers.

 What can I do?

Choose accommodation with a local sourcing policy, at least for food

Be adventurous: try local dishes on the menu

Ask your hosts if they could source more locally

Boost the demand for regional crafts and produce by visiting nearby markets and shops and eating at local restaurants

Philanthropy and ownership

Many travel companies have traditionally supported schools and hospitals in their destinations and encouraged guests to donate money and supplies. Increasingly, that model is changing in favour of joint or complete local community ownership to increase income and consultation and remove any tinge of paternalism. This is not without its own challenges, particularly in the areas of customer service and administration.

 What can I do?

Try to stay in accommodation at least part owned by local communities

Be patient and open-minded when booking and during your stay

Conservation and development

"Green tourism has often neglected and sometimes denied the importance of development for communities," explains Harold Goodwin, professor of responsible tourism at Leeds Metropolitan University. Yet conservation of natural resources cannot be sustainable unless local communities can find viable incomes elsewhere.

 What can I do?

Ask your hotel or tour operator what they are doing to involve local communities in conservation and tourism work

Go on village tours and buy local handicrafts

Cultural integrity

Tricia Barnett of Tourism Concern warns that cultural integrity is a less visible issue. "The most difficult thing is that green tourism often runs into environments managed by indigenous people who are very vulnerable and can be ignored," she says. Pioneering schemes such as the Mara Triangle Maasai Villages Association in Kenya (maratriangle.org) and the Thailand Community-based Tourism Institute (cbt-i.org) are working with communities to develop an awareness of the tourist value of cultural tours and help to market them internationally. Sometimes, local people underrate the value of their culture.

 What can I do?
Check your hotel and tour operator's ownership and relations with local people
Choose responsibly handled cultural tours and performances
Purchase traditional handicrafts, foods and drinks

Construction

The best eco-friendly properties employ local tradesmen for building and maintenance work, use locally sourced and sustainable materials, minimise their impact on the local landscape and maximise energy-efficient design and architecture. The worst developments can leave the local landscape scarred, deforested and prone to coastal erosion. Cement production is particularly carbon-intensive, producing 5% of global manmade CO_2 emissions.

 What can I do?
Choose accommodation which has a stated responsible construction policy
Ask your hosts about the materials used to construct the buildings and if local
    people worked on the construction

Seven steps to more responsible travel

Fly less

Taking a flight will dwarf all other elements of your holiday in terms of carbon emissions. Use sites such as carbonresponsible.com to calculate the footprint of a particular journey and see how long it would take you to make the equivalent carbon saving by cutting down on car journeys or using low-energy lightbulbs. Sites such as seat61.com and sailanddrive.com help you plan breaks by rail and ferry as alternatives to short-haul flights.

Find green accommodation

There are more than 20 'green' accreditation schemes in the UK and more than 100 worldwide. Look out when choosing a holiday for members of the Green Tourism Business Scheme (green-business.co.uk); Legambiente in Italy (legambienteturismo.it); the Certificate in Sustainable Tourism in central America; and Australia's Ecotourism Certification programme (ecotourism.org.au). The greener hotels in package holiday brochures should now display the 'Travelife' logo.

Find a green tour operator

The Association of Independent Tour Operators (aito.co.uk) has a rating scheme for members. If you decide to book directly and bypass tour operators, charity Tourism Concern (tourismconcern.co.uk) has 300 vetted community-run trips on its website.

Play detective

All the schemes and badges in the world can only tell you so much. The most reliable advice is to make your own enquiries - ask the hotel management directly what they are doing to become more sustainable in terms of carbon emissions, energy and water use and waste minimisation. Does your holiday provider or accommodation employ local people and buy food and other supplies from local producers where possible? The more people raise the issue with managers, the more they will listen. Establishments with the best records will be happy to tell you all about them.

Liane Katz and Richard Hammond; photo: shutterstock/stoyanvassev

Report bad practice

If you spot hotel staff ignoring environmental policies, report it to the management. A written sustainability policy is only worth something if implemented properly. Similarly, if you encounter exploitative practices in destinations or among tour operators, complain to the company you booked with and write a review on a site such as irresponsibletourism.info. You can report animal exploitation via the Born Free Foundation's Travellers' Alert campaign at bornfree.org.uk/TAA.

Take good habits with you

If you diligently do your recycling, avoid unnecessary car journeys and take care not to waste water at home, take these habits on holiday with you. Use public transport once you are at your destination, keep heating, lighting and air-conditioning to a minimum and take showers rather than using the bath. Many island and mountain destinations have very limited waste and recycling facilities, so it is worth leaving all the unnecessary packaging that comes with holiday purchases at home. Environment-friendly suncreams and toiletries, such as the Dr Hauschka and Lavera ranges, can also limit your pollution of sensitive eco-systems.

Consider volunteering

Offering your time and skills for the benefit of a developing country can be a very rewarding experience, though it pays to do your homework before deciding where to go. The most responsible voluntary tourism operators focus on the environmental and developmental benefits of their projects, rather than providing an excuse for a holiday in the sun. Often the best projects are those that originate within the destination, where local people have sought specific help from volunteering agencies. The website ethicalvolunteering.org has some useful tips on how to choose the right agency, depending on how much time you have to give. See page 188 for tips on ethical volunteering.

IS THERE ANYWHERE WE SHOULDN'T VISIT?

Everest
More than 30,000 people were estimated to visit Everest in 2006. Most will only have trekked as far as Everest base camp on the Nepalese side of the mountain but increasing numbers are climbing up the world's highest peak. Conservationists say the area is at risk of turning into an ecological disaster yet tourism can bring much-needed income to the surrounding mountain communities.

Unlike other popular treks, such as the Inca Trail, there are no restrictions on how many tourists can visit Everest base camp. To avoid the crowds consider going to other spectacular unexplored treks in the Himalayas. If you do go to Everest base camp, make sure you take kerosene or gas for cooking rather than relying on wood-fired stoves (deforestation is a major concern) or if you're booking with a travel company, make sure it employs sufficient numbers of local porters to carry all the food, tents and fuel in and out of the park. KE expeditions (keadventure.com) employ up to 50 porters for a group of 16 people camping. Himalayan Kingdoms (himalayankingdoms.com) no longer runs camping trips to Everest base camp; instead the company arranges for you to stay in tea houses en route so that the money from your trip directly benefits local people.

Antarctica
During the 2007-2008 season, almost 35,000 tourists stepped ashore from their cruise ships in Antarctica, according to the International Association of Antarctic Tour Operators (IAATO). Just 6,704 tourists went ashore in 1990.

There are rising fears over the impact of these visitor numbers on the planet's last great wilderness, with the UN environment programme and British Antarctic Survey expressing concern. In addition, the projected retreat of sea ice is likely to lead to an expansion of tourism activities, as more sites will become accessible by sea and the season will lengthen.

"On the smaller boats, where there are lectures on geology and science, passengers feel a sense of ownership of what is going on in Antarctica," says Dr John Shears, an environmental expert at the British Antarctic Survey. "That is less likely to happen when you're on board a huge cruise ship." He recommends travellers book with a member of the International Association for Antarctic Operators (iaato.org), which sets guidelines that ensure environmentally sound travel. As well as Peregrine Adventures, other UK-based IAATO members include Journey Latin America (journeylatinamerica.co.uk) and Wildwings (wildwings.co.uk).

Galápagos Islands
Before 1968 there were no flights to Galápagos. The only way to get to the islands was by boat – either your own or the local supply boat, the Cristobal Carrier. The trip took about a week each way and you had to share space with dried salt fish and live cows, the islands' only economic exports.

Now there are up to five flights a day and we are seeing the advent of cruise ship tourism. Around 100,000 visitors every year come to marvel at the natural wonders of the archipelago. But the islands – the first area to be declared a Unesco world heritage site – could lose this status because of invasive species such as rats inadvertently introduced by tourists. It is now on Unesco's "world heritage in danger" list.

And yet Galápagos was a pioneer in the development of ecotourism. In 1968 the Galápagos National Park Service (PNG) set limits on the size of vessels and the number of passengers (90) that they could carry. Specific areas were designated for tourist visits and some were reserved for smaller boats carrying 16 passengers or less. As a result, the impact of well-controlled tourism has, until recently, been modest.

The arrival of cruise ships with 500-or-so passengers could put this at risk. You cannot realistically disinfect a large passenger boat, its passengers and crew. The additional arrivals could also overload these sites and diminish the experience for everyone. And of course, the real danger is that the number of such cruise visits will be allowed to increase.

Sustainable tourism is vital to Galápagos; the people of Galápagos need it as their main economic activity and the wildlife needs it as a means of conservation. But the Galápagos ecosystem and its tourism operation simply does not have the capacity or resources to handle such a sudden influx of visitors.

Burma

Some tourist attractions in Burma (Myanmar) have been built on forced labour while the money generated from tourism largely goes into the pockets of its military leaders. Organisations such as Amnesty International have highlighted the disturbing connections between tourism development and human rights abuses. That much most people will agree. But there is fierce argument between those who refuse to visit Burma in protest at the regime and those who oppose such a boycott. People who choose to visit Burma say that isolating the regime has not weakened it, that maintaining contact with Burma gives hope to its people and that some tourist money can trickle down to locals. Those who support a boycott argue that the opposition leader Daw Aung San Suu Kyi asks tourists not to visit her country until democracy is restored. Groups such as Tourism Concern have launched campaigns to ask tour operators to stop visiting Burma – some no longer do – and for Lonely Planet to withdraw its guidebook to Burma. The Rough Guide does not publish a guide to Burma nor does the website responsibletravel.com feature holidays there. The boycott debate perhaps evokes the situation during the apartheid era in South Africa – if you were not happy to go South Africa under apartheid, perhaps you wouldn't be happy to visit Burma now.

Richard Hammond, Leo Hickman, Polly Pattullo and Julian Fitter

HOW SHOULD WE BEHAVE ON HOLIDAY?

Gifts for children

It feels like the generous thing to do – pack a few small gifts into your hold luggage to hand out on your travels – but does this kind of travellers' philanthropy encourage a dependence on rich tourists?

The type of present and the manner in which it is given can make a big difference to how beneficial the present will be. While it may be tempting to hand out gifts yourself, it can encourage children to expect all tourists to bring something for them, so it's better to give your gifts discreetly to someone in authority, such as the local schoolteacher, who can distribute them appropriately. And while watches and electronic toys may go down well with children at home, schools in poor areas often lack access to the most basic classroom equipment, so pens, pencils, chalk, rulers, jigsaws and colouring books are often the most welcome gifts.

There may also be local charities that take contributions, such as clothes or medicines at the end of your holiday, or financial donations. The more responsible travel companies work with local NGOs and charities and should be able to advise which are the most appropriate. For example, Nomadic Thoughts (nomadicthoughts.com) works with New Life Mexico, which focuses on the rehabilitation of street children in Puerto Vallarta. Save the Children (savethechildren.org.uk) accepts financial donations (rather than presents) for children worldwide.

To haggle or not to haggle

In the local markets and souks of north Africa, the Middle East and Asia, haggling is considered honest trade and often the only acceptable way to buy goods. Yet arguing about the price of a cheap bracelet can seem unfair when you're splitting hairs over a couple of pence with a small trader who earns a fraction of your salary. Pay too much, though, and you risk encouraging market traders to inflate prices beyond what others are prepared to pay.

A general rule of thumb is to knock down the quoted price from between a third to half and then negotiate up to a fairer price. Initial quotes may be way too high, however, so it's worth shopping around beforehand to get a rough idea of what other sellers are asking, particularly if you're buying a more expensive item such as a carpet or piece of furniture.

Friendly haggling is a fine art and all part of the experience of visiting a local market; it's not meant to be a battle. And it's worth putting the deal in perspective – what may seem small change to you can make a big difference to the income of the trader. Remember the person selling is a professional salesman who will have a fixed price under which he or she won't go. The trick is to get as close to this as you can without compromising on what you're prepared to pay. Walking away empty-handed will usually determine if the final offer really is the last.

The bottle mountains

The rubbish caused by plastic water bottles is bad enough at home, but the problem is a thousand times worse in countries where there may be no waste management or recycling facilities to deal with piles of garbage. Yet, forgo buying bottled water and you risk illness from drinking unsafe local water.

If you're staying in a place where there will be a safe water source, such as a bulk water dispenser in the hotel, it's much better to pack a reusable water bottle that you can refill rather than buy bottles of water that you'll dump when you're done. Collapsible plastic pouches are easy to pack, while sturdy aluminium bottles with canvas coats keep the water cool and can be re-used for years.

Responsible travel companies that run trips to Africa and Asia, such as Exodus, KE Adventure and Dragoman, advise clients against buying bottled water and instead provide their own supplies of filtered/boiled water.

Dress Code

Stripping off or going topless on the beach seems a harmless enough holiday pleasure. But it is not always so simple. Tunisia for example has beaches where women go topless – yet it is a Muslim country, which suggests that it is the tourists who make up their own rules. "When in Rome" etc is a useful benchmark.

Photography

Signs that say "leave only footprints, take only photographs" warn about environmental damage. But taking photographs can also be damaging – to people. The women of the Kayan Padaung tribal group in northern Thailand wear brass coils around their necks and spend their days having their photographs taken by western tourists who pay local businessmen to visit the "giraffe women". The United Nations has described the women as living in a "human zoo". In southern Ethiopia, photographing the tribal peoples, including the women of the Mursi tribe who have plate lips, has also become an entirely commercial and nowadays often an antagonistic exchange. These are some hardcore examples of how people become exhibits to satisfy tourist curiosity.

Under such circumstances it is not hard to believe that story of how some cultures believe that if you take their photographs you steal their spirit. But wherever you are on holiday, it makes sense to ask permission before you take a photograph of people or their homes or sacred places. Remember to ask children, too. Not to ask is intrusive and rude and can cause distress, if not hostility. If people decline, accept that decision. Or, if they ask for money, perhaps that is the price you have to pay for the very unequal relationship between guest and host especially in the poorest parts of the world.

Richard Hammond and Polly Pattullo

Eco-labelling

There is currently no internationally accepted standard for green tourism. In the UK alone there are more than 20 independent accommodation eco-labels, including Green Dragon (Wales), Green Leaf (New Forest), the Green Acorn (Cornwall), the Green Island (Isle of White) and the Green Tourism Business Scheme (England and Scotland). Worldwide, there are more than a hundred labels; a bewildering mixture of regional, national and international schemes. Yet there is no single, international regulatory body responsible for providing a standard by which they operate; the result is that you can't compare like with like.

What's in a label?
The term "eco-label" is also applied differently throughout the world. In South America and Asia, ecotourism is often used to market wildlife tourism, regardless of whether there is any environmental benefit from the trip. The popular South American ecotourism website planeta.com cites John Noble, editor of Lonely Planet's Mexico guidebook, who said: "What you call ecotourism in Latin America, in Europe we call a walk in the country." Julian Mathews, founder of Discovery Initiatives, which runs holidays that support conservation in more than 30 countries, says "in India's travel industry, ecotourism simply means going into the outdoors". While Patricia Barnett of Tourism Concern has said that the ecotourism label can be "used by anyone at anytime for anything from a small-scale locally run rainforest lodge where the money goes to support a community, to a large, luxury, foreign-owned resort which has little community involvement and uses masses of natural resources".

Xavier Font, a specialist in responsible tourism certification at Leeds Metropolitan University, argues that hotels also have to take both social and environmental factors into account if they are to market themselves as green: "In this day and age, it's no longer just about how a hotel deals with energy, waste and water. To be genuinely sustainable, a hotel has to demonstrate it has proper labour conditions and emplyment rights for its workers, such as provision for single mothers, people with disabilities and so on."

Cheeky marketing
The hijacking of the "eco" label by tourism businesses riding cheaply on the green wave means that nowadays you're unlikely to see the word ecotourism used in British tour operators' brochures. Harold Goodwin, professor of responsible tourism management at Leeds Metropolitan University says: "Ecotourism has no marketing utility because people just don't believe it anymore."

Greenwashing comes in various guises. In some cases it can be little more than cheeky marketing – a golf course claiming it is green because its lakes attract wildlife is commonplace. But there is a more serious side to greenwash, especially at the sharp end of poverty, such as when tribal people are evicted from their traditional land to make way for so-called "eco-resorts".

But ecotourism – and greenwashing – are no longer confined to developing countries. Just as the green agenda has gone mainstream, from city breaks to summer holidays in the Med, so we start hearing about so-called eco-friendly spas that do little more than sell Fairtrade bananas in the bistro. This undermines the genuine article. But there are hotel chains, such as Scandic that are going the extra mile to green up their operations by doing much more than simply asking guests to put their towels out for washing less frequently; often it involves a fundamental change to the way they run their business, from ensuring that any new hotels are designed using the latest green techniques to investing in more efficient technologies that minimise their use of electricity and water.

Is it really green?

Judging whether your holiday really does benefit the environment and satisfy ethical scrutiny requires a technical expertise beyond the call of most holidaymakers. After all, who wants to spend their holiday poking their noses into recycling bins and checking whether local guides are paid above the minimum wage? Yet it's difficult to find independent, reliable advice to help you make ethical decisions about a holiday.

Given the fact that over 26m holidays are booked through travel agents each year, you might think the travel industry would be the first port of call for guidance. Yet not one high street travel agent in the UK specialises in eco travel. Only specialist tour operators offer that kind of service according to the Association of British Travel Agents (ABTA).

They are referring to the likes of alternative holiday specialist Sunvil, which for years has sold holidays that take visitors to places where local communities really benefit from ethical tourism. Sunvil is a member of the Association of Independent Tour Operators (AITO), which represents about 150 UK tour companies. AITO runs its own "responsible tourism" classification, awarding its highest three-star grade to 31 of its members which offer holidays that use locally owned accommodation and that try to minimise the impact of their holidays on the environment.

But these small specialist companies only skim the surface of the travel industry. The travel giants, Thomas Cook and TUI Travel, are not, historically, known for giving advice on where to go green. Yet things are beginning to change: the Federation of Tour Operators (FTO) – whose members carry around 18m UK package travellers annually – has developed a common environmental standard for its members' hotel suppliers, known as the Travelife Sustainability System. First Choice, Virgin Holidays and Thomas Cook now include Travelife logos in their brochures for hotels that have achieved bronze, silver and gold accreditations.

While TUI believes the move to flag up green hotels is a significant development in response to consumer demand for ethical purchasing in general. Jane Ashton, head of sustainable development at TUI Travel, says: "Travellers are becoming more interested in green products so it's becoming increasingly important to define what being green actually means."

Whereas in other industries you can rely on accredited eco-labels to point you in the right direction, in tourism, it's not so straightforward. "More or less anyone can set up a scheme," says Ed Gillespie of the green communications specialists Futerra. "Respected eco-labels in other sectors, such as the Marine Stewardship Council for seafood, or Fairtrade for coffee, tea or sugar are trusted and have rigorous criteria that need to be fulfilled before a company can use their logo on its products. But in tourism you can practically buy an eco-label and slap it on your website or marketing materials, and there are so many out there that punters have little or no idea how much substance lies behind the claim."

Green travel schemes demystified

One of the largest and best-known green tourism certification schemes is Green Globe, and even it was criticised in its early days in an independent report commissioned by the World Wildlife Fund (WWF) for promoting "confusion rather than clarity", by not distinguishing clearly enough between companies that had simply pledged to undertake its certification system from those that had actually achieved certification.

In Africa, there is no pan-continental certification system. Some countries have their own ecotourism associations, such as the ecotourism Society of Kenya (ecotourismkenya.org), which currently awards its gold rating to just two lodges: Basecamp Maasai Mara and Campi ya Kanzi. Fair Trade in Tourism in South Africa assesses travel businesses on criteria such as wages and working conditions. Elsewhere, it can be hard to separate the green from the greenwash. Leading tour operators, such as Rainbow Tours, Expert Africa, Tribes and Discovery Initiatives carry out their own vetting procedure. Tribes now publishes an "eco-review" of 25 lodges based on their environmental performance and social responsibility. So far, the best-performing lodges are Chole Mjini and Chumbe Island Lodge in Tanzania, and Kenya's Amboseli Porini (tribes.co.uk).

Closer to home, VisitBritain's Green Start programme (visitbritain.com) is designed to help hoteliers prepare for entry level to a recognised certification scheme, such as the UK's Green Tourism Business Scheme (GTBS). This scheme has vetted over 1,500 places to stay, from B&Bs to luxury five-star hotels and visitor centres in England and Scotland. The scheme requires owners to provide details on more than 160 criteria, ranging from energy, waste and local transport, and sends out an environmental auditor to visit each property before awarding them a bronze, silver or gold rating. Owners can only apply for membership if their properties already qualify for one of the UK's quality assurance schemes, such as the AA, Scottish Tourist Board or VisitBritain's.

"Quality and Tourism"

Other recognised eco-labels include: the Green Key, which has certified accommodation in France, Sweden, Greenland and Estonia; the Nordic Swan, which has certified 125 hotels and youth hostels throughout Scandinavia; and Legambiente, which has certified over 100 properties in Italy.

Outside Europe, Australia's Ecotourism Certification program has built up a comprehensive list of accredited accommodation and attractions in the country, while the best-known scheme in central America is the Certificate in Sustainable Tourism, which has certified 55 hotels in Costa Rica – a country that Tourism Concern says "has made pioneering strides to promote sustainability."

Britain's GTBS also assesses the local economic and social benefits of tourism, something that most green travel schemes don't do, according to Polly Pattullo, author of the *Ethical Travel Guide*. However, the Fair Trade in Tourism South Africa (FTTSA) scheme is showing the world how this can be done. It assesses travel businesses on fair trade principles, such as whether they provide decent wages and working conditions for their staff, and has certified over 30 businesses, including a downtown backpackers' hostel and a luxury lodge in the African bush.

The Fair Trade Labelling Organisation, Tourism Concern and several other European NGOs are looking closely at the scheme to see how fair trade principles can be applied in tourism on a wider scale. Harold Goodwin thinks this has potential: "British people are used to getting fair trade coffee because they buy into the idea that it is good for local producers, yet tourism has the advantage that when you've bought the product, you then go and see it in action." In other words, seeing is believing.

Richard Hammond

photo: shutterstock/Mark Gabrenya

Arenal volcano, Costa Rica

High above the Apennine Mountains, Italy
photo: shutterstock/ligio

FLYING

"There is no point being environmentally concerned all year and then bingeing on holiday," points out Harold Goodwin, director of the International Centre for Responsible Tourism at Leeds Metropolitan University. However much we all choose to cut our greenhouse gas emissions, we should not conveniently forget the portion contributed by our travels.

In fact, Britons produce more carbon emissions from air travel per capita than any other country – at 603kg per year, according to a 2007 study by market research firm Global TGI, which blamed our bingeing on a series of wetter summers and our predilection for low-cost flights. Alongside the burgeoning short-haul sector, we are also taking more and more long-haul flights, which account for a disproportionately high percentage of UK aviation emissions. And it is this pace of growth that worries scientists and environmentalists the most.

"The future of aviation is complex and no one knows what an environmentally safe level is, but what is absolutely certain is that the increases projected by the UK industry and sanctioned by government are completely unsustainable," warns Charlie Kronick of Greenpeace. Scientists at the Tyndall Centre for Climate Change Research echo that if aviation is allowed to grow at rates even lower than those being experienced today, the UK could see aviation accounting for between 50% and 100% of its total carbon budget by 2050 under climate change stabilisation agreements.

But do we really have to give up flying, or simply cut down? Just how bad is flying and will the scientists come to our rescue with a "technofix"? Are there any ways to cut or compensate for our emissions if we do fly – and if we do make the switch, is it always better to take the train or can driving a car full of passengers compete on fuel efficiency? Can we really make a difference by cutting down on our flying while China's air market has nearly tripled since 2000? Can we fly if we don't drive a car?

On the following pages, the *Guardian's* specialist writers on science, the environment and ethical living unravel the complex facts behind different modes of transport to enable you to understand your carbon footprint and choose the best option for your next trip.

Just how bad is flying?

Fasten your seat belts, there is turbulence ahead. More than 2.5m scheduled flights take off worldwide every month, and the 300m plus passengers inside all those pressurised cabins are part of a modern success story that threatens to turn into an environmental disaster.

Demand for cheap flights continues to rise, and nations across the world are scrambling to increase airport capacity to share in the bonanza. The UK government predicts that passenger numbers through Britain's terminals will double to 490m a year by 2030. In 1990, it was just 100m.

Worldwide, forecasts by the aviation industry say passenger traffic will climb by about 5% for the next decade and a half at least. As the number of flights increases, so does the industry's carbon footprint. Like all fossil fuels, jet fuel releases carbon dioxide when burned.

In 2005, the UK government estimated total UK aviation emissions as 37.5m tonnes of CO_2 — more than 90% of which was down to international flights. If included in national totals, this would have represented about 5.9% of total UK carbon dioxide pollution, compared to less than 1% in 1970. By 2050, the government expects total UK aviation emissions to reach between 53 and 67m tonnes of carbon dioxide.

Internationally, the Intergovernmental Panel on Climate Change estimates that flights were responsible for 2% of world carbon emissions. What worries scientists and campaigners is the rate of growth, at a time when the world is supposed to be slashing carbon pollution. EU aircraft emissions alone have risen 87% since 1990. Official industry forecasts presented at an aviation conference in Barcelona in 2008 predict international carbon dioxide pollution from aircraft will reach 1.2bn to 1.4bn tonnes by 2025, up from 610m tonnes now.

Officially, aircraft emit a lot less pollution. Almost none in fact, because they are excluded from official figures. As jetting between countries is classed as an international activity, the greenhouse-gas pollution of aircraft is missed out when countries tot up their emissions. That means the UK government can claim our carbon dioxide output is about 5% lower than in 1990. But take emissions from flights and shipping into account, as scientists at the Tyndall Centre for Climate Change Research have done, and Britain's carbon footprint has actually grown since 1990.

Unlike other sources of emissions, with aircraft, the carbon accounting does not tell the whole climate story. Uniquely, aviation emissions are spewed into the atmosphere at high altitude and this can make flights worse for the environment than their carbon signature alone would indicate. Nitrous oxide, another greenhouse gas, also comes from the business end of a jet engine, and so does water vapour, which quickly condenses in the freezing air to form the tell-tale condensation trails (contrails) left behind in the sky, which are believed to have a global warming effect. Particles of soot and sulphate also contribute.

The scale of this extra "radiative forcing" effect is controversial, and depends on a number of factors including the location in the world and local weather conditions, but is usually counted as amplifying the carbon impact by 2.5 times, so the true climate damage caused by a flight is more than double that suggested by its carbon emissions alone. Taking this into account, the impact of aviation jumps to more than the industry is usually keen to admit: about 3.5% of all man-made global warming in the early 1990s, and almost 10% of Britain's total climate change emissions in 2005.

So just how much more polluting is a flight compared to other forms of transport, such as trains? Comparing the direct emissions of air and rail journeys is complicated by the mixture of power sources used by trains (in the UK, some 40% of the network is electrified) and the different occupancy rates at different times of the day — as well as the amplification effect described above.

After muddling through these issues in April 2008, the government's environment department, Defra, calculated that UK rail journeys produce the equivalent of 0.06kg of carbon dioxide per passenger kilometre and Eurostar produces 0.02kg. For long-haul flights it is 0.11kg, while short-haul flights produce 0.10kg and domestic flights 0.18kg. That would make a domestic flight on average three times worse than a train journey and a flight from London to Paris about five times as polluting as travelling by rail. Although, long-haul flights are better per kilometre than domestic routes, the huge distances involved with intercontinental travel means such flights end up being far more damaging per journey.

In 2008, Robert Noland and a team of transport researchers at Imperial College London analysed the pollution from all flights that leave Britain during a typical day. Of the 3,900 departures, the scientists found that an astonishing 26 produced almost 10% of the carbon dioxide. And just 243 flights, none of which landed within Europe, accounted for half the total daily emissions.

However, there is some good news for eco-aware air passengers: taking a flight at certain times during the day can lower its carbon footprint. Scientists at the University of Leeds have found that the warming effect of aircraft is much greater when they fly in the dark, because of the effects of those contrails they leave behind. They say aircraft contrails enhance the greenhouse effect because they trap heat in the same way as clouds. During the day, their warming effect is not as pronounced because contrails reflect sunlight back into space, which helps to keep the planet cool. The experts say the government could reduce the impact of aviation on climate by ensuring that more people fly during the day. It will not solve the problem, but it could make that in-flight meal taste just a little less sour.

David Adam

WHY I DON'T FLY

I stopped flying away on holiday in 2003 . I don't think leisure travel by plane is really defensible once you're in possession of all the facts. The train is infinitely classier, and budget airlines, particularly on short-haul routes, are doing a good job of making aviation about as unglamorous and uncomfortable as possible.

My most difficult journey without flying was probably crossing the Pacific Ocean from New Zealand to Mexico on a rusty Chinese-built cargo ship. The journey took 16 days and the sense of isolation midway was quite something. My favourite was the Trans-Siberian Express: crossing the thousands of miles of tundra and birch forest was meditative and mind-blowing. There's a whole different experience possible if you just give up the aluminium sausage!

Ed Gillespie, Slow traveller and founder of Futerra (lowcarbontravel.com)

I talk so much about carbon footprints that I am trying hard to massively cut back on flying. I went to the south of France and Frankfurt by train in 2007, in both cases with serious benefits – such as getting to know beautiful Strasbourg, largely ignored by British travellers because there is no nearby airport. I don't pretend for one minute that train travel is cheap – though it can match air travel on many routes – but I do think that trains create a proper "journey". And they don't get diverted because of fog.

Alastair Sawday, publisher of Special Places to Stay and Go Slow England

I stopped flying four years ago, as an experiment. I reasoned that if I (no relatives abroad, no need to fly for work, no yearning for hot countries) couldn't give up flying, then no one could – or would. When I first made my decision, I was wary of telling people about it on the grounds that it came across as pious and holier than thou. Those I did tell were generally baffled; a few were downright aggressive. Now, just a couple of years on, people are supportive and interested. The ground has shifted. For me, it's an absolute ban. The only exception I can imagine is flying to the US

Flying in numbers

610m

tonnes of CO_2 emissions from global aircraft in 2008

300m

number of global air passengers per month in 2008

2.5m

number of global flights per month in 2008

100m

air passengers using UK airports in 1990

photo: istockphoto/Frank van den Bergh

490m

air passengers forecast to be using UK airports in 2030

18.4m

Chinese domestic flights in 2007

6.4m

Chinese domestic flights in 2000

40%

aviation's share of global tourism emissions

90%

international flights' share of UK aviation emissions in 2005

at some point. Having never been, and very much wishing to go, I had planned to travel there by container ship. However, I've just had a baby and that scheme now looks somewhat impractical.

Sarah Crown, editor of guardian.co.uk/books

Giving up flying was initially an easy decision for me. I wasn't an especially intrepid traveller and recent trips abroad only served to remind me how little I knew about my home country. But then one of my best friends invited me to be a bridesmaid at her wedding in Brisbane, Australia. With only a small amount of research I knew that I couldn't fly. Not wanting to miss the occasion I was determined to find another way, a slow and more fun way, using buses, boats, bikes and trains. Flying, especially short-haul, is another symptom of our modern, fast-paced world gone mad. There is so much more to see and experience overland. You meet real people, you slow down and relax and it is often cheaper too.

Barbara Haddrill, environmentalist and author of Babs2 Brisbane

I haven't stopped flying altogether, but I've managed to avoid being tempted by any "recreational flights" since about 1995, and have substantially reduced my flights for work. It's not a self-imposed, absolute ban, but an effort to cut down on my own, excessive, carbon footprint. Without exception, all the road/rail journeys I've undertaken instead of flying, have been more fun than suffering the stress and discomfort of air travel. I'm not against flying, but understand that the planet's carbon sinks cannot keep pace with current CO_2 emissions, and that the cost of runaway climate change is unthinkable. I take the view that it's better for 10m people to make a small effort, than for 10m people to stick their heads in the sand – or in an in-flight magazine.

Nicholas Crane, presenter BBC Coast and Great British Journeys

WHY I DO FLY

I'm no lover of aviation – I live below the Heathrow flight path – but flying is still the cheapest, fastest, most practical way to visit most places abroad. The train may be a more civilised experience but, once you're past north-west Europe, it still costs far more and takes days to arrive: luxuries few can afford. The argument for flying to emerging destinations has an ethical as well as practical dimension – responsible tourism can play a hugely positive role in developing economies, so your flight can bring vital revenue and opportunities to the Latin American farmer or African conservationist. Fly less, by all means, but not to fly at all is simply counterproductive.
Dan Linstead, editor of Wanderlust magazine

I have reduced the amount that I fly and drive a car; I travel more by rail. However, there is no individual solution to the problems of greenhouse gas emissions and climate change – we have to find and implement collective solutions. At the moment, aviation is being made a scapegoat: it is easier to campaign against flying than it is to address the way we heat and light our homes and power our economy. For many of the world's poorest countries, tourism is the only industry that offers any way of engaging in the global economy and addressing poverty: our governments do not put up tariff barriers against tourism. So as we develop tax instruments to reduce flying, we need to remember that our holidays make work for many.
Harold Goodwin, professor of responsible tourism management, Leeds Metropolitan University

I really don't understand the "don't fly" argument. There are just not enough people willing to forgo the enjoyment of a foreign holiday to pressurise airlines into reducing the number of scheduled flights. So, the planes are going to fly anyway, whether or not the concerned individual is on board. What is so exciting is that each person can make a difference to the host country through projects such as stuffyourrucksack.com. This simple idea is the brainchild of TV presenter Kate Humble: local charities, schools and

603kg
average carbon emissions per capita in UK

0.10kg
Defra's figure for CO_2 per passenger km on short-haul flights

0.11kg
Defra's figure for CO_2 per passenger km on long-haul flights

0.06kg
Defra's figure for CO_2 per passenger km on rail journeys

6.3%
aviation's share of UK CO_2 emissions

photo: istockphoto/Paul Senyszyn

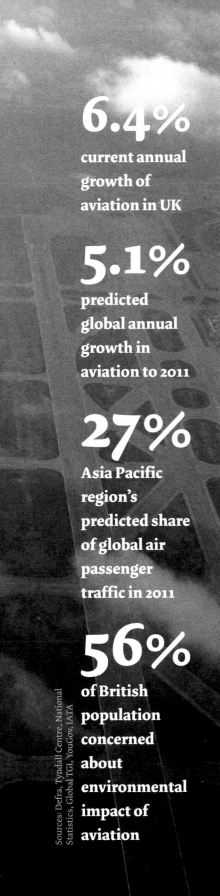

6.4%

current annual growth of aviation in UK

5.1%

predicted global annual growth in aviation to 2011

27%

Asia Pacific region's predicted share of global air passenger traffic in 2011

56%

of British population concerned about environmental impact of aviation

Sources: Defra, Tyndall Centre, National Statistics, Global TGI, YouGov, IATA

other organisations in the developing world badly need goods ranging from quality pens or books to laptop computers, and travellers are flying out to these places with half-empty rucksacks. The website puts the traveller in touch with the charity. Travellers love having the opportunity to travel positively in this way – they just need to know how to do it.

Hilary Bradt, travel writer and founder of Bradt guides

I fly because I have to, but I don't really like it, never did, and feel that given the environmental concerns, you should always look for an alternative if there is one. If this means discovering new parts of Europe by train, or spending more time in the UK, then that's an upside. But what we mustn't do is turn our backs on the huge benefits that I believe travel brings – to us, to the places we visit, and to the world in general – and that means occasionally we have to get on a plane.

Martin Dunford, co-founder Rough Guides

For me, it's about "cut and switch". I am a strong believer that we should all be reducing the amount of flights we take, as aviation is the fastest-growing contributor to climate change. We need to start holidaying closer to home and take the train for short-haul journeys when we can. And when we do fly long-haul, it's more important than ever that we choose holidays that benefit local communities and environments as much as possible. This kind of responsible tourism is very important for the creation of jobs and livelihoods around the world, especially in developing countries where tourism is growing fastest. We need to balance our need to reduce our carbon impacts with the need to sustain communities around the world.

Justin Francis, co-founder of responsibletravel.com

WHY WE NEED TO CURB BINGE FLYING

When did spending more than 14 hours in a plane over a long weekend suddenly become enjoyable rather than a punishment that befalls only the hardiest of business travellers? Are airport queues no more? Has in-flight dining suddenly become a gastronomic delight? Does everyone now get a fully reclining seat and limitless leg room? Have they found a cure for deep-vein thrombosis? Is there a pill to pop to nullify jet lag?

We have now entered an era where "long-haul minibreaks" are becoming the norm for a well-heeled section of British society. According to a survey by Halifax Insurance in 2007, 3.7m Britons chose to fly to destinations seven hours away or more in the pursuit of leisure. The travel insurer predicted an increase of a third in 2008 meaning that 4.9m tourists from the UK would be jetting off to places such as Hong Kong, New York, Vancouver, Dubai, Las Vegas and Rio de Janeiro for the weekend, on so-called "breakneck breaks".

"Better airline quality, the lure of winter sun and cheaper long-haul flights have created a boom in demand for long-haul minibreaks, with millions of us enduring long flights for a weekend on the other side of the globe," said Paul Birkhead, a senior manager at Halifax. Other factors are also promising to make this form of entertainment more attractive, such as the "open skies" agreement for routes across the Atlantic and the proposed new runways at Heathrow and Stansted.

Countering these new developments are environmentalists – and increasingly a wide coalition of other groups who are fighting hard to rein in this growth in aviation. They are often told that they are trying to "stop the poor from flying". In fact, as Civil Aviation Authority data shows, there is very little evidence, if any, that the era of low-cost carriers has suddenly "democratised the skies" for one and all, as the airlines and their lobbyists would have you believe.

The fight to stop airport expansion isn't about stopping those who fly once a year to the Med for their annual two-week holiday; it's about curbing the still relatively small section of society that is now addicted to "binge flying" – those who fly three or more times a year for leisure. These are the people who are driving much of the growth in aviation in the UK – and its resultant emissions, which in 2008 accounted for about 13% of the country's overall greenhouse gas burden.

Friends of the Earth were quite right to label such journeys as "indulgent".

CAN YOU CHOOSE A GREENER AIRLINE?

Despite what some airlines would like us to believe there is no such thing as a green airline. In fact, the words "green" and "airline" should not really be in the same sentence – except this one. But, as with all forms of transport, there are varying shades of grey. These differences are most pronounced in domestic and short-haul routes. It doesn't take much research to find out on an airline's website what type of planes it typically uses.

Flybe, for example, was one of the world's first low-cost carriers to use turboprop planes rather than jets. It uses some Bombardier Q400s and Embraer 195s in its fleet which are about 20% less polluting per passenger kilometre than the jets used by rivals such as the BAe146s or A319s. Turboprop planes also tend to fly at lower altitudes meaning the radiative forcing impact of their emissions is reduced. When it comes to long-haul journeys, though, there is little difference between the airlines as all tend to use long-range jets, such as the Boeing 747-400.

Leo Hickman

If you fly ...

- Avoid short-haul flights
- Fly direct
- Fly economy
- Choose airlines with modern fleets and high capacity
- Avoid night flights
- Avoid winter flights
- Fly less, stay longer
- Keep luggage to a minimum

WILL THERE BE A TECHNOFIX FOR AVIATION?

Don't hold your breath. There is technology on the horizon that can shave incremental percentage points off the carbon footprint of flying but none seem to be on their way quickly enough to stem the huge rise in emissions predicted as air travel grows this century. Alice Bows, of the Tyndall Centre for Climate Change Research at the University of Manchester, says that while passenger miles are growing at around 6-7% per year, efficiency improvement in airplanes is only rising by 1% per year. This leaves a net annual increase in the carbon emissions from aviation around the world.

There are some promising ideas to make planes better, such as carbon composite materials to make lighter airframes. "Airbus and Boeing have been using bits of this for a long time but the latest Boeing Dreamliner has the most carbon composite material within its airframe," says Bows. "It makes it considerably lighter and the lighter it is, the less fuel it needs."

Another idea is to use open-rotor or turboprop engines. The technology is not new as such, but they are far more fuel efficient than standard jet engines as the rotor blades can accelerate a bigger mass of air producing significant additional thrust without using any more fuel. They have been sidelined in the past because of complaints of excessive noise but, as oil prices continue to rise, this might become less of an obstacle.

Alternative fuels also present a way for airlines to close the carbon loop. Biofuels mixed with aviation fuel have already been tested by both Virgin and New Zealand Airlines. But, as with the more general issue of biofuels in transport, there are issues around sourcing good biofuel plants that do not displace the growing of food crops.

More radical ideas involve redesigning planes entirely – several teams have come up with the "blended wing" concept. This replaces the traditional design of a plane – a metal tube with wings – to something that looks more like a manta ray. Engineers claim the improved aerodynamics could be more fuel efficient and also quieter.

Talk to engineers and there are plenty of ways to make planes more efficient, the problem lies in implementing the technologies in a meaningful way. "Planes haven't changed much for decades so we're quite sceptical that these technologies are actually that close to coming into operation," says Richard Dyer, aviation campaigner for Friends of the Earth.

Developing a new plane can take decades and even designing new wings or engines can take many years. The problem is that we need to start cutting carbon emissions now.

Air travel might be painted as environmental pariah but the industry seems to understand its image problem and is making moves to deal with it. In 2007, Giovanni Bisignani, chief executive of the International Air Transport Association (IATA), admitted that a growing carbon footprint was no longer politically acceptable. "Climate change will limit our future unless we change our approach from technical to strategic. Air transport must aim to become an industry that does not pollute — zero emissions." He added that the industry had a good record in making environmental improvements to air travel. "Over the last four decades we have reduced noise by 75%, eliminated soot and improved fuel efficiency by 70%. And the billions being invested in new aircraft will make our fleet 25% more fuel efficient by 2020. This will limit the growth of our carbon footprint from today's 2% to 3% in 2050."

Quentin Browell, of IATA, points to increasing fuel efficiency of planes as a measure of the technological improvements in the industry. The average fuel used per 100 passenger kilometres at the moment is four litres. Newer planes reduce this to around 3.5 litres while the Airbus superjumbo is aiming for just three litres. "For our industry, fuel equals environment," he explains. "The less fuel you use, the less emissions you produce. With fuel prices soaring, that's the biggest incentive for the industry too to keep fuel use, hence emissions, down."

There are also ways to cut emissions that are less obvious to passengers. The Intergovernmental Panel on Climate Change argues that there is an inefficiency of up to 12% in the routes planes fly. "There are quite a lot of areas that are grossly inefficient in terms of air traffic management," says Browell. "The European area is one example: you have 34 air traffic control authorities across Europe. In the US, for an area of much the same size, you've got one." This means that planes flying over Europe tend to zigzag from one air traffic control system to another – longer routes mean more fuel is used.

Browell estimates that streamlining routes could save 12m tonnes of CO_2 a year. Last year, IATA shortened 395 routes across the world, which, it says, saved 3.8m tonnes of CO_2.

Browell also points to "green teams" that IATA sends to airlines to help save fuel. "They advise on everything from saving on the weight of seats, trollies and the amount of potable water on board. Last year, those teams saved 7m tonnes of CO_2 across airlines – between 2-14% of those airlines' fuel bills."

Dyer says that while the air industry is certainly aware of the environmental problems it faces, it has a blind spot with how fast it can grow sustainably. "There doesn't seem to be any acceptance that there might have to be curbs on their growth. There seems to be a belief that technology will come along in the future and solve the problem for them. I think it's quite a reckless way of looking at things."

WHAT IS THE UK GOVERNMENT'S POLICY ON AVIATION?

Ministers say the demand for aviation is increasing rapidly and is of vital importance to UK plc. The Department for Transport issued a white paper on the issue in December 2003 looking ahead to the requirements of 2030, which predicted a potential tripling of demand for UK airport capacity. A progress report in December 2006 forecast a rise in the numbers of air passengers using UK airports from 228m per year in 2005 to 490m in 2030. In principle, the government backs the expansion of airports, provided "strict environmental conditions are met". Ministers believe the south-east in particular needs two new runway:, one at Stansted and one at Heathrow.

However, environmental groups and an increasing number of local councils and MPs are voicing opposition. A consultation in 2007-8 on expanding capacity at Heathrow, including a third runway and a sixth terminal, generated 70,000 responses and 3,000 noisy protesters. In 2006, Stansted's initial application for a second runway, which would increase passenger numbers from 24m a year to 68m by 2030, was rejected by Uttlesford district council forcing a public inquiry.

In May 2008 the Sustainable Development Commission and Institute for Public Policy Research called on the government to halt all airport expansion plans pending an independent inquiry into the true economic benefit and environmental impact of aviation.

In tax terms, the government announced at the pre-budget report in 2007 that it intended to replace air passenger duty with a duty payable per plane, rather than per passenger. This reform will take place on 1 November 2009. The government claims the change will send better environmental signals and ensure that aviation makes a greater contribution to covering its environmental costs, while maintaining a "fair level of revenue" from the sector.

Opposition parties had earlier mooted the same idea. In August 2007 the Liberal Democrats proposed adding £10 per person to the price of domestic flights in a bid to reduce global warming. Two months later, at the Conservative party conference, shadow chancellor George Osborne announced that his party would follow the recommendations of a report commissioned from John Gummer and Zac Goldsmith: to replace air passenger duty with an airline pollution duty, which would mean "empty planes will pay the same as the full ones", and newer, cleaner planes would pay less.

HOW GREEN IS THE A380 SUPERJUMBO?

The first commercial flight of the new A380 took off from Singapore in October 2007 headed for Sydney, with a bellyfull of passengers, some donating up to $10,000 to charity for their place in aviation history. If this really was a paradigm shift in flying then it might have warranted all the fanfare, but in reality it illustrated to me just how little we've travelled in terms of aviation innovation since 1970 when the Boeing 747 "Jumbo Jet" first took to the air.

There will be many who marvel at this new plane's engineering prowess, but what really counts is can this plane get as many people from A to B using as little fuel as possible? Much has been made of the A380's green credentials and most of it, sadly, has been vastly overblown. The plane's basic principle is sound – if something is going to take to the air it might as well have as many people on board as possible to maximise the fuel used. But on closer inspection, the Airbus claims lose a lot of their lustre.

Airbus's website says that the plane will burn 2.9 litres of fuel per passenger for every 100km travelled, or, put another way, it will emit 75 grammes of carbon dioxide per passenger kilometre. This, says Airbus, is a better fuel efficiency than a hybrid car. But how did it arrive at that figure? I couldn't find an explanation on the website, and no one from the UK office returned my call. So I'm reliant on the National Centre for Public Policy Research in the US, which did manage to extract the details from Airbus. Airbus told them that the measurements were based on the A380 carrying 555 passengers at a cruising speed of 900km – but with no luggage or cargo on board.

Singapore Airlines has said that its A380s will be set up in the traditional three-class configuration, but will be carrying less than 480 passengers. This is because it wants to give passengers more space – including those paying big bucks to travel in its much-heralded "12 ultra-luxurious suites". (The A380 can, in theory, carry 853 passengers, but it is highly unlikely that any airline will utilise this, except perhaps on some short-range internal routes in, say, China and Japan.) Given that most of these passengers will have hand luggage and a suitcase or two, you can safely assume that the quoted fuel efficiency is going to be less impressive than it first appears. And don't forget that it is rare for a passenger flight to take off without cramming commercial cargo on board too – or that carrying capacity among the so-called legacy carriers who are ordering up these planes is lucky to ever break through the 80% barrier.

This could seem to be unnecessary nit-picking, but for me the far bigger concern is that Airbus predicts these planes will be in service for 40-50 years. With other airlines also investing heavily in Boeing's rival Dreamliner, which has its own much-puffed "eco" claims, we can safely assume that these two planes will be the principal workhorses of the skies for the next several decades. These are the planes that will serve the huge growth that is predicted for the aviation industry over this period – and is what has triggered the huge concern about aviation's fast-increasing environmental impact. This goes a long way to quashing any realistic talk of some huge technofix lying just around the corner – blended-wing designs, hydrogen fuel cells and so on – that would mean we would be able fly without a thought for the atmosphere that our plane carves through.

The truth is that while these tweaks in efficiency are welcome don't believe the hype that they are anything more than just tweaks. That flight from London-Sydney, or wherever, will still come at a considerable carbon cost, whichever plane you are travelling in. Somehow getting fewer people into the skies is the key, not beckoning people on board with inflated eco claims.

Leo Hickman

FLIGHTS IN CONTEXT

**a return
London-Sydney flight
with Qantas via Singapore
emits**

4.63 tonnes
of CO_2 per passenger

according to
carbonresponsible.co.uk

**a return
Edinburgh-Barcelona flight
with British Airways
emits**

0.58 tonnes
of CO_2 per passenger

according to
carbonresponsible.co.uk

**to save this amount of CO_2 by day-to-day
actions at home you would need to:**

reduce your car use by

22,322 km,

wash at 30 degrees for

over 71 years

use energy efficient light bulbs for

2,767 days,

or

wait 676 days

**for your solid wall insulation
to save on heating emissions**

reduce your car use by

2,795 km,

wash at 30 degrees for

over 9 years

use energy efficient light bulbs for

346 days,

or

wait 85 days

**for your solid wall insulation
to save on heating emissions**

A VIEW FROM AFRICA...

Climate change is a result of the rich world's inability to live sustainably and, as with the ozone hole, we in the developing world suffer the worst consequences. The average European emits 9,000kg of CO_2 a year, the average American emits 22,000kg and the average African emits about 1,000kg. This means that while the rich world must decrease its average CO_2 emissions drastically, we Africans are entitled to increase ours moderately as we pull ourselves out of poverty. We are the forest, you are the factory, so why should we be penalised for your smoke?

I help to run Bulungula Lodge, a community-owned lodge in one of the poorest, most remote amaXhosa villages in South Africa. The village has no school, no clinic, no road, no electricity, no shop, no piped water and no toilets. The lodge runs on solar energy, uses compost toilets and recycles its grey water through a lush banana circle. It offsets CO_2 emissions from its vehicles by planting 50 slow-growing forest trees per year and we will soon offer guests the opportunity to offset their airplane emissions by planting three trees of their own.

The community not only jointly owns the lodge, but also runs the activities that allow guests to immerse themselves in the cultural and natural environment: you can walk through the forests with a herbalist learning about traditional medicines; ride horses on the beach; canoe up the Xhora river; or just hang out at the local shebeen, where the traditional umqombothi beer never runs out.

More than 40 jobs have been created by the lodge and associated businesses, which include guided hiking, village cultural tours, a solar restaurant, honey projects, a nursery, a low-pressure, drip-irrigated veggie farm supplying the lodge, guided fishing, and craft-

making. This means that almost half the families in the village have moved on from subsistence farming and now have an income (and thus money for medicines and other essentials).

If this lodge were to close, the only other realistic source of income for local people would be the rich titanium deposits found on the beaches and primary dunes of this coastal paradise. The mining companies have already begun tempting communities with lucrative deals.

I believe the fair way to attribute CO_2 emissions generated by holiday travel is to "give" them to the destination country. In South Africa, we have 1 million foreign tourists flying here annually, each emitting about 2,300kg of CO_2 in the process. When divided by our 45 million population this would raise our average emissions by a mere 51kg per person per year. It would be utter hypocrisy to demand that South Africa reduce its average emissions by 51kg a year when Africa is by far the least polluting continent on Earth, and in the process destroy its tourism economy creating widespread poverty. Instead of increasing our emissions by building factories, we prefer to fly tourists to our continent. You wouldn't dispute our right to build a factory, so why complain about these flights? This isn't "creative" accounting, this is fair accounting.

Yes, cancel your holidays to Europe, Australia and the US, countries that have grown rich from climatic destruction/ industrialisation. Cancel your business trips (use video conferencing) and holidays to the rich world (by train, plane or bus), and save up for a worthwhile holiday to the developing world. Your CO_2 emissions are on us!

Dave Martin

Maasai reserve, Kenya
photo: shutterstock/franck camhi

JUST HOW BAD IS IT TO...

So it's sorted, then. Travelling by train or coach is greener than going by car. Similarly, driving yourself to a destination is greener than flying there. As a rule, yes, but let's apply the brakes a little. Not all journeys are directly comparable, as our journey map on page 78 shows. Rail typically wins the day in terms of lower carbon emissions, especially on journeys that pass through France due to the nuclear factor. But there are some anomalies. The greenest choice can vary depending on how many people are travelling and which mode of transport allows the most direct route. For instance, travelling from Newcastle to Amsterdam, going by ferry can actually be the least polluting way to go – but only by a whisker – because it allows a more direct route as the crow flies than going by train.

Pack the car

The most important variable is the number of passengers in the vehicle when choosing to go by car. When just one person is in the vehicle, going by car suddenly becomes comparable to travelling by plane in terms of carbon emissions per passenger kilometre. However, if the car is occupied by more than two people the improved efficiency is considerable. In fact, in some situations, four or more people in a car can even start to compete with travelling on a diesel train over the same distance. For example, on the Edinburgh to Bristol route, four or more people in a car comes out as the least polluting option per passenger journey. Good news, perhaps, for large families seeking an alternative to the hell that is the modern-day airport. (See page 208 for games to keep kids entertained on long journeys!)

Is high-speed train always a green option?

Yes, if you're "only" concerned about your carbon emissions. But things are never that simple. The high-speed intercity network that services France (and includes Eurostar) is largely powered by electricity produced by nuclear power stations and hydroelectric dams. Nothing divides environmentalists quite as much as nuclear power, but only the most principled environmentalist would refuse to travel through France by train because of the still unresolved issue of what is to be done with nuclear waste. It would be wrong, though, to describe high-speed trains, without hesitation, as the "greenest" option. It's more accurate to describe them as the most carbon-efficient form of high-speed transport.

The fine detail

We compare seven typical holiday journeys from around the UK, and calculate the best transport options for individuals, couples and families. But comparing emissions between various modes of transport always comes with some important caveats and footnotes. For example, those with a beady eye will probably wonder why the lowest carbon emissions for travelling by car are listed as 170g of CO_2 per passenger kilometre (CO_2/ppkm) when the most efficient cars on the market boast emissions rates closer to 100g CO_2/ppkm. Forum for the Future, the sustainability charity which collated these figures, explains that this is because "well-to-tank" emissions have been included to better reflect the true environmental impact of travel. These are the emissions created getting the various fuels – petrol, diesel, marine or aviation fuel – out of the ground and to the fuel tank. Typically, this adds about 17-19% to each CO_2/ppkm calculation. Forum for the Future also stresses that real life emissions tend to be higher than those obtained in official tests and that their motoring figures represent the most widely used high- and low-emission cars rather than the best and worst performing models. In addition, all emissions figures for flying have been doubled to account for the "radiative forcing" impacts of aviation (see p.60-61 for more on radiative forcing).

Leo Hickman

Source: Forum for the Future

Carbon emissions (kg CO_2/km)		
	Low	High
🚗 Car	0.18	0.35
Car – 2 people	0.09	0.18
🚌 Intercity coach	0.03	0.11
Urban bus	0.09	0.12
🚆 Local rail UK	0.05	0.09
Intercity rail UK	0.048	0.14
Eurostar	0.01	0.02
Intercity rail EU	0.003	0.14
⛴ Ferry	0.06	0.14
✈ Domestic flight	0.22	0.49
Short haul int'l	0.19	0.42
Long haul int'l	0.23	0.26

FLY

Aircraft engines are powered by burning kerosene, which emits gases and particles into the atmosphere during flight. As well as releasing carbon dioxide (CO_2), aircraft emit water vapour, oxides of nitrogen (NO_x), oxides of sulphur (SO_x) and soot. Water vapour is a greenhouse gas that, like CO_2, absorbs heat being emitted from the Earth's surface. Subsonic aeroplanes (the majority) fly at altitudes between nine and 13km. At this level, NO_x increases the concentration of ozone, another greenhouse gas that contributes to global warming. Meanwhile, particles of sulphate from sulphur oxides and soot act as surfaces for water vapour to condense onto when hot air from the engine hits the colder air at altitude. This is how contrails (condensation trails) form and if the air is moist these can create cirrus clouds. Contrails and cirrus clouds reflect some solar radiation, causing cooling, but they also absorb radiation, emitting it back downwards and helping to warm the Earth. Scientists believe that the various actions caused by the cocktail of emissions from aircraft contribute to warming the atmosphere at a magnitude of two or three times greater than the effect of carbon dioxide alone.

Modern aircraft are 70% more fuel-efficient than those designed four decades ago and biofuels may offer a way for airlines to reduce their greenhouse gas emissions, though these are not without their own controversies.

DRIVE

In addition to emitting CO_2, petrol, diesel and alternative-fuel engines release carbon monoxide (CO), NO_x, un-burnt hydrocarbons and fine particles. Carbon monoxide reduces the blood's ability to carry oxygen to organs. At high concentrations it can be fatal; lower levels can pose a health risk to people with heart disease. At ground level, NO_x can cause or exacerbate respiratory problems. It also contributes to smog and acid rain, damages plants, contributes to forming ozone, (which acts as a greenhouse gas at ground level and also irritates the lungs when breathed in) and can contribute to forming fine particles. Fine particles cause various lung problems. The World Health Organization estimates that 100,000 deaths a year in Europe may be related to fine particles.

In 2008 the EU set a target to reduce carbon emissions to 130g/km for 65% of new cars by 2012, rising to 100% of new cars in 2015. Hybrid petrol-electric cars are becoming more widespread, as are fuels containing a percentage of biofuels. Since April 2008 all petrol and diesel sold on forecourts in the UK has had to contain 2.5% biofuel. There is a proposed EU-wide target for fuels to contain 10% biofuel by 2020. This was intended to be a lower-carbon fuel, but there is now great uncertainty over the carbon savings delivered by biofuels, and they have also been accused of pushing up food prices in the developing world.

TAKE A TRAIN

Trains run on electricity or diesel. The exhaust from diesel-powered trains contains nitrogen oxide (NO_x), sulphur dioxide (SO_2) and particles. NO_x and particles can cause or exacerbate respiratory problems. Older trains use iron block tread brakes. Heavy braking on these trains emits a fine iron dust which sticks to land, buildings and cars close by. Electric trains do not release air pollutants at the point of use but production of electricity from fossil fuels contributes to global warming and acid rain. However, rail is still a relatively eco-friendly transport option. According to Friends of the Earth, although rail carries 7% of UK traffic, it contributes only 0.2% of carbon monoxide, 2%

of nitrogen oxide and 2.5% of sulphur dioxide emissions.

Emissions of CO_2 per passenger km have fallen 22% on passenger rail in the UK since 1995/6, over twice the improvement in car emissions. However, this has mostly been achieved by the greater number of passengers using trains and changes in the carbon intensity of the national electricity generation mix. Some train companies have committed themselves to improving their environmental record further. For example: Virgin launched the UK's first biofuel train in 2007; Southwest Trains has achieved the ISO14001 award for sustainability at all its traincare depots and is switching to low-sulphur fuel, and Eurostar has pledged to reduce its CO_2 emissions per passenger km by 25% by 2012. FirstGroup aims to reduce CO_2 emissions from its UK rail division by 10% on 2006 levels by 2012.

TAKE A FERRY

Ferry engines emit significant amounts of NO_x along with SO_x, hydrocarbons and particles.

Although most ferries use marine diesel which is lower in sulphur than the fuel used by container ships, there is still room for improvement. One ferry that had a catalytic converter fitted and switched to using ultra low-sulphur fuel, New York's Alice Austen, reduced its annual emissions of nitrogen oxides by 16.5 tons and particles by 25%.

TAKE A BUS/COACH

Like cars, bus and coach engines emit carbon monoxide, hydrocarbons, oxides of nitrogen and particles. Buses that sit with their engines idling emit considerable concentrations of these pollutants. Urban buses tend to travel in lower gears, stop more often and be less full as they operate in off-peak hours. Intercity and international coaches are extremely carbon efficient as they are usually well filled and spend more of their journeys in higher gears, cruising at steady speeds. Perhaps surprisingly, intercity buses actually have the best carbon footprint of all, after French trains.

The EU has laid down increasingly stringent emissions standards for diesel-engine buses and lorries since 1992. Meanwhile, London has introduced a low-emission zone.

TAKE A CRUISE

Cruise ships emit the same pollutants as ferries (see above) and more besides. Essentially floating towns, they are major polluters. Typically carrying 2,000 passengers and 900 crew, a single cruise ship can produce 25,000 gallons of human waste and 143,000 gallons of greywater (this is waste water that can contain detergents from cleaning, bleach and other toxic chemicals) per day. Cruise ships can legally dump raw sewage when only three miles from shore. There are very few controls on where ships dump greywater. Onboard facilities such as laundries, restaurants, cinemas and swimming pools are all energy-intensive.

In 2005, new legislation was introduced requiring all new cruise ships to be fitted with a sewage treatment plant and other disinfecting and waste treatment systems. Existing ships have until 2010 to fit the required equipment. The World cruise ship has a full UV sewage treatment plant onboard.

Carolyn Fry

THE GREENEST WAY TO GO...

Rail is usually the greenest option but this can can vary depending on the route, the type of fuel and the number of people travelling.

Edinburgh – Bristol

		CARBON KG/GROUP	
		LOW	HIGH
✈	1 person	114	252
	2 people	228	504
	4 people	456	1008
🚆	1 person	29	81
	2 people	58	162
	4 people	116	324
🚗	1 person	106	212
	2 people	106	212
	4 people	106	212

London – Barcelona

		CARBON KG/GROUP	
		LOW	HIGH
✈	1 person	213	327
	2 people	425	654
	4 people	851	1308
🚆	1 person	19	46
	2 people	38	91
	4 people	75	183
🚗	1 person	259	520
	2 people	259	520
	4 people	259	520

DATA AND ANALYSIS COURTESTY OF

forum for the future
action for a sustainable world

WWW.FORUMFORTHEFUTURE.ORG

Newcastle – Amsterdam

	CARBON KG/GROUP	
	LOW	HIGH
✈ 1 person	97	149
2 people	194	298
4 people	388	596
🚆 1 person	35	58
2 people	70	117
4 people	141	233
🚗 + ⛴ 1 person	35	86
2 people	64	160
4 people	124	308

London – Budapest

	CARBON KG/GROUP	
	LOW	HIGH
✈ 1 person	276	425
2 people	552	850
4 people	1104	1700
🚆 1 person	52	219
2 people	104	438
4 people	208	876
🚌 1 person	51	185
2 people	102	369
4 people	204	738
🚗 1 person	302	608
2 people	302	608
4 people	302	608

London – Geneva

	CARBON KG/GROUP	
	LOW	HIGH
✈ 1 person	140	215
2 people	280	430
4 people	559	860
🚆 1 person	7	8
2 people	14	16
4 people	27	33
🚌 1 person	29	105
2 people	58	210
4 people	117	419
🚗 1 person	170	342
2 people	170	342
4 people	170	342

Manchester – Florence

	CARBON KG/GROUP	
	LOW	HIGH
✈ 1 person	268	413
2 people	537	826
4 people	1074	1652
🚆 1 person	44	76
2 people	87	151
4 people	175	302
🚗 1 person	334	670
2 people	334	670
4 people	334	670

Birmingham – Nice

	CARBON KG/GROUP	
	LOW	HIGH
✈ 1 person	264	584
2 people	528	1168
4 people	1056	2336
🚆 1 person	18	37
2 people	36	74
4 people	72	148
🚗 1 person	278	558
2 people	278	558
4 people	278	558

A 'pavilion' pod at Whitepod
eco-camp, Monthey, Switzerland

photo: Whitepod

CARBON OFFSETTING

The average Briton is responsible for emiting 10 tonnes of CO_2 per year. This compares with almost 20 tonnes per US citizen, but scientists say that a sustainable annual quota for the planet's 6bn inhabitants is more like two tonnes each. So we all need to give some serious thought to reducing our carbon footprints. Although China has now overtaken the US as the world's largest producer of CO_2 – creating 24% of global emissions compared to 22% by the United States – most of the world's population has some way to go before reaching levels anywhere near as dangerous as those in developed countries. China's emissions per capita are still at 5.1 tonnes while India produces just 1.8 tonnes per person.

The first step towards reducing your footprint is to calculate it, and carbon calculators are springing up for this purpose all over the web. Bear in mind that even the best ones will only provide you with an estimate rather than a cast-iron calculation. Next you will need to find ways to reduce your direct and indirect consumption of fossil fuels. (The *Guardian* has extensive ethical living tips at guardian.co.uk/environment/ethicalliving.)

But what about the emissions – such as those from travel. Step forward the offsetting companies, which offer to "neutralise" your emissions by funding carbon-saving projects elsewhere in the world. There is much debate over whether these schemes are a valid tool in the fight against climate change, and here we explore this issue in detail, as well as recommending the best online calculators.

Offsetting – the great debate

The idea of carbon offsetting is simple enough. Each time you fly, drive or hop on an energy-guzzling cruise, you calculate the amount of carbon your action will generate and then pay a company to save the equivalent amount of carbon from reaching the atmosphere elsewhere. There are now more than 60 companies and charities providing offsetting services in the UK, including ClimateCare, Carbon Footprint and Pure – the Clean Planet Trust. They use a wide range of mechanisms to "neutralise" our use of carbon. These include: protecting mangrove swamps in Madagascar by providing alternative building materials for locals, thus preventing the release of carbon dioxide that would happen if the mangroves were cut down; capturing methane that would otherwise be released from a disused coal mine in Pennsylvania; and conserving virgin cloud forest in Ecuador that would release vast amounts of carbon dioxide if logged.

The concept of carbon offsetting dates back to 1989, when US company Applied Energy Services sought to build a new coal-fired power plant. It got the go-ahead thanks largely to its proposed "mitigation project", which involved planting 50m pine and eucalyptus trees in Guatemala. Trees use carbon dioxide (CO_2) from the atmosphere, along with sunlight and water, to produce the carbohydrates they need to survive. Therefore, while they are thriving, they suck CO_2 out of the atmosphere. The project was later deemed a "dismal failure", because it criminalised activities such as gathering firewood, used inappropriate species for the region, promoted conflict over the rights to trees and did not achieve the anticipated offset level.

In 2002, the rock band Coldplay helped raise the profile of the industry when they opted to offset emissions from their album A Rush of Blood to the Head by planting 10,000 mango trees in Karnataka, India. However, many of the trees died from insufficient water; a combination of drought and poor management were blamed for the scheme's failure. Subsequently, a study by scientists in California concluded that forests' usefulness in helping combat climate change depends on their latitude. Only trees below 20° latitude cool the planet, by around 0.7°C. This is because water evaporating from trees in the humid tropics increases cloudiness, which has a cooling effect. Elsewhere, the solar energy absorbed by dark tree canopies and radiated back out as heat either balances the cooling effect of removing carbon from the atmosphere or exceeds it. In 2006, WWF, Friends of the Earth and Greenpeace released a joint statement declaring that they do not support forestry projects for offsetting carbon emissions.

Today, most offsetting companies have diversified from tree-planting to offer schemes spanning conservation, renewable energy, waste processing and low-carbon technologies. However, calculating the exact carbon savings from individual projects is still an inexact science. For example, achieving the projected long-term carbon saving from replacing traditional light-bulbs with low-energy ones in a township might only happen if the people given new bulbs can afford to replace them with low-energy ones when they run out; monitoring is vital (see page 88 for a 2007 survey of 13 offsetting company websites by Which?).

A recent study conducted by Defra found that people remain suspicious about offsetting projects. Although 65% were aware of the concept, only 7% claimed to have contributed to an offsetting project. The government hopes to rectify this with its code of best practice, which was drafted in February 2008. Offsetting projects that meet the requirements of the Clean Development Mechanism – the means by which developed nations finance projects in developing countries to reduce greenhouse gases under the Kyoto Protocol and receive a Certified Emissions Reduction certificate for each tonne of CO_2-equivalent saved – will be able to apply for accreditation and, if successful, display a kitemark.

The Tourism Industry Carbon Offset Service (TICOS), which aims to help travel and tourism companies reduce emissions and boost levels of sustainability in their operations, has criticised the code for being limited to Kyoto-compliant projects; it believes that there are many high-quality projects that achieve benefits but that cannot be accredited because they are outside of the regulatory market. Defra is encouraging such non-Kyoto scheme providers to develop their own standard, as less formal voluntary offsets, termed

VERs. These may, in time, be incorporated in the code. At present, there are two major accreditation schemes for such "voluntary" offsets: the voluntary gold standard launched by WWF in 2006 and the voluntary carbon standard, developed by the Climate Group and the International Emissions Trading Association.

There is no doubt that offsetting is becoming an accepted means by which people and industries can compensate for emissions caused by taking holidays. As well as launching TICOS for businesses, the travel industry is making efforts to help individuals become greener when they go on holiday through its reducemyfootprint.travel website. ABTA (The Travel Association) and AITO (Association of Independent Tour Operators) have jointly set up the site to advise individuals and businesses on ways to reduce carbon emissions as well as providing offsetting services in conjunction with the Travel Foundation and TICOS.

Nonetheless, environmental groups remain concerned that offsetting schemes promote the idea that people can continue to emit greenhouse gases guilt-free by apparently "neutralising" them. The International Institute for Environment and Development and the New Economics Foundation hope to address such criticisms with its new scheme ADMit. The programme aims for people to reduce emissions first and foremost but then to contribute money to projects to help the hardest hit nations begin adapting to the effects of climate change. The scheme shifts the emphasis from "paying money to carry on polluting" onto making compensation payments to countries likely to be hardest hit by climate change.

photo: David Mansell

A plane in flight near Stansted airport viewed from Hatfield forest in Hertfordshire. The ancient woodland is under threat from the expansion of the airport.

THE CASE FOR OFFSETTING:

The voluntary carbon market is built on a desire to do the right thing. The principle is that together we take a world view, recognising that emissions generated in one place will be felt in another. Once we have reduced our impact at home, we can then take another step: offsetting the value of carbon we use in the UK to fund projects that will reduce emissions elsewhere in the world.

Many ask: wouldn't we be more effective by focussing all our efforts (and money) nearer home? There is much to be done in the UK and this government is committed to some tough targets. They must be held to account for those, but it's not the job of the voluntary market to make it easier for them; our work must be "in addition to" that of the state.

And when you consider that £12,000 for solar panels on an average house in the UK will save 40 tonnes of carbon over 50 years, providing one family with a warm home – compared to £12,000 to buy 400 fuel-efficient cooking stoves to replace open fires, saving 1,200 tonnes over three years, and benefiting 2,500 Ugandans – the logic seems simple.

Carbon offsetting is a pragmatic part of a bigger solution. Our message is "do offset, but don't just offset". We know that some critics think offsetting is a dupe – suggesting that people can "wipe out" the damage they cause by writing a cheque. ClimateCare prefers to talk to customers about becoming "carbon responsible" precisely because there is nothing neutral about carbon, and such loopholes in language allow room for misunderstanding.

When ClimateCare began in 1997, the simplest way to express the idea of putting a price on carbon and investing in environmentally sound projects to reduce emissions was to talk about offsetting, and the account-book language of being "carbon neutral" was born. Today, as climate change is more clearly understood by consumers and businesses alike, our responses have become more sophisticated – and it's time for the language of offsetting to catch up.

Edward Hanrahan, executive director, ClimateCare

The debate around offsetting is too often framed in black and white – proponents can oversell its benefits, whereas opponents often reject it outright. The reality is somewhat greyer. The concern that offsetting enables us to carry on with behaviours that are inherently unsustainable cannot be easily dismissed. But, conversely, offsetting – if done well – can be the first entry point for individuals to start thinking about their own contribution to climate change.

And the best offsets not only result in genuine emissions reductions, but can also have positive secondary benefits by providing employment, protecting biodiversity, or by increasing the reliability of electricity supply.

That said, the responsible traveller cannot simply turn to offsets, they must also look for actions further up what we call the "carbon management hierarchy". The avoidance of emissions, their reduction through energy efficiency and the replacement of high-carbon energy sources with low or zero-carbon alternatives must come first.

This means holidaying closer to home (distance travelled, rather than the method of travel, is often the real source of carbon emissions); looking for lower-carbon alternatives to flying; and taking fewer, longer trips when we do fly. It might also mean embracing a cyclic approach to holidaying, whereby any long-haul holiday is followed in succeeding years by a regional, and then a local holiday.

Iain Watt, principle sustainability adviser, Forum for the Future

THE CASE AGAINST OFFSETTING:

Fundamentally, offsetting is an accounting trick. Investing in a good scheme or project isn't an intrinsically bad thing to do. It just doesn't actually "offset" emissions over here. There is no such thing as "carbon neutrality". Any tonne of carbon in the atmosphere is there for its lifetime and no investment – no matter how worthy – in better cooking stoves or low-energy lighting in the developing world will make it go away.

In addition, citizens of developed countries making investments in the south can increase opportunity costs for those communities – if we make the cheap investments now, they are potentially left with more expensive ones in the future, at the same time the climate change will have increasingly significant impacts on vulnerable communities.

Advocates – and salesmen – of offsets will tell you offsetting raises awareness of climate change. Perhaps that is true, but if you're looking at a global situation where carbon emissions must peak in the next seven years and then dramatically reduce, awareness-raising is no longer an adequate response.

It sends the misleading message to the consumer that offsetting is a meaningful response to climate change – and it's not. Offsetting won't make a damned bit of difference as long as airports continue to expand, aviation spirit is untaxed and governments continue to encourage growth in aviation.

At the moment, the governments in this country and elsewhere in the developed world are counting on markets in carbon to solve this problem. The idea is that we can buy "carbon reduction credits" somewhere, anywhere in the world cheaper than we can achieve them here. In reality, we need to reduce emissions here and elsewhere. Reducing all efforts to control climate change to the level of a transaction, that is, a richer person buying a credit from a poorer person to continue their polluting lifestyle appears superficially attractive, but is inadequate – and dishonest.

Charlie Kronick, Greenpeace

"What if I told you that for £2.50 you could cheat on your girlfriend and then offset the damage by paying someone else to be faithful?"

"That doesn't make any sense, you're not offsetting anything, the only difference it makes is in our minds."

This is a conversation I had with a man while shooting the short film CheatNeutral. CheatNeutral told people that infidelity was no longer something they had to feel bad about – it was something they could offset. In just the same way, it is possible to "offset" the carbon emissions from a flight by paying a company to reduce emissions somewhere else.

People who took CheatNeutral seriously were outraged. They were disgusted that we were encouraging people to forget about their cheating and not address their relationship problems. "That's terrible, you're just encouraging people to cheat more!" a US radio phone-in listener told me. But this is exactly how the real carbon offset companies work. Although they claim they encourage us to reduce our emissions, the message of the companies is very much "pay and forget". Their primary aim is not to help us find ways of reducing our emissions – but to sell us offsets.

Offsetting also produces real problems in less developed countries. Getting development right is difficult. When a project has to produce carbon reductions to generate offsets, the chance of providing genuine benefit to a community is small. Community benefit is no longer the primary aim of the project if it is funded by offset money.

So what can you do instead? What is really needed is political action. Climate change is a global problem that needs coordinated action from all governments. They need to cap global emissions at a safe level and share the rights to those emissions fairly. There are lots of things you can do to change government policy. First find out more about climate change and the kind of policies needed to tackle it. Then use your influence as a citizen to change things: join pressure groups, write to your MP, attend marches and take part in peaceful protests. Talk to your friends and family and explain why you're concerned and what you're doing about it.

Alex Randall, the Centre for Alternative Technology

HOW TO MEASURE YOUR CARBON FOOTPRINT

In a matter of years, the term "carbon footprint" has gone from being an obscure phrase to being an entry in the Oxford English dictionary. It is defined by carbonfootprint.com as "a measure of the impact human activities have on the environment in terms of the amount of greenhouse gases produced, measured in units of carbon dioxide".

There are two ways in which we consume greenhouse gases. First, we directly use up fossil fuels when we draw on electricity and gas to heat and power our homes; when we fill up our cars with petrol and diesel; and when we fly. Second, we indirectly contribute to greenhouse gas emissions through energy that is "embedded" in the items we buy and the leisure activities we participate in.

Calculate your footprint

The first step towards reducing your impact is to calculate the size of your footprint. Carbon calculators vary widely in how they measure your footprint and the level of accuracy they offer.

For an all-round estimate of your direct greenhouse consumption, the government's Act on CO_2 calculator (actonco2.direct.gov.uk/carboncalc/html/) is a good starting point. It uses data and factors verified by government departments to calculate the carbon footprint generated by your travel as well as your household's heating, lighting and use of appliances.

Carbon Footprint provides a similar calculator, but theirs also makes an estimate of your indirect footprint, taking into account basic information on food choices, recycling, leisure activities and shopping habits.

A more in-depth carbon calculator is that offered by Resurgence (resurgence.org/resources/carbon-calculator.html). This requires you to provide more detailed information, such as your electricity use for each quarter in kilowatts (provided on your bill), and the mileage of different journeys taken by road, rail and air. It also attempts to include some indirect greenhouse contributions in sections such as "fuel-intensive leisure activities". This calculator was developed by Mukti Mitchell, the pioneer of low-carbon living, who designed the zero-emission yacht, Explorer.

Flight emission calculators

With aviation being the fastest-growing source of greenhouse gas emissions, many offsetting companies have set up dedicated flight emissions calculators. These estimate the footprint of your holiday flights, then show you how to offset them by contributing to carbon-reducing projects, such as schemes supplying fuel-efficient stoves in Uganda or installing wind turbines in China. Climate Care (climatecare.org/), a corporate partner of Guardian News & Media), and the CarbonNeutral Company (carbonneutral.com/cncalculators/flightcalculator.asp) both offer this service.

Be warned that there is great variation in the figures provided by flight emissions calculators. One of the better ones is ChooseClimate's emissions calculator (chooseclimate.org/flying/mapcalc.html), which enables you to specify the type of ticket, model of plane and occupancy rate. It displays its findings as kilograms of fuel used, kilograms of CO_2 generated, and the total warming effect. The latter takes into account other emissions from aviation, such as nitrogen oxides and water vapour, and the fact that CO_2 emitted at high altitude has an enhanced warming effect.

Calculators for other types of travel are beginning to become available. The website CO2balance.com enables you to calculate emissions from some rail and car journeys. Meanwhile, transportdirect.info provides a means to compare the emissions made by a small car, large car, train, coach and plane for a set distance. It is likely to be some time, however, before we can accurately compare travel to a wide range of destinations by train, plane, ferry, car and coach.

Carolyn Fry

THE OFFSETTING SCHEMES TO TRUST

In April 2008, *Which? Money* magazine investigated the UK offsetting market and published its concerns over the discrepancies in emissions calculations and offset costs. It also cricitised some companies' lack of verifiable projects and clear audit trails for customers' payments. The companies that *Which? Money* felt gave the most relevant and easily accessible information were: Climate Care, Blue Ventures Carbon Offset, Pure, and the World Land Trust.

In the table below, the magazine's researchers rate 13 UK offsetting companies on various aspects of their service from website ease of use to transparency over funding. The total emissions figure is based on a couple living in a two-bedroom semi-detatched house in west London, spending £500 and £300 a year on gas and electricity respectively, driving a petrol-engine Ford Focus 8,000 miles a year and taking one return flight each year from London Heathrow to Barcelona.

>> CARBON OFFSETTING WEBSITES COMPARED

Company	Examples of what it does with your money	Website ratings — Ease of use	Website ratings — Project details	Website ratings — Financial data	Offset calculators on site	Tips on cutting CO2	How much CO2? (tonnes)	Cost to consumer (£)
Blue Ventures Carbon Offset	Development projects mainly in Madagascar	★★★★	★★★★★	★★★★	Flights. Recommends Defra calculator otherwise	✓	6.44	77.28[a]
Carbon Clear	Kyoto-compliant and voluntary schemes	★★★	★★★★	★	Flights and cars	✓	6.58	49.35[b]
Carbon Footprint	Renewable energy projects and tree planting	★★★★	★★★★	★★	Flights, public transport, cars and household energy	✓	3.358	25.19–58.75[c]
The CarbonNeutral Company	Renewable energy work in India; restoring English forests	★★★	★★★★★	★★	Flights, cars and household energy	✓	10.5	78.75–147.00[c]
Carbon Offsets	Fire efficiency and windfarm projects	★★★	★★★	★	Flights, public transport, cars and household energy	✓	8.1	56.70–[c] 157.95[d]
Carbon Responsible	Funding UK tree planting	★★★	★★★	★	Flights and vehicles	✓	7.815	66.43–176.93[b]
Climate Care	Efficient stove and rainforest reforestation schemes	★★★★	★★★★★	★★★★★★	Flights, cars and household energy	✓	7.41	55.55
CO2 Balance	Supplying solar ovens in Africa; planting forests in UK	★★★	★★★★★	★★★	Flights, public transport, cars and household energy	✓	9.98	79.84–99.71[c]
Equiclimate	Buying and retiring Kyoto-compliant carbon credits	★★	★★★	★★	Flights, cars and household energy	✓	7.996	156.40
Flying Forest	Planting indigenous trees in southern Africa	★★★	★	★	No – flat donation per flight of £5 or £10	✗	n/a	n/a
The Offset Carbon Company	Supplying energy-efficient stoves to Nepal	★★★★	★★	★	Flights, cars and household energy	✓	8.18	77.72
Pure – The Clean Planet Trust	Kyoto-compliant projects in India, China and Brazil	★★★★	★★★★★	★★★★★★	Flights, cars and household energy	✓	9.5	124.45[e]
World Land Trust	Conservation work, including tree planting	★★★★★	★★★★★	★★★★	Flights, daily travel and household energy	✓	8.85	132.75[d]

a Defra calculator used for gas, electricity and car emission calculation b Defra calculator used for gas and electricity calculations c Range of products available. Prices vary d Gas and electricity figures converted to usage in Kwh e After Gift Aid

Source: "Is carbon offsetting worth the money", *Which? Money*, April 2008. which.co.uk

CAN YOU MEASURE A HOTEL ROOM'S CARBON EMISSIONS?

Yes, thanks to a unit of measurement invented in 2008 known as the CarePar, or Carbon Emission Per Available Room. A CarePar score is based a room's physical dimensions as well as the emissions created by the direct and semi-direct operations of the hotel. So routine energy use and staff business travel are taken into account, while food miles, staff commutes and the embedded carbon in building materials are not.

"This scheme is specifically about carbon. It's the one area you can accurately measure," explains Peter Ducker, who dreamed up the idea after a career in the hotel industry. "In a couple of years' time I wouldn't be surprised if we hadn't extended our remit to other considerations such as water." Currently, a simple gold, silver or bronze rating ranks a hotel's less quantifiable policies on recycling, grey water and the environmental impact of their suppliers.

CarePar scores are available for both overnight stays and half-day meeting room hires in participating hotels. The idea is that leisure and business travellers compare emissions between hotel brands and venues before booking in, thereby encouraging hotels to reduce their CarePar scores through efficiency measures.

According to Ducker, a UK hotel room scoring 30kg per night is "doing very well" as most will be at 35-45kg. "Down at a Mediterranean resort it might be lower," he explains, but "a hotel in New York will be higher than in London" because the ambient temperature is more variable.

The Hotel Carbon Index Company, which developed the scheme with involvement from the Carbon Consultancy, aims to integrate its CarePar scores with a number of online booking engines to increase visibility.

Hotels pay £300-500 per year to be CarePar rated and must submit their own data every six months. Though they are not physically inspected, they face spot checks of utility bills at random or if their figures seem suspicious.

Old steam locomotive in Brocken, Germany

SECTION TWO

WAY TO GO...

BY TRAIN OR BUS

Travelling by coach or electricity-powered train are two of the most carbon efficient modes of transport and offer our most viable alternatives to flying around the UK and Europe. Fares can also be very competitive if booked ahead, while overnight services relieve you of a hotel bill. Encouragingly, recent upgrades to high-speed rail links are beginning to change our travelling patterns. Eurostar recorded a 21% rise in bookings in the first quarter of 2008, following the opening of the 186mph St Pancras-Channel Tunnel line. The coach industry is equally bullish about the future, predicting that spending on overseas coach holidays will increase by 45% by 2011.

 **Why I love ... train journeys**

You've heard of the magician's code, right? Well, the rail code is even more secretive. We don't want just anyone discovering the joys of a weekend rail break, and clogging up the dining cars. Not when everyone is seemingly so content to be herded around by the no-frills airlines. But it's time to break the code. Partly because of climate change, but, to be honest, I just can't keep it to myself any more. Not when I keep seeing footage of people screaming at some poor woman behind a counter because their flight has been cancelled, especially when she's clearly still traumatised by the orange smock she's being forced to wear.

There's the two-hour check-in and being forced to wait in a hangar where you're bombarded with casino lighting. Then you have to re-enact a pitch invasion with your fellow detainees and wrestle your way to a seat. After that, the doors are sealed, everyone gulps and finally you end up being dumped in an airport miles from where you actually want to be.

A weekend break is not supposed to be book-ended by the kind of false experience and strain that makes you down six vodkas to calm your nerves before and after you've landed. The journey is not supposed to be an ordeal for you to whinge about with a mutter under your breath.

The argument in favour of it, so it seems to me, is that anything that takes a bit more time isn't as good as something that's quick. Hmm, well not when you're talking about sex, obviously, or food, or friendships, or when you stop and think about it, most of the other experiences that make being human such a delight. If you decided to go out for a walk, would you take the quickest route alongside a motorway or spend a few more hours to get there by ambling through beautiful countryside?

So it is with long-distance trains, especially in Europe. Compared to flying, it's an effortless and rewarding experience. You've got the luxury of the dining car, and the comfort of a cabin to sleep in, not to mention being able to wander about and meet people. But the real joy of the experience is not dependent on the class of ticket you buy.

When in your life are you literally forced to do nothing but sit and think? You could mull over the problems troubling you. Or even spend some time watching the memories of your life that make you smile behind your eyes (try doing that at 35,000ft with the drone of the engines and the buzz of Hollywood around you).

Immerse yourself, languidly, in your own hopes and dreams for a change. Fight back against the rituals of the modern world and try taking your time. Before you know it, you'll be away from it all in body and mind.

(Just don't tell anyone I told you, OK?)

Dan Kieran

A corridor on a Polish passenger train

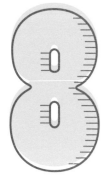

Weekend breaks by train

BARCELONA AND FIGUERES

Head south from London on Friday on the 3pm Eurostar to France. There's just time for a vin rouge in a Parisian cafe before boarding the "trainhotel" to Barcelona. Dinner in the diner, a night snuggled in clean sheets in your sleeper, fresh croissant and coffee in the trainhotel's cafe-bar, and before you know it you're in central Barcelona, arriving 8.30am on Saturday. After a weekend rambling on the Ramblas, gasping at Gaudí and tasting the tapas, the 9pm trainhotel on Sunday night will get you back to central London at 11:55am on Monday. For something different, leave the trainhotel at Figueres, two hours short of Barcelona, find a cafe for breakfast then check out the remarkable Salvador Dalí museum. You can visit Dali's equally remarkable house on the coast at Cadaques a few miles away by bus or taxi. Eurostar to Paris starts at £59 return, trainhotel fares from Paris start at £60 each way in a four-bed sleeper, £92 each way in a two-bed sleeper. There are no airport taxes, no extra to pay to get to and from remote airports, and morning arrivals and evening departures mean a smaller hotel bill than when you fly.

The Trevi Fountain at sunrise, Rome

photo: shutterstock/ MASSIMO MERLINI

BERLIN AND COLDITZ

Leave Waterloo on the 6pm Eurostar to Brussels, and switch to a modern German sleeper train which will whisk you overnight to the newly reborn capital of Germany. A knock on the door next morning announces coffee and croissant delivered to your compartment, in time for a city centre arrival at 8.30am. For something different, head south and visit the infamous castle at Colditz, an hour beyond Leipzig by bus. Fares from around £117 return with couchette or £249 return in a two-bed sleeper. See seat61.com/Germany.htm or call German Railways on 0871 8 80 80 66.

BRUSSELS AND AMSTERDAM

Inclusive fares from London to Amsterdam start at £69 return. Take the Eurostar to Brussels and the hourly InterCity train on to Amsterdam, total journey time three hours. You can break your journey for up to 24 hours in Brussels, making it possible to hop on a Friday night Eurostar to Brussels for some moules et frites in the Grande Place, then move on to Amsterdam at your leisure on Saturday morning. A Sunday afternoon train from Amsterdam will get you back to London that night.

KRAKOW AND AUSCHWITZ

Leave London on Thursday evening by Eurostar and the sleeper to Berlin, then take the EuroCity train "Wawel" from Berlin across Poland to Krakow, arriving Friday evening. Spend Saturday exploring Krakow and its royal castle, and on Sunday visit Auschwitz, an hour to the south by local train. Take the Sunday night sleeper from Krakow to Berlin, then comfortable high-speed trains back to Waterloo arriving on Monday night. Eurostar to Paris starts at £59 return, fares from Paris to Berlin start at £33 each way with a basic couchette or £67 each way in a 2-bed sleeper. Berlin-Krakow starts at £25 each way.

MUNICH AND SALZBURG

If you're a fan of The Sound of Music, head for the hills around Salzburg. The 5.40pm Eurostar to Paris connects comfortably with the excellent German sleeper train to Munich, arriving at 9am next morning. A connecting EuroCity train will get you to Salzburg by 11am. Fares from around £117 return with couchette or £265 return in a two-bed sleeper. Munich-Salzburg is about £20 each way.

PRAGUE

The same 6pm Eurostar and sleeper to Berlin make a convenient connection with the EuroCity train to Prague. It's a relaxing scenic ride along a pleasant river valley with lunch in the restaurant car, arriving in Prague early afternoon. The sights of Prague are all the more special when you've made the effort to get there overland. Berlin-Prague starts at £25 each way.

ROME

The Eternal City is as alluring as ever. Take a lunch-time Eurostar and change in Paris for the 'Palatino' sleeper train to Rome. Linger over dinner in the restaurant car, retire to your sleeper or couchette for the night, and wake to a classic Italian landscape. You'll catch glimpses of the dome of St Peter's as the Palatino skirts the city and arrives at the Stazione Termini in the heart of Rome at 9.40 next morning. Eurostar to Paris starts at £59 return, fares from Paris to Rome start at £30 each way with a basic couchette or £119 each way in a 2-bed sleeper.

VENICE AND VERONA

For sheer romance, few European cities compete with Venice, and there's no more romantic way to get there than by sleeping-car. Take a lunchtime Eurostar to Paris and climb aboard the "Stendhal" sleeper to Venice. There's a restaurant car for dinner with views of rural France swishing past in the moonlight, sleeping-berths in couchettes or more comfortable private sleepers, and an arrival across the causeway into central Venice at 9.30 next morning. Eurostar to Paris starts at £59 return. Fares from Paris to Venice start at £30 each way with a basic couchette or £119 each way in a two-bed sleeper. This can easily be made a two-centre trip, combining a stay in Venice with a day or two in Verona, with its Roman a(mphitheatre and pleasant piazzas.

Mark Smith, seat61.com

View from the fort into the bay, Collioure, France

photo: shutterstock/Carole Castelli

European beaches by train

DE HAAN, BELGIUM

Make the most of the free 24-hour rail travel to any station in Belgium available when you buy a Eurostar ticket to Brussels. De Haan is a seaside resort on the Flemish coast that you can reach in just over an hour from the capital. It has wide sandy beaches that are excellent for kitesurfing and horseriding. The Manoir Carpe Diem is a family-friendly four-star hotel, 300m from the sea (+32 59 233 220, manoircarpediem.com): B&B from €125. Eurostar to Brussels from £59 return (eurostar.co.uk, 08705 186 186), then train to Ostend to get the coastal tram to De Haan for €1.6.

PLAGE DE LOZARI, CORSICA

Take advantage of the fast ferry from Nice to Corsica and bask on the island's dazzling white beaches. Plage de Lozari is a wild, semi-circular sweep of white sand, a short bus ride east of the ferry port at L'Ile Rousse. Stay inland at Auberge de Tesa (+33 4 95 60 09 55, aubergedetesa.com), a chambre d'hôte renowned for its Corsican food. Rooms €59, dinner €38. Train London-Nice (via Paris) from £109 return (0844 848 4070, raileurope.co.uk) then ferry to L'Ile Rousse from €128 (+33 4 95 32 95 95, corsicaferries.com). Bus from L'Ile Rousse to Lozari €5 (corsicabus.org). For information on ferry travel, visit sailanddrive.com.

COLLIOURE LANGUEDOC-ROUSSILLON, FRANCE

There are three beaches to choose from in the Mediterranean fishing port of Collioure on the Catalan coast. French Travel Service runs a "holiday by rail" trip to Collioure – staying at Hotel Madeloc, a family-run hotel 500m from the centre of Collioure – followed by a train ride up to the Cerdagne plateau. The Catalan Experience trip costs from £510pp, including three nights' B&B in Collioure, three nights' half-board at Hotel Saillagousse and all train travel from London via Paris or Lille (08702 414243, f-t-s.co.uk).

MIMIZAN AQUITAINE, FRANCE

If the breakers are just as important to you as the beach, pack your surf bag and head to Mimizan, south of Bordeaux on the Atlantic south-west coast. One of the unofficial surfing capitals of Europe, Mimizan is also beginner-friendly with plenty of space to find your own rhythm along six or so miles of surf. Rosco's Surf Lodge just outside town has surfboard storage (020 3239 8181, surfnlodge.com), B&B, £20pp. Surf lessons £20 (for groups of up to 8) or £40 for a private lesson. Train from London to Bordeaux (via Paris) from £99 return (raileurope.co.uk, 0844 848 4070) then bus to Mimizan for €27 return (cars-jarraud.com, +35 5 58 09 10 89).

PLAGE DE LA COURTADE, PORQUEROLLES, FRANCE

Porquerolles is the largest (and the nearest to the mainland) of the three islands in the Hyères gulf, just east of Toulon on the French Riviera. Plage de la Courtade is one of several long sandy beaches close to the island's only village on the north coast where you can stay at L'Arche de Noé, a fish restaurant with rooms and a large terrace (0033 4 94 58 33 71, arche-de-noe.com), from €210 half-board per room for two. Train London-Hyères (via Paris) from £138 return (0844 848 4070, raileurope.co.uk) then ferry to Porquerolles, £10.70 return (+33 4 94 58 21 81, tlv-tvm.com).

SCUBA DIVING, SOUTH OF FRANCE

Diamond Diving is a small, family-run company that picks up clients from Nice or Toulon stations for the short transfer to one of their hotels (two-stars) in the south of France. They will also arrange transfers from either the hotel to a dive centre in Nice, Sainte Maxime, St Raphael, Le Londe or Antibes. Divers will see healthy sealife including barracuda, grouper and lobster. Temperatures hover around 25C in July and Diamond (01908 234 030, diamonddiving.net) also offers diving courses. From £199 for a three-night, three-dive weekend or £229 for a four-night, five-dive weekend (excluding train fares). The train from London to Nice (via Paris) costs from £109 return (0844 848 4070, raileurope.co.uk).

VERT BOIS, ILE D'OLÉRON, FRANCE

Ile D'Oléron off France's west coast is much flatter than its neighbour Ile de Ré and has an extensive network of cycle paths. Vert Bois is a long, sandy beach on the south of the island, bordered by dunes and pine forest. Stay at Habitation Léonie, a small B&B with a tennis court and pool near St Giles. (+33 5 46 36 88 42, oleron.org), rooms from €75. Train to La Rochelle (via Paris) from £99 return (0844 848 4070, raileurope.co.uk), then ferry to Boyardville, €19 one way (inter-iles.com).

SYLT, GERMANY

The island of Sylt is a favourite holiday resort for Germans, but rarely visited by Brits, though for no good reason when it has wide sandy beaches, 200km of walking and cycling trails and dozens of seafood restaurants in its pretty towns. The Long Island House Sylt (+4651 9959 550, sylthotel.de) in the main town Westerland is a good example of the island's laid-back style. Rooms from €78. Eurostar to Brussels (from £59 return, eurostar.com), change to Thalys high-speed train to Cologne (from £79 return, raileurope.co.uk). Train to Westerland from Cologne around €90 return (bahn.hafas.de).

ES TRENC, MAJORCA

One of Majorca's few remaining undeveloped beaches in the rural south-east of the island. The only access is on foot or by bike. It's a far cry from the Palma crowds; just a few huts, dunes, pine and juniper trees line two miles of sandy coastline. Nearby is Es Torrent (+34 971 650 957, estorrent.com), an agrotourism country estate with a barbeque terrace and pool. B&B from €88 per room. Take the overnight train to Barcelona (via Paris) from £167pp return in a four-berth couchette (0844 848 4070, raileurope.co.uk), then fast ferry (within walking distance from the train station) from Barcelona to Palma, a four-hour journey, from €128 (trasmediterranea.es), then taxi to Es Torrent.

PLAYA LA VEGA, ASTURIAS, SPAIN

Your reward for the long ferry trip across the Bay of Biscay is this wild beach with its spectacular mountainous backdrop. Inland is Posada del Valle, a 19th-century farmhouse, organic farm and eco-hotel. If you want to work up a sweat before cooling off in the sea, walk to the beach on tracks that pass through the hills (+34 985 841 157, posadadelvalle.com), doubles from €62. Portsmouth-Bilbao ferry from £324 for car plus two, including cabin (08716 645 645, poferries.com).

Richard Hammond

photo: shutterstock/Mandy Godbehear

A deserted stretch of Es Trenc, Majorca

Long-haul train journeys

CHINA, JAPAN, VIETNAM, THAILAND, SINGAPORE

The Trans-Siberian railway is no mere curiosity, it's a working railway linking Europe with Asia. Two direct trains link Moscow with the Chinese capital Beijing every week, one via Mongolia and the Gobi desert (7,620 km), the other via Manchuria (9,050 km). Booked through local Russian agencies, fares for the six-day journey start at around £240 one-way including sleeper. Add a London-Moscow train ticket (£160-£260 one-way) and you're all set for an overland trip to the Far East. In fact, there's a twice-weekly train from Beijing to Hanoi in Vietnam, and with onwards train and buses and the time to spare, you can reach Saigon, Bangkok or Singapore. Or how about Japan? The "Rossiya" runs from Moscow to Vladivostok every second day, 9,900 km in seven days, around £296. A weekly ferry links Vladivostok with Japan taking two nights, from £200 one-way with cabin berth. London to Tokyo takes around 14 days, depending where and for how long you want to stop off on the way.

FINLAND

Take an evening Eurostar to Brussels and change on to the excellent City Night Line sleeper train to Berlin, arriving next morning. A three-hour train ride to Rostok later, and you're boarding the daily Tallink ferry for the two-night cruise across the Baltic to Helsinki and the Land of the Midnight Sun. London to Rostock starts at around £167 return including couchette; Rostock to Helsinki around £205 return with cabin berth.

GREECE

Greece is a fabulous destination and only two nights away, without flying. Take an afternoon Eurostar to Paris and the "Palatino" overnight sleeper to Bologna. A connecting train speeds along the Adriatic coastline to Bari, arriving mid-afternoon, where you've time to wander round the pleasant old town before catching the overnight ferry to Patras in Greece. Sailing past Ithaca and Cephalonia next morning, across deep blue water under equally blue skies is the nicest part of the trip, a world away from cramped plane seats. London-Bari by train starts at £190 return, Bari to Patras by Superfast Ferries starts at £87 return with reclining seat or £127 return with cabin berth. Patras-Athens takes four hours by train, £14 return.

A passenger train waiting in Moscow station

photo: shutterstock/Holger Mette

ISTANBUL, SYRIA AND JORDAN

The Orient Express may no longer run there, but Europe's most oriental city is still an epic three-day train ride from London, contrasting cities such as Vienna, Budapest and Bucharest with tiny Balkan villages nestled in pretty river valleys. But why stop at Istanbul? A weekly sleeping-car links Istanbul with Aleppo in Syria, through great scenery including a dramatic descent from the Taurus Mountains. From Aleppo, Damascus is a five-hour train ride, and Amman in Jordan just four more hours by bus. Three weeks is enough to visit Vienna, Budapest, Istanbul, Aleppo, Damascus and the incomparable Petra, without flying. London-Istanbul from around £470 return; Istanbul-Damascus £35 each way.

MALTA

It's perhaps the friendliest island in the Med and easy to reach plane-free. Head for Sicily by train, then take a fast ferry to Valetta, Malta's capital. Virtu Ferries sail regularly to Valletta from Pozzallo (90 minutes) or Catania (three hours), from £60 return.

MOROCCO

St Pancras to Morocco is an overland adventure which takes just 48 hours. Catch an afternoon Eurostar to Paris, where the overnight 'trainhotel' to Madrid awaits. Dinner in the diner, then off to bed in a cosy sleeper. Next morning brings views of distant snow-capped mountains, arriving in Madrid after breakfast. You've a day to explore (and maybe take in the famous Prado museum) before an evening high-speed express whisks you south to Andalusia. Spend the night in Algeciras or perhaps across the bay in Gibraltar, then ride the morning ferry to Tangier. From here, the real Marrakech Express heads south across Morocco to the foot of the Atlas Mountains. London to Madrid starts at £179 return including sleeper; Madrid to Algeciras, from £34 return. Ferry to Tangier £52 return; train to Marrakech £26 return.

SICILY

Take an afternoon Eurostar to Paris and the "Palatino" sleeper to Rome. After pasta and chianti in the restaurant car, you retire to your sleeper and wake up in Italy. Change in Rome on to an air-conditioned InterCity along the coast to Catania, Siracuse or Palermo. The train crosses the Straits of Messina aboard a train ferry – one of the few places in Europe where this still happens, an experience in its own right. London to Sicily by train starts at £190 return. You can stop off in Paris, Rome or Naples on the way – it costs no more.

TUNISIA

Tunisia is also just 48 hours away, with a cruise thrown in. Take a lunchtime Eurostar from St Pancras, one easy change in Lille and you reach Marseille before bedtime. Next day, your ferry sails past the Vieux Port and the infamous Chateau d'If (think Count of Monte Cristo) into the wide blue Mediterranean. More cruise liner than ferry, next morning it enters the warm, green waters of the Bay of Tunis, with the ruins of classical Carthage on Byrsa hill to your right. London to Marseille starts at £109 return; Marseille to Tunis starts at £280 return including cabin berth.

UKRAINE AND THE CRIMEA

UK citizens no longer require a visa so there's never been a better time to visit Ukraine. Leave London on an evening Eurostar for Brussels and change there on to the City Night Line sleeper train to Berlin. You've a full day to explore Berlin before catching the daily "Kashtan" to Kiev, which conveys a direct sleeping car to Odessa and Simferopol in the Crimea several times a week. The sleepers come complete with patterned carpet, frilly curtains and hanging baskets (plastic!) in the corridor. Stand in the Livadia Palace courtyard in Yalta where Churchill, Roosevelt and Stalin were photographed side by side, or wander the countryside round Balaclava to find the battlefield where the Light Brigade charged. London to Simferopol costs around £327 return including sleeper.

Mark Smith, seat61.com

Famous train journeys on the cheap

CAPE TOWN TO PRETORIA

The Blue Train – a gentleman's club on rails with post-prandial cognacs – charges around £580 (bluetrain.co.za) for a 27-hour luxury journey. But you can enjoy exactly the same scenery for just £23 including a sleeper, aboard the regular four-times weekly Shosholoza Meyl train from Cape Town to Johannesburg. Shosholoza Meyl passenger trains link major South African cities and have to be one of South Africa's best-kept travel secrets. Comfortable, cheap and safe, they have basic sleepers (shared two and four-bed compartments, with a hot shower at the end of the corridor) and a restaurant car selling meals, snacks, beer and South African wine. The train isn't air-conditioned, so the windows open for great views of Africa, up-close-and-personal. Bring your own cigar! (seat61.com/SouthAfrica).

For a touch of luxury that's still five times cheaper than the Blue Train, a twice-weekly "Premier Classe" train also links Cape Town with Jo'burg, with private sleepers, lounge car and restaurant, for £107 per person including meals (premierclasse.co.za).

SINGAPORE TO BANGKOK

Once a week, the ultra-luxurious Eastern & Oriental Express leaves Singapore's 1932-built art deco railway station, bound for Kuala Lumpur, Penang and Bangkok. Prices for the two-day trip start at £1,100 including meals. Regular daily trains ply exactly the same tracks, and a seat on an air-conditioned express from Singapore to Kuala Lumpur is yours for £12 one-way. Or hang the expense, go first class for £24. Another £6 train ride and you're in Penang. A sleeping-berth on the international express from Penang to Bangkok costs just £19, with fresh, clean sheets and curtains for privacy, like those used by Marilyn Monroe in Some Like It Hot.

RAJASTHAN TOUR

If you've £1,500 to spare, you can live like a Maharaja aboard the Palace on Wheels on a seven-day tour of Rajasthan (palaceonwheels.net). If you haven't, an IndRail pass costs £68 for seven days, £93 for 15 days, giving unlimited air-conditioned travel across the whole Indian Railways network. If you're sure of your itinerary, the excellent family-run SD Enterprises in Wembley (020 8903 3411, indiarail.co.uk,) can pre-book some or all your trains for you free of charge. Delhi, Varanasi, Agra, Jaipur, Jaisalmer and Simla makes a great two-week itinerary, contrasting desert cities with cool hill stations, a holy city on the Ganges with princely Rajasthan. Overnight sleepers between many cities save both time and hotel bills. Forget images of overcrowded trains with passengers hanging out the doors – in air-conditioned class you'll have your own reserved berth, clean bedding provided, and plenty of room. With every journey you'll experience the real India, with cries of "chai, chai, garam chai" (wonderful hot sweet tea) from attendants walking the train, and hot cheap curries (veg or non-veg) served at your seat. You can also book Indian train tickets online, at irctc.co.in.

TRAILBLAZER

Eurostar

What? High-speed rail company operating through the Channel Tunnel since 1994.

Where? Services link London St Pancras, Ebbsfleet and Ashford with Paris, Brussels, Lille, Calais, Disneyland Paris, Avignon and the French Alps.

What's their big idea? Eurostar's Tread Lightly programme, launched in 2007 with advice from Friends of the Earth, pledged to cut CO_2 emissions per passenger journey by 25% by 2012. It's 10-point plan also set sustainability targets throughout the company, from recycling staff uniforms to sorting and recycling on-board waste, replacing damaging air-conditioning refrigerants and sourcing Fair Trade and local on-board food produce.

Track record: Current emissions are offset at no cost to passengers. All cups, bags and napkins in the bar-buffet are biodegradable and where possible made from recycled material. Most cold food is organic, locally-sourced and seasonal and hot drinks are ethically sourced. Since the opening of the St Pancras terminal and High Speed 1 line passenger numbers have risen 21%.

The long view: The company is focusing on expanding capacity and cooperation with other national rail networks to encourage strong growth in regional passengers booking through tickets beyond Eurostar terminals. It also plans to reduce paper usage by switching to e-tickets and bar-code ticketing downloadable to mobile phones.

Awards and schemes: *Guardian*, *Observer* and guardian.co.uk best train company award 2002 & 2003, Responsible Tourism best mode of transport award 2004, Network Rail Environmental Award 2005

More information: eurostar.com/environment

Why I love ... bus travel

On 31 March 2008, I paid my last ever fare on a local bus: £4 to go from Penzance to Land's End. The subsequent journey of 600 or so miles to Lowestoft cost nothing. As soon as my friend and I read about the government's free bus scheme for the over-60s, we wanted to set ourselves the challenge of travelling the longest distance in a straight line in England without paying for transport.

This was not a see-how-fast-you-can-do-it trip, nor were my friend Janice and I aiming to spend as little as possible on our holiday. What the buses offered was the opportunity to see the English countryside and its hidden villages at a slow pace. We wanted to look. We carried only small rucksacks so we could hop off on to footpaths in the prettiest counties, and we built in some special treats along our route from England's most westerly point to its most easterly.

I enjoyed the 574 bus so much that I was reluctant to get off. Our driver had to reverse to let cars pass on the narrow lanes; we rattled over cattle-grids, brushed past high banks drenched in primroses and passed signposts to Cornish villages with names like Siblyback, Minions, Dobwall and Crow's Nest.

People chat at bus stops. You start on the weather, speculate on whether the bus will be on time, then move on to more substantial things. Sometimes it gets a bit out of hand. We missed a connection as a result of a woman being intent on finishing her story despite the arrival of our bus ("No, it's not that one …"). Not that it really mattered. We were heading for Glastonbury and still had the afternoon for exploring. Buses may run late but there's no such thing as a missed connection, just an opportunity to explore a new town.

So will I use my bus pass regularly now? You bet. Not if I'm in a hurry, but for holidays, preferably ones with no specific plan. Buses complement rail travel. While trains often offer the best views of passing countryside, if you sit in the front seat on top of a double decker, England unfolds in front of you. Slowly, with time to look.

Hilary Bradt

Golden rules of bus travel
- Carry a mobile phone
- Go to the loo whenever you get the chance
- Ask the bus drivers for advice; they are a good source of information
- Tourist offices are usually helpful and have bus timetables
- The first concessional bus of the day – not before 9.30am – often runs late
- Allow at least 15 minutes for connections

Travel information

Traveline (0871 200 2233, traveline.org.uk) is particularly helpful in the south-west of England: its journey planner allows you to specify local buses rather than coaches in your search. Visit Britain (visitbritain.co.uk) is a worthwhile planning back-up in other regions. The transportdirect.info website also has a "find a bus" journey planner with nationwide information.

How to get a free bus pass

To get a concessionary bus pass, apply to your local district council or go to direct.gov.uk and follow the links. Since 1 April 2008, free bus travel in England has been available to those over 60, or to disabled people, between 9.30am and 11pm. Some councils allow earlier or later travel in their region, and extend the concession to carers accompanying disabled people.

For younger travellers

You don't have to be a pensioner to enjoy bus travel. All local buses are inexpensive and many bus companies offer day "rover" tickets allowing unlimited travel.

10 Long-haul bus trips

LONDON TO ROME

Insight Vacations is aimed at travellers who want a bit of comfort in between stops, with good standard hotels included in the package. Their London to Rome journey stretches over eight days, with the most interesting bit sandwiched in the middle. After leaving Paris, the coach travels through the vineyards of Burgundy, crosses the Rhine at Basel and heads for Lake Lucerne. From there, it's on to Italy; through the Italian Lake District and south to Milan, then into the fertile plains of the Po Valley and across the Apennines towards Florence, from where the final road leads to Rome. From £700 including hotel accommodation (01475 741203, insightvacations.com).

LONDON TO PRAGUE

Kumuka's seven-day London to Prague tour ploughs a course through central Europe twice a month throughout the summer. The Prague Express trip includes a single fare on Eurostar to Paris, where two days of sightseeing are helmed by the Kumuka crew. Onwards to the thrill-seeker-friendly Interlaken where those wanting to skydive, hang-glide and paraglide will have their fix. If you time your trip right, the bus will roll into Munich during Oktoberfest before finishing in Prague. The Prague Express trip is from £435 including accommodation, tours, six breakfasts and three dinners (kumuka.com).

EUROPEAN NETWORK

If you want to visit Dubrovnik and the southern Dalmatian coast, the forests of north-east Estonia or the southern beaches of Turkey, don't bother with an InterRail pass. European train passes are a backpacker staple, yet there are huge swathes of the continent that only a bus can reach. Eurolines is Europe's biggest coach network, grouping together 32 coach companies and more than 500 destinations. Its 30-day passes – £205 for adults and £159 for those under 26 – are considerably cheaper than a rail pass and even include Morocco. If nothing else, Euroline's website is a travel planner's goldmine, collating bus timetables from across the continent (01582 404511, eurolines.com).

photo: shutterstock/ Peter Zurek

Early morning on the Charles Bridge, Prague

LONDON TO SYDNEY

The inaugural OzBus journey played out like a soap opera on wheels. Before it had reached halfway there were on-board feuds and love affairs, the bus was stripped of its logo in Turkey before it shuddered to a halt in Tehran where beer-starved tempers frayed. But after 84 tumultuous days, it somehow made it to Sydney. Seats on subsequent departures sold out. If you want as much of an experience on the bus as off it, this one is difficult to beat, for £3,850 including accommodation and most meals (020 864 11443, oz-bus.com).

DRAGOMAN OVERLAND

Dragoman Overland's journeys are the philosophical opposite of the OzBus's whizz-bang approach to overland adventure. The company was founded in the 1960s, and is run by an experienced troupe of guides whose expertise covers Africa, Asia, South and North America. Their most interesting projects are their most epic, including an 11-week journey from St Petersburg to Beijing via the Russian and Kazakh steppe, southern Siberia, Mongolia and the Gobi desert. As Dragoman's multi-terrain truck heads east, accommodation options progress from yurts to yurtas, and the trip takes in the nomadic settlements of reindeer herders and traditional hunters. From £236 per week (01728 8611 33, dragoman.com). Getting to St Petersburg: Eurostar to Brussels, overnight train to Berlin (b-rail.be), then Moskva Express to St Petersburg (bahn.hafas.de).

TURKISH TREEHOUSES AND BEYOND

Not many Brits know about the Fez Bus, but these tours are hugely popular with antipodean backpackers wanting to visit Gallipoli and beyond. Their 15-day Shoestring Turkey tour starts in Istanbul before heading west along the Sea of Marmara's coast, then south to the Mediterranean beaches and the treehouses of Olympos. The final leg swings inland through Cappadocia (with an optional extension into Turkey's wild eastern countryside) before making its way back to Istanbul. From £299 half-board (020 7099 92077, feztravel.com). Getting to Istanbul: Eurostar to Brussels, Thalys train to Cologne (Thalys.com), CityNightLine sleeper Cologne-Vienna (bahn.de/citynightline), Avala train to Belgrade (oebb.at), then Balkan Express to Istanbul (serbianrailways.com)

MOROCCAN MOMENTS

Busabout offers a variety of tours around Europe and beyond, but its 15-day All Morocco trip is its most exotic option. The bus starts in Tangier before making its way to Fes via Chefchaouen in the Rif mountains. Then it's into the desert, setting up camp at the Meski oasis, trekking through the Sahara on camels and staying at a traditional Berber camp. Two more days are spent travelling in the Todra gorge before visiting Marrakech and Essaouira and returning to Tangier. From £399 plus local payment of €220 including all accommodation and food (020 795 01661, busabout.com). Getting to Tangier: Eurostar to Paris, trainhotel Paris-Madrid (elipsos.com), train Madrid-Algeciras (renfe.es) and ferry to Tangier (no advance booking necessary).

TRANSYLVANIAN EXPLORER

Top Deck's Transylvanian Explorer trip covers the less-trodden south-east corner of Europe, setting off from Budapest and arriving in Bucharest nine days later. After allowing a day for guests to sample the night-time pursuits of the Hungarian capital, the bus heads towards the Baroque town of Eger, known for its castle and Bull's Blood wine. The Romanian leg begins in the university town of Cluj Napoca before moving on to the Unesco heritage city of Sighisoara then calling at Bran castle, former home of Dracula and winding up in the capital. Costs £719 including tours, accommodation and half board (0845 2575212, topdecktours.co.uk). Getting to Budapest: Eurostar to Brussels, Thalys train to Cologne (thalys.com), CityNightLine sleeper Cologne-Vienna (bahn.de/citynightline), then Avala Train to Budapest (oebb.at).

RIGA TO STOCKHOLM (VIA RUSSIA)

The more geographically aware will notice a few peculiarities with this route. First of all, Russia isn't between Riga and Stockholm. This is because Contiki's route goes a fair few miles east before finishing across the Baltic in Sweden. The Russian stretch of the trip includes both Moscow and St Petersburg, but also takes in the less visited cities of Velikiye Luki and Novgorod. The second problem is an aquatic one – getting from Helsinki to Stockholm. Luckily, an overnight cruise is included. Contiki's tours have something of a reputation for alcohol-fuelled tourism for the 18-30 crowd, but this one's scope makes it stand out from the rest. Price is £1,004 including accommodation and most meals (020 8290 6422, contiki.co.uk). Getting to Riga: Eurostar to Brussels, Thalys train to Cologne (thalys.com), EuroNight sleeper to Warsaw (bahn.de), Eurolines bus to Riga (eurolines.pl).

SCANDINAVIAN JOURNEY

Trafalgar Tours' 15-day trip begins in Copenhagen with arranged excursions and plenty of time to enjoy the evenings. The grand loop begins on day three, driving west to the Jutland peninsula via the island of Funen and Odense, Hans Christian Andersen's birthplace. After crossing the Skagerrak into Norway, the coastal highway north of Stavangar is one of the most spectacular drives in Europe, passing dozens of fjords and islands on its way to Bergen. From here the trip heads inland, rides the Flåm railway through mountains and waterfalls and crosses into Sweden for two nights in Stockholm before returning to Copenhagen. But don't choose this route if you're looking for rowdy times on the bus – Trafalgar's tours are generally aimed at the discerning older traveller. From £1,525 including hotel accommodation, breakfast and seven three-course dinners (020 7828 8143, trafalgartours.com). Getting to Copenhagen: Ferry Harwich-Esbjerg (dfds.co.uk), then train to Copenhagen (dsb.dk).

Benji Lanyado

BY BOAT

For too many of us, a holiday on the water means an all-inclusive cruise – environmentally damaging and of limited benefit to the destinations so fleetingly visited. Yet from sailing yachts to barges and kayaks, there are hundreds of ways to explore UK waterways or take a more scenic route overseas. Ferries connect many corners of Britain to European escapes, while a canal or river barge holiday provides the ideal excuse to go slow and delight in the little places usually missed along the way. Cargo ships, though not very green in themselves, produce no additional emissions for your journey, and can be a viable non-flying option for the time-rich traveller.

 **boat trips**

Coming into harbour, the easterly wind picks up, scalping white caps off the heads of waves. Ahead a fishing boat, rusty and battered around the bows, punches into the chop of water, then turns south. The radio crackles to life on the bridge of our boat, the Glen Massan, and the engines are cut back, allowing time for a ferry to dart out of the narrow harbour entrance.

A pair of seals bobs up near the rocks to watch our progress towards the pretty waterfront, the brightly painted houses and the ruined and overgrown castle. Behind us are snow-peaked mountains, hillsides drizzled with golden gorse and lined with sunlight, then below in the water is the sudden leap of a porpoise.

This is a cruise, I remind myself, but not one of those anodyne luxury hotels on water, rather a true salty experience with itineraries that change with the winds and a trawl-net of wonderful experiences. No need, either, for planes or airports since we're sailing into Tarbert on the Kintyre peninsula, unbelievably just 40 miles from Glasgow.

Our boat is a converted fishing trawler, one of two belonging to local outfit, the Majestic Line. This 85ft hunk of Irish oak has been stripped and rebuilt for passengers with an elegant saloon, well-appointed cabins and a little suntrap of a sundeck behind the bridge. But there is a great deal more to the Glen Massan than smart panelling and soft cushions, and once she was tied securely to Tarbert harbour wall I scouted around and discovered the first clues. They were up on the bridge, sitting behind the charts and binoculars, a little pile of treasure: three leather-bound volumes filled with careful looping handwriting, the unpublished memoirs of a man looking back on his youth.

I began reading, "In the year 1842, I was in command of the brig, Mary, and returning from Egypt with a cargo of cotton bound for Liverpool ..." I settled on the stool and placed the book on the chart: "... had been following us closely for some days and I decided, when the opportunity arose, to harpoon the beast." A tale emerges of an impetuous young sea captain who spears a shark, only to get his leg tangled in the harpoon rope which then flips him overboard. He ends up dangling, like bait, in front of the angry shark – a potentially fatal situation if not for a crew member who spots the captain's unlikely predicament and rescues him.

Scot Atkinson, our own captain, returns to the bridge after a chat with the harbourmaster. "Those are the diaries of Captain Andrew Smith," he tells me, "great-grandfather of the co-owner of this boat, Andrew Thoms."

The Majestic Line is nothing if not steeped in maritime history and tradition. Four years ago, lamenting the senseless breaking-up of good wooden fishing boats, Thoms and a friend, Ken Grant, hatched the idea of refitting the vessels as luxurious cruising boats that would tour the Western Isles and the long, narrow fingers of sea lochs that tickle the coast from Campbeltown to Ardnamurchan. It is an area they had sailed all their lives, and despite it being so close to Glasgow, they knew that most people had no idea of its beauty when seen from the sea.

It was not always like that. At the end of the 19th century, 1.5m tonnes of shipping were launched every year on the Clyde and the river was thick with pleasure craft. Every resident of Glasgow knew the route "doon the watter", catching one of the many steam packets for day trips. Competition in those days did not just mean low prices: the boats had fine dining saloons and German oompah bands to entertain. And the islands, though losing population for decades, had inhabitants who needed transport and supplies.

The Majestic Line's Glen Massan and Glen Tarsan may not have the oompah bands of yesteryear, and they are certainly not steam-driven, but they do match the elegance of old-fashioned service in other departments. Catering for 10 passengers at most, the order of play is to tour the more beautiful bits of coast, putting in at pretty little ports like Tarbert. When passengers want to walk, they disembark, tramp along a shore or over a hill, and get picked up. Meals are taken at one large convivial table and the food is excellent – lobster fresh from the ship's creels with a bit of luck, or a line-caught mackerel in summer.

The Glen Massan sails from Inverary to Dunoon, and the Glen Tarsan out of Oban to the waters around the Isles of Mull and Islay. Three-night cruises £650pp, six nights £1,285, including all meals and wine with dinner (0131 623 5012, themajesticline.co.uk).

Kevin Rushby

Waterborne breaks

SAIL TO VINEYARDS, BORDEAUX

You would expect that seven days of hard sailing might deserve a reward, wouldn't you? The sea crossing from Dartmouth to La Rochelle, after all, is no route for the faint-hearted. But if you have the experience necessary, the exhilaration of the open sea voyage is followed by a week cruising up the Gironde river in Bordeaux, visiting vineyards and chateaux. The boat is a Dufour 485 and passengers are required to have a RYA Competent Crew standard (which can be done in five days if you are a complete novice). Once on the Gironde, you tour Médoc vineyards such as Château Cos d'Estournel, Lynch-Bages, Haut Brion and Vieux Châteaux Certan, with plenty of stops for wine-tasting. £1,475pp including on-board accommodation, all food and soft drinks and a vineyard tour. Return via high-speed train La Rochelle-Paris, then Eurostar. Nonstop Sail (01803 833 399, nonstopsail.com).

SEA KAYAKING, SCOTLAND

Sea kayak enthusiasts Stuart Hood and Ben Dodman set up Rockhoppers four years ago to cater for demand for trips out to the beaches and islands west of Fort William. The speed and silence of the kayaks ensures close contact with the natural world of otters, seals, dolphins and birds. Rockhoppers use single or two-person expedition craft which are stable and fast – into these go all the camping equipment and food. Three-day trips start at Loch Moidart and move out to sea visiting various small islands and beaches. Nights are spent under canvas with a campfire. Beginners are welcome. Rockhoppers can pick you up from Fort William station. Two days for £160 or £220 for three days (07739 837344, rockhopperscotland.co.uk).

PADDLE AND CAMP, NORFOLK BROADS

Paddling along the Norfolk Broads by canoe gives you access to areas that cannot be reached by larger boats: nature reserves, shallow waters and secret side channels. Mark Wilkinson runs guided canoe adventures with overnight stops in B&Bs in some of the prettier villages such as Horning and Coltishall. Canoeing is by far the best way to spot the elusive freshwater otter; other delights include kingfishers, bitterns and marsh harriers. If you prefer a hardier trip, Mark also runs bushcraft voyages where you camp in woods alongside the broads.

A two-night guided bushcraft canoe trail costs £150pp, including camping and food. A two-night guided B&B trip (including lunches) costs from £175 (07810 838052, thecanoeman.com).

CREATE YOUR OWN CRUISE, FAROES AND ICELAND

Spectacular and unusual, the 18 islands of the Faroes can be visited by boat from Britain by taking the Smyril Line's new route from Scrabster in the far north of Scotland to the capital Tórshavn, a 13-hour journey on board the MV Norröna. Once there, you can use MV Norröna's routes between the Faroes, Iceland, Norway, Denmark and Scotland to construct your own mini-cruise with stopovers where you wish. The ship is a large comfortable cruiser with restaurants, bars and panoramic viewing lounges. Scrabster–Tórshavn from £57pp one-way. Runs from May until September (scantours.co.uk/smyril, 020-7554 3530).

BUILD YOUR OWN CANOE, LEICESTERSHIRE

This mini-break not only scores well on the green-o-metre, it's also practical. You come back with a clean conscience and a boat, a wooden Canadian-style canoe to be precise, that will fit on to a car roof rack. John Clohesy runs three-day courses at his riverside home in the Wreake Valley, Leicestershire, where you build a lightweight plywood canoe and two paddles while camping in his garden (or there are rooms available). No woodworking experience or special talent is required. £600 for a three-day course including materials, camping on site with hot meals, and, of course, your canoe. See one of John's boats at tinyurl.com/44z04q (07922 164061, birchcanoes.com).

photo: Wilderness Scotland

The yacht 'Sealgair', Scotland

JOIN THE RESISTANCE, IRELAND/BRITTANY

One of the more unusual consequences of the second world war was a sailing club, Les Glenans, established by former members of the French resistance to promote friendship, love of the sea and adventure. Les Glenans is a small archipelago off the Breton coast where much of the activities occur, but there is also an Irish branch that teaches cruiser sailing at centres in Baltimore, West Cork, and Collanmore Island, near Westport. The Glenans approach is to offer tuition but it also encourages sharing of duties. You can find yourself cooking lunch aboard for six crew, alongside learning to sail. It's a great method, especially if you fancy the idea of owning your own boat one day. Weekend (two days) from €190 a week from €575, full board, Glenans Irish Sailing Club (+353 1 661 1481, gisc.ie).

BARGING IN STYLE, LOIRE

There are barges and there are barges. Renaissance is a 128ft converted barge with spa pool, crew of five and touring bikes for all eight passengers. Starting at Paris, the boat explores the Upper Loire over a week with lots of opportunities to hop off and go exploring – by hot air balloon if you like. Candle-lit dinners are served in the panelled 13m saloon. If all the luxury makes you feel guilty, then comfort yourself with the knowledge that Renaissance uses less fuel in an entire season than the average jet gets through in one hour. From £2,700pp for six nights, includes all meals, wine, open bar and excursions (01784 482439, gobarging.com).

MAIL SHIP TO ST HELENA

Intrepid travellers with solid sea legs can join the 128-berth RMS St Helena, a mail ship which sails from Portland to Cape Town twice a year (May and October), stopping en route at St Helena, an unspoilt, lost-in-time island in the south Atlantic. This is not a voyage for anyone in a hurry – it takes about 24 days to reach the island and another five or six to Cape Town – nor is it the kind of cruise that offers swimming pools and luxurious cabins. The "casino" allows a maximum bet of 20p. This is an old-fashioned marine experience with comfortable cabins, decent food and entertainment provided by you and your fellow passengers. How much longer this anachronistic but wonderful service might last is uncertain – a St Helena airport is planned. From £1,501pp full-board (plus surcharges). Andrew Weir Shipping (020 7575 6480, aws.co.uk, rms-st-helena.com).

FOLLOW A CANOE TRAIL, NORTHERN IRELAND

Northern Ireland has some particularly well-organised canoe facilities, including five marked trails. The river Bann trail goes from Lough Neagh northwards through the wildlife-rich area of Lough Beg and on to Coleraine via campsites and B&Bs. Alternatively, head south from Lough Neagh along the river Blackwater, passing through rural Tyrone and Armagh, or explore the bays and islands of Lough Erne. For canoe hire centres, guided trips and places to stay: canoeni.com.

Kevin Rushby and
Chris Moss

CREW A YACHT, CHANNEL ISLANDS

Don't have a spare half-a-million to buy your own yacht? Never mind – you can sail one for under £300. Portsmouth-based Tall Ships Adventures has launched a series of trips – for 16 to 75-year-olds – on board its new fleet of four 22m yachts, previously used for round-the-world races. No experience required (023-9283 2055, tallships.org).

5 Weekend breaks by ferry

POOLE TO JERSEY

Get back to nature with Jersey's easily accessible attractions – sunbathe on a different beach every day, cycle through the country lanes, explore the island's numerous landscaped gardens and walk across fields and cliff-tops. It's also a great destination for history buffs – visit the medieval castle of Mont Orgueil or walk through the Jersey war tunnels. Journey time is three hours. From £107 return. Condor Ferries (0845 609 1024, condorferries.com/uk/home.aspx).

HOLYHEAD TO DUBLIN

Dublin has to be one of the ultimate city break locations, with its 18th and 19th-century architecture, art galleries, bars and restaurants. If you've been before and fancy something a bit more off the beaten track, take a walk along the city's quays to discover where the hidden river Poddle meets the Liffey, view the bones of St Valentine in the Carmelite Whitefriars Street church, wander through the open-air Boulevard Gallery where artists sell their work during summer weekends, sit in the Morrison bar overlooking the river and stay at the Dylan, a renovated Victorian nurses' home. The four daily crossings take less than two hours on Dublin Swift, or three and a quarter hours on the cruise ferry Ulysses. Operator is Irish Ferries (08705 171 717, irishferries.com) with prices of £23 one way per person (for foot passengers) or £79 one way for a two-night mini-cruise break.

NEWCASTLE TO AMSTERDAM

Visit the Van Gogh museum and Rijksmuseum, wander around the old city houses, and linger in cafes, navigate your way through the canals, floating flower market and diamond

UK Island Hopping

SHETLAND

Best for: Otters, cliffs and the country's longest midsummer's day.

Highlights: If you want to see an otter fishing for its dinner, then Shetland is the place. On a trip to the island of Yell, with otter devotees John Campbell and Terry Holmes, it took literally two minutes to spot one in their telescope. Dramatic cliff scenery in Eshaness, in Shetland's northwest mainland, makes for excellent hiking. Visit Shetland runs a festival of walks in summer and early autumn. For a free taste of what life would have been like in Shetland in the "olden days", don't miss the superb new Shetland museum.

Getting there: Rail is cheaper and faster than coach. Take the Aberdeen-Lerwick ferry with Northlink Ferries.

Staying there: Lerwick youth hostel (islesburgh.org.uk) opens April-September. On Unst: Gardiesfauld hostel (gardiesfauld.shetland.co.uk). Across Shetland there are basic but comfortable bothies, known as bods. Book one through camping-bods.com.

Tourist information: visitshetland.com

SKOMER ISLAND, PEMBROKESHIRE

Best for: Puffins, wildflowers and comfy eco-accommodation.

Highlights: Go to Skomer to see portly puffins on the cliff edges right next to the footpaths. They're not shy and throughout June and July will be flying back to their burrows (often stolen from an unfortunate rabbit family) with beaks stuffed full of silvery sand eels to feed their growing chicks. May and June is the best time to see enchanting swathes of pink and purple wildflowers covering the island. Guillemots and razorbills perch on sheer cliff faces, fluffy gull chicks squawk from stony outcrops in the island's interior and seals bask on rocks in the sun at low tide.

Staying overnight in the island's eco-accommodation is a special treat. Built out of reclaimed stone and powered by solar electricity, a stay here is the only way to hear the screaming call of the rare Manx shearwater as thousands of them stream back to their burrows at night. The eaten-out corpses of shearwaters caught by prowling greater black-backed gulls can be seen strewn over the paths in the morning. Take food if staying the night – there's nowhere to buy it on the island, so it's BYO, scavenge or starve.

Getting there: From Fishguard take bus 404 to St David's, then the 400 to Marloes. Timetable at gobybus.net. The ferry departs from Martin's Haven, a three-mile walk or hitchhike further on.

Staying there: 01239 621600 to book eco-accommodation. If you volunteer with the Wildlife Trust of south and west Wales for a week you stay for free.

Tourist information: visitpembrokeshire.com

HOLY ISLAND, NORTHUMBERLAND

Best for: Peace and quiet, religious ruins and a heady alcoholic aphrodisiac.

Highlights: Home of the splendidly ornate Lindisfarne Gospels (though only replicas can be seen here – the originals are in the British Library), Holy Island is the place to go if you need a bit of downtime. Attached to the mainland by a causeway, you have to time your trip carefully as the road is completely covered by the sea at high tide. The ruins of Lindisfarne priory are a must-see. A place of pilgrimage for centuries, it continues to draw people in search of spiritual solace.

Then there's the local tipple: St Aidan's Winery is where Lindisfarne mead is made from grapes, honey and herbs. In an ancient Norse custom, newlyweds were practically force-fed the stuff for a month in the belief it would make them more fertile.

Getting there: From Berwick upon Tweed take bus 477 to Holy Island: this runs daily in summer, less frequently out of season.

Staying there: Crown and Anchor Inn (holyislandcrown.co.uk) overlooking the harbour and castle. Alternatively, the Open Gate (lindisfarne.org.uk) is a Christian retreat house of Tudor origin, open for group or personal retreats, guided or non-guided.

Tourist information: visitnortheastengland.com

ALDERNEY, CHANNEL ISLANDS

Best for: Making sandcastles on wide, empty beaches.

Highlights: This remote island is just 3.5 miles long and 1.5 miles wide and is still remarkably undiscovered, with most visitors to the Channel Islands making for Guernsey or Jersey. The safe sandy bays are great for water-sports including sailing, waterskiing and surfing. Watching racing yachts battle it out around the island during the July Alderney International Sailing Regatta is a completely free thrill. The August Alderney Wildlife Festival is a chance to take guided boat trips by experts to the tiny islets of Burhou to see glossy white gannets, seals and storm petrels. St Anne, Alderney's capital, is full of higgledy-piggledy cobbled streets lined by colourful painted cottages and Georgian townhouses. Because of a much-feared French invasion in the 19th century there are forts aplenty to explore around the rest of the island. You can even stay in one: the Landmark Trust has renovated Fort Clonque, which sits on a large group of rocks south west of the island.

Getting there: Weymouth to Guernsey on Condor ferries (condorferries.co.uk), then on to Alderney with manche-iles-express.com. Alderney is so small that hiring a bike is the perfect way to get around. Try Pedal Power at Les Rocquettes (01481 822286) or AFS Bike Hire (01481 823352) at Braye Harbour.

Staying there: The campsite behind the sand dunes of Saye Bay is cheapest, with fully equipped tents available for hire. Or stay at the Town House, High Street, 01481 824897.

Tourist information: visitguernsey.com; alderney.gov.gg

centres. Or escape on an afternoon train to Castricum on the coast, hire a bicycle and follow a path through the woods and down to the sea. Daily crossings (except December 24/25) depart Newcastle (North Shields) at 5.30pm, arriving the next morning and departing Amsterdam (IJmuiden) at 6.00pm. A short coach transfer from the port to Amsterdam is included in the price. DFDS Seaways (dfds.co.uk) charge from £55 return per person for a two-night mini cruise break.

ABERDEEN TO LERWICK

Lerwick is Britain's most northerly town and the main port of the Shetland Islands. Although small (the population numbers less than 6,500), it has plenty of charms and attractions, from the free Shetland museum to the annual Up-Helly-Aa fire festival, where a full-size Viking longship is set ablaze in midwinter. The daily 12-hour crossing departs from Aberdeen at 7.00pm and from Lerwick also at 7.00pm. With NorthLink Ferries (0845 6000 449, northlinkferries.co.uk), from £21.40 one way per person (low season) while mid-season prices start at £27.10 and high season at £32.70.

LIVERPOOL TO ISLE OF MAN

With its short crossing time from Liverpool, the Isle of Man is perfect for a relaxing weekend away – within hours of finishing work on Friday, you could be paddling in the sea on Douglas Beach or bedding down in the peaceful surrounds of a country farm stay. Outdoor pleasures range from fishing and whale watching to a round of golf on Castletown's clifftop course. It takes two and half hours out, and three and a half hours back. Twice daily crossings, departing Liverpool at 11.15am or 7.00pm and departing the Isle of Man at 7.30am or 3.00pm. Steam Packet (0871 222 1333, steam-packet.com), at £17.50 one way per person (£12.50 for children).

Sarah Bourn

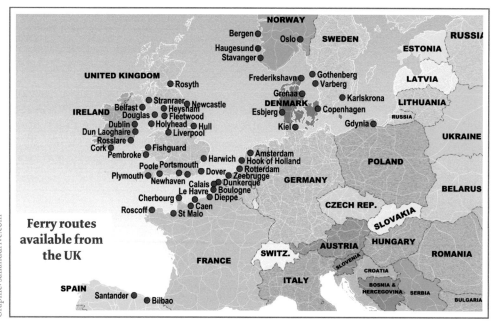

Graphic: sailanddrive.com

Cargo Ships

Imagine yourself slipping slowly through the limpid waters of the Sargasso Sea, the surface calmer than the proverbial mill-pond, azure skies overhead and just a handful of fellow passengers and several thousand tonnes of Caribbean fruit to share the experience. This is cruising but not as you may know it, on board a working cargo vessel shipping fruit from Central America to Europe to give us this day our daily bananas.

I love cargo ships, and, having recently travelled right the way round the globe without flying, I've now been on a few. For those who seek the serene isolation of the open seas without several hundred other passengers and an entertainment itinerary of crap cabaret and cocktails, a voyage on a working cargo ship is just the ticket. The divine and humbling experience of being hundreds of miles from the nearest land, and the sense of freedom that accompanies it are, for me, the real joys of ocean travel. A "cargo cruise" allows you to enjoy this sensation without the slightly forced holiday camp jollity of a regular cruise vessel.

So how do you pass the time in the absence of the usual distractions? With trans-oceanic trips typically taking around two weeks or more, time is definitely not in short supply and this is a wonderful thing. Travel by sea returns us to a more sedate pace, with thinking space and time to properly relax. My partner Fi and I devoured books we had meant to get round to for years, took a Spanish course on our way across the Pacific before reaching Mexico, and developed some mean table-tennis skills playing against burly Ukrainian crew members.

Cargo ships vary hugely depending on the company that owns and runs them, the nationalities of the working crew on board and the route they serve. Comparing them is a bit like comparing trains in China and France – the technologies are similar but the comfort levels and ambience are rather different. French ships serve fantastic food with complimentary wine, Russian officers can be a little stern and even dour, whilst Croatians are relatively garrulous and Filipinos positively ebullient. We've sung karaoke with the ship's bosun, watched whales breaching from the bridge and every voyage includes a tour of the gargantuan engine room in which the oily behemoth rumbles along 24/7 to drive you through the sea whatever the weather.

Ah, the weather. Crossing oceans does put you somewhat at the mercy of the elements and this in itself can be enough to put off potential sailors. However, a 30,000 tonne cargo ship is usually relatively stable in all but the most extreme conditions. The irony of our trip was that despite crossing notorious stretches of water such as the Tasman Sea and the Atlantic in early March, the most ferocious weather we encountered was the very first leg of our journey on a car ferry from Portsmouth to Bilbao in northern Spain.

The single biggest excuse people give for not travelling by sea is a lack of time. Well, all I can say is that if you can possibly make the time, be it through a sabbatical, between jobs or an extended holiday, you'll get a chance to revisit a modern version of a mode of travel centuries old. Unfortunately, the opportunity is in danger of disappearing thanks to increasing security and immigration restrictions at various ports around the world. So rediscover the romance of the sea by getting out on it in a cargo ship while you can. You'll not regret it (as long as it's calm).

Ed Gillespie

HOW TO PLAN YOUR OWN CARGO VOYAGE

Where should I start?
There's a lot of information available online from various shipping companies that offer passenger bookings, but it's not all in English and it can be confusing trying to compare what's out there yourself, so the best way to book is through a specialist agent. Among the best is cargo ship guru Hamish Jamieson at freightertravel.co.nz. In the UK, try Strand Travel strandtravel.co.uk (0207 010 9290) and the Cruise People, cruisepeople.co.uk (0207 723 2450). Both have excellent websites, and Strand Travel's boasts an interactive map showing possible routes.

What does it cost?
Travelling by cargo ship works out more expensive than flying but your food and lodging are included in the price. The Cruise People estimate that it costs around £70 per day per person.

How does the cost compare with that of a cruise?
Cargo ships will work out cheaper, although perhaps not by as much as you might expect. Routes vary, but there's a regular weekly ferry service to North America from Liverpool via Antwerp and landing in Montreal. 12 days from £11465 for a double cabin. Once on board a cargo ship things are very cheap too; drinks are duty free and not usually marked up. Unlike cruise ships, there are rarely single-supplements on cargo ships, which can make a huge difference.

Where can you go?
Options range from short journeys to the Med, to transatlantic and transpacific voyages or epic, multi-port journeys. The longest voyage Strand Travel features is a 124-day round-the-world trip leaving from Hamburg and travelling via the Suez Canal, China, Japan, the Panama Canal and the US, which costs £9,155 per person. One of the shortest is a 10-day round trip from Goole in Humberside to Sweden, via Denmark and Germany, from £870. On most of the longer itineraries, it's usually possible to join the ship for part of the route, and it's common to fly one way, or return on another ship.

A cargo ship entering San Francisco Bay

What's included?

Three meals a day plus snacks are included, as well as accommodation. You'll have to pay for drinks and anything else you want on board. Bed linen and towels will be changed regularly and there will be a self-service launderette for personal items. You'll need to arrange your own insurance, too.

What are the ships like?

A variety of freight ships will take passengers, but most are container ships. Accommodation is of a good standard. Facilities vary greatly but there's likely to be a lounge, with TV, DVD and CD player and a selection of films and books, shared with officers and sometimes crew. There's usually a bar and a fitness room. Cabins are generally quite spacious, tend to be on the outside of the ship, and usually have en suite facilities. Compared with the average cabin on a cruise ship, you're likely to have more space but less luxury. Generally, ships will have swimming pools too, mostly outdoor.

What's the food like?

It tends to be simple but good, often reflecting the nationality of the ship. Passengers generally have their own table, which is usually in the officers' restaurant.

How many passengers are there likely to be?

Usually just five or six, but you could be the only one. There will rarely be more than 11 because if a ship has more than 12 passengers it's legally required to have a doctor on board.

What nationality will the crew be?

The shipping companies are of different nationalities, and the captain is usually the same nationality as the ship's owners, but the crew is likely to be a real mix, from anywhere around the world.

Are you expected to tip staff?

It is usual to tip the steward who looks after you. He'll generally clean your cabin and serve you at mealtimes.

Will I be able to see much in port?

You'll probably only have time for the most whistle stop of tours. Most ships will spend 10-12 hours in port, but bear in mind that you could be arriving at 10pm.

Can anyone join a cargo ship?

Most companies won't accept anyone over 80. Passengers with chronic health conditions are generally not accepted.

Will I arrive on the expected date?

Departure and arrival dates are very likely to change because of weather conditions, cargo requirements, even strikes, so it's not for those with fixed schedules.

Jane Dunford

A cruise ship nearing Istanbul

photo: shutterstock/Faraways

Cruises

Flying may be the villain of climate change, but British and European ministers stress that we are only just waking up to the problem of emissions from shipping.

For travellers, the good news is that green concerns seem to have come to the fore in the cruise industry's latest shipbuilding projects. Less reassuring is a chequered history that has left many observers sceptical. As mass tourism, cruising in Britain is only lately catching up with the enormous popularity it enjoys in the US: now well over a million people from Britain take a cruise each year, making it one of the most rapidly growing sectors of the travel market. But concerns around the industry have longer been apparent in the US.

The environment was espoused as a cause by some of the biggest cruise lines as far back as the 1990s; unfortunately it was to emerge that while, for example, Royal Caribbean was promoting its Save the Waves campaign to passengers, its ships were regularly dumping oil and toxic waste at sea, before getting slapped with multimillion dollar fines. Public pressure in California and, most notably, Alaska has forced cruise companies operating there to re-examine their water and airborne emissions in response to local concerns. To some extent, such issues have been eclipsed lately by safety, with new laws passed after campaigns by relatives of passengers who have been assaulted, died or gone missing on board.

The most obvious pollution from ships has been in waste water, although the fuel oil used is also of a lower grade than in cars, containing high levels of sulphur. While international treaties (such as Marpol) restrict what can be dumped at sea and protect the coastline, policing is often by self-regulation.

Critics have also argued that cruises take tourists into previously inaccessible and pristine areas. Even if the pioneering operators are often self-described environmentalists and conservationists, with a vested interest in protecting the waters they sail in, it's not certain that all who follow will share the same zeal. The first large cruise ship only reached the unique ecosystem of the Galápagos islands in 2006. Then fears for wildlife in Antarctica were raised when the Explorer ran ashore and eventually sank, leaking oil, in 2007.

While the Passenger Shipping Association calculates that on an average ferry journey the CO_2 emissions per passenger km (0.12kg) are far lower than flying, this is not the case on a luxury liner where staterooms, enormous meals and high staff-to-passenger ratios are the norm. George Monbiot cites a study by the Climate Outreach Information Network which shows that crossing the Atlantic by cruise ship produces 7.6 times as much CO_2 per passenger than taking a plane. That is perhaps an unfair comparison: many ships are now, as the brochures say, "floating resorts" where people eat and sleep (not to mention ice skate, and have spa treatments), so the cruise might be best compared to the total footprint of another holiday. But then again, many passengers will also be flying to and from their ship.

Questions have also been asked about the impact of cruise ships on the ports they visit. While many have vied in the past to attract them, plans to create harbours big enough to accommodate huge liners have been resisted from Australia to the US. A ship can indeed bring many visitors, but these may often, for example at Caribbean ports, be offloaded at jetties with international franchises and straight on to tours run by the cruise company before they reach the locals or their businesses. Residents in Alaska recently showed they weren't convinced of the net benefit by voting to impose an extra $50 tax per head on every cruise visitor.

Jobs on board remain highly sought after in developing countries, but there are evident tiered systems of labour and pay, with many drawn from Asia and Latin America working long hours (under western officers) on extended, bonded contracts for very low wages plus tips. Arguably, this does no more than mirror globalised labour (and on far more equitable terms than, say, the textile industry) but such racial divides become obvious when gathered on the same ship.

This and other environmental and economic concerns are far from unique to the cruise industry, which argues its record stands proud compared to shipping at large and life on land. The two giant corporations which dominate cruising globally, Royal Caribbean and Carnival (owning British brands such as Cunard and P&O), have put an environmental officer on every ship, reduced disposable packaging and claim high recycling rates. The megaliners they have recently launched or have under construction will be equipped with advanced waste water management systems that virtually eliminate pollution by treating discharges to a high standard (comparable, executives claim, with branded bottled water). Cleaner fuels are being investigated and cruise companies have responded to concerns about anti-fouling paint used on ships' hulls, which was toxic to marine life. There have even been efforts to reduce the occasional, accidental skewering of humpback whales.

But many cruise ships still in service were constructed in days when tipping rubbish overboard or pumping out sewage was barely questioned: often a cruise company's "new" flagship is the repainted and renamed cast-off from another fleet. It will be some years before the cleanest models become the norm.

Cruise companies complain, with some justification, that they are being held to a higher standard than exists on shore. Some aspects are improving. For the individual traveller, the company, ship specification and itinerary chosen can make one cruise holiday f(ar greener than another.

Gwyn Topham

TRAILBLAZER

Ra solar-powered boat, Norfolk Broads, UK

What? The UK's first purpose-built, solar-powered passenger boat, named after the Egyptian sun god. The futuristic vessel offers up to 12 passengers (including wheelchair users) a high vantage point from which to enjoy the restored environment of the Barton Broad nature reserve.

Where? Barton Broad, Norfolk. A similar solar-powered craft is now in service on The Serpentine, in London's Hyde Park.

What's their big idea? To foster sustainable recreation and tourism in an area traditionally known for diesel-powered boating. "Quiet enjoyment is the watchword," says Sam Bates, visitor services manager for the Broads Authority. "It's an ideal opportunity for people to see nature and wildlife with an expert commentary, while not actually damaging the thing they've come to see."

Track record: Ra is one of a fleet of four electric boats, which are quieter as well as cleaner than diesel-powered launches, meaning less disruption to wildlife. Tickets are priced to make the experience as accessible as possible and do not return a profit. The craft was purchased as part of the Clear Water 2000 project to dredge the Broad and improve public access.

The long view: The Broads Authority is working with the regional tourist board to encourage green accreditation in area.

Awards and schemes: The Norfolk Broads is the first area of the UK to gain a European charter for sustainable tourism.

More information: Trips on Ra run daily from June to September and on weekends, bank holidays and local half term in April, May and October. Telephone 01603 782281 to book (in season) or 01603 610 734 for general information, broads-authority.gov.uk.

BY BIKE

Cycling leads the way in zero-carbon travel, with the chance to travel great distances free of cost, guilt and timetables. It's a healthy choice that can lead you to some of the world's most stunning landscapes. Whether you cycle directly from your front door or pick up a bike when you arrive, getting around on two wheels is a great way to reduce your holiday footprint. Look out for self-service schemes such as Vélib' in Paris and Marseille and Cyclocity in Brussels. In this section we hope to inspire you with classic rides the world over, and a few in your backyard too.

Why I love ... cycling touring

It is quite tricky to pinpoint, when you factor in bleeding buttocks, unidentified insect life crawling in panniers and ridiculous, permanent tan lines, exactly what makes travelling by bicycle such a profound joy. Certainly, anyone who would rather don a pair of padded shorts than loll on a sun-drenched beach should be treated with a respectful amount of caution.

Sweating, aching, chaffing do not a holiday make. Especially when they are in the service of a destination which you reach just as it's time to go home. But within all great madness there is a touch of logic. My friend Chris, who, after one particularly arduous day in the saddle, unexpectedly found himself sipping vodka in a sauna with three chaste Finnish girls, would probably be able to argue very convincingly in cycle touring's favour.

He'd start by saying one of the most amazing things about life on a bike is that you literally never know what the day is going to bring. This starts off horribly – usually involving something like being marooned in the middle of a motorway while you pull 13 thorns out of your back tyre. But after getting used to, it provides the physical translation of the saying, "It's not the destination that's important, it's the journey." Perhaps a friendly motorist will come to your aid and you finish the day munching home-cooked meatloaf with some new friends.

Forget plans. As soon as you leap eagerly into the saddle, the road unravels before you on a minute-by-minute basis. It's a sense of freedom we don't usually get to experience. And the best bit is, because you are totally self-sufficient, because you carry everything you need to survive with you, suddenly life becomes a heady clash of opportunities. Do you go left or right? Stop for the night where you are, or see what's over that hill? Have another drink with this strange-looking man or with that group of Finnish girls?

As long as you keep your body fuelled – honestly if you ever needed an excuse to eat a gallon of Neapolitan ice cream, cycle touring is it – there is no where you can't go. And every place you pass through, you taste, smell and feel so much more acutely than if you had sped through in a soft-top at 70mph. Small towns, friendly faces, simple pleasures you get to see them all. Unless you're gasping for breath on a grass verge, which does occasionally happen.

Relaxation doesn't necessarily mean spa retreat in Thailand. Moving slowly upon Earth – waking when the sun rises, sleeping when your body is tired – brings you into a peaceful rhythm with nature which is incredibly soothing for the soul.

Susan Greenwood

photo: JC Decaux, operators of the Vélib' scheme

Using the Vélib' bike hire scheme, Paris

International bike trips

PORT PHILLIP BAY, MELBOURNE, AUSTRALIA

Port Phillip Bay is like a great seawater lake, with a coastline 160 miles long. But this does not mean dodging bikini-clad rollerbladers on flat boardwalks: basalt plains give way to granite hills, tortuous ascents and "Crikey, mate!" views of the bay and Bass Straight.

Where to stay: Elwood Beaches just outside St Kilda, a suburb of Melbourne, is a gorgeous boutique B&B with one room available for A$150 a night.

UYUNI SALT FLAT, BOLIVIA

For wide, open spaces, choose Uyuni salt flat: nothing can prepare you for riding over its swathes of white salt, baked hard under a fantastically blue sky. This is a landscape just waiting for your imagination to paint it. Moreover, there is a bonus in the title – salt flat. The ride can be done in a day, which is probably advisable as night-time temperatures sink to around -20°C (-4°F). Make sure you have fat tyres not road ones.

Where to stay: the Jardines de Uyuni (+591 2 693 2989) is a little inn favoured by honeymooners. Rooms from £15 a night.

ALPE D'HUEZ, FRANCE

Twenty-one switchbacks, a 1,120m vertical climb on a gradient ranging from 7.7% at the lowest to 12%, over a distance of 14km. This is the most famous climb in cycling history. Cyclists who do it wear the T-shirt with pride. The view is great, too.

Where to stay: Hotel L'Ancolie (+33 476 111 313). Rooms from €52.

GORGES DE LA JONTE, CEVENNES, FRANCE

The vultures circling above are not encouraging, but ride this road the right way – from Meyrueis to La Rozier – and the delicious downhill gradient will ensure it is not you they divebomb. In autumn the trees clinging to the steep sides of the Jonte gorge put on a riotous display of colour. The ride out and up is pretty brutal but the brief, blissful escape in the gorge makes it worthwhile.

Where to stay: take a trip back in time at the Château d'Ayres (+33 466 456 010), a 12th-century monastery. Rooms from €60 a night.

LANGKAWI, MALAYSIA

Not only a cycle route but an entire island to explore. Think water buffalo grazing, back roads leading to secluded waterfalls, white sandy beaches and verdant jungle. Apart from flies hitting your face like bullets when you gather speed, Langkawi makes for pretty laid-back riding. Add a bit of spice by hauling yourself up Gunung Raya, which at 881m is the tallest point on the island. The annual Malaysian cycle race is known as the Tour de Langkawi.

Where to stay: Frangipani Langkawi Resort and Spa, standard rooms from £47 a night. (+60 4 952 0000)

JOTUNHEIMEN NATIONAL PARK, NORWAY

The Lord of the Rings might have been filmed in New Zealand, but Norway was surely a strong contender. Jotunheimen, the highest mountain area in Scandinavia, offers endless options for the strong of thigh. As evening approaches, the high mountain road is enveloped in an icy beauty that is out of this world. The ride is a steep climb but crystal views of still mountain lakes along the way make it worthwhile. If you prefer fewer hills, try the Sognefjord Cycle Route between the towns of Borluag and Turtago: it combines mountains and fjords without causing your muscles to cannibalise themselves.

Where to stay: Sogndal B&B (+47 913 00 946) in Sognefjord, with single rooms from £33 a night and doubles from £45.

WHITEHAVEN TO SUNDERLAND, UK

From sea to shining sea – this classic ride traverses England (admittedly across its thinnest point). It goes from coal-mining country, through the northern Lakes before hitting the Pennines and going on through the dales. At around 140 miles, hardened cyclists could do it in a couple of days but that would leave time for about one post-ride pint of ale, and where would be the fun in that?

Where to stay: you could camp but, this being England, it would rain. Instead, stop in Keswick, halfway along the route. There are B&Bs aplenty with rooms starting at around £24 a night.

LONDON TO HEVER CASTLE, UK

Included here because this is such a classic Sunday ride. Drop down into the Weald of Kent: the rolling hills are gentle at first but you know you have Westerham Hill ahead, which keeps the legs pumping. Kent in the sun is a pretty, pastoral patchwork, and even in the rain it is never miserable. Stop off at Hever Castle for a quick history lesson before heading to the Swan pub, in west Peckham, for a home-brewed ale. With so many little roads linking up, you get a taste for an older England without ever having to do the same route twice.

Where to stay: Wendy Wood's B&B in Seal (0173 276 3755), which has single rooms from £30 a night.

DUBOIS, WYOMING, TO GRAND TETON NATIONAL PARK, US

Sometimes you have to put in to get out. Just think of the climb over Togowotee Pass as an investment – you get to splash out later. Stock up on some calories at the Cowboy Cafe in Dubois before tackling a series of cruel uphill sections that undulate as they rise. But the descent into Teton is the magnificent payoff: first hugging the mountainside, then screaming along the valley floor – the Teton mountains constantly dominating the horizon like kings. This is wild country, and you are riding it.

Where to stay: Colter Bay Village (+1 406 862 8190) on the shores of Jackson Lake. You can camp for as little as $5; rooms in the lodge start from $40.

HIGHWAY 12 FROM LOLO PASS TO LOWELL, IDAHO, US

By the time you reach the summit of Lolo Pass, on the border between Montana and Idaho, your body has passed the pain barrier and entered the realms of rigor mortis. Highway 12, a graceful, twisting, solitary road, is like the kiss of life. Completed in the early 1950s – before that, access to the valley was by donkey – it still offers a glimpse of an untouched wilderness. This is 80 miles of mesmeric riding through thick carpets of forest, chasing the racing Lochsa river to the left.

Where to stay: Three Rivers Resort, Lowell (+1 208 926 4430). Camp on the shores of the river for £5 per person per night or treat yourself to a motel room or cabin from £30pp per night.

Susan Greenwood

photo: shutterstock/Harry H Marsh

The Grand Teton mountains from the shore of Jackson Lake, Wyoming, US

# European cycling holidays

MÉRIBEL, FRENCH ALPS

In summer, the ski slopes of Méribel in the Trois Vallées become the largest mountain bike course in the world, with 100km of trails to suit every level. If you're more into adrenalin than sweating, the gondolas are equipped to carry the bikes so you can enjoy super-long downhills and also link with neighbouring valleys. For hardcore cyclists, Méribel hosts one of the world's toughest mountain bike challenges, the annual VTT (es3vallees.com/3vtt). Unlike the rest of Europe, accommodation prices in the Alps plummet in summer, so you can stay in a large six-berth chalet (meribelapartments.com, for example) for as little as £300 per week.

More accommodation options and general info at meribel.net. Bike hire and guided rides: meribike.com. Raileurope.co.uk to Moutiers Salins from £99 return. Taking your bike by train to Europe is complicated and expensive, especially if you have to change trains. The easiest way is to take off the wheels, handlebars and saddle, put it in a bike bag and carry it on board as luggage.

WESTERN LOIRE, FRANCE

"Cyclopedia" claims to be the first GPS handheld guide for cyclists, holding a database of places of interest along the 65km trail from Gennes to Montjean-sur-Loire. The GPS is free and in English – to borrow one you have to leave a €250 deposit at one of seven local tourist offices on the Loire à Vélo route, clip the device to your bike and off you go. A series of Accueil Vélo hotels linked to the scheme offer high-energy breakfasts, secure bicycle parks and breakdown assistance: some of the best are in Angers, which is served by the high-speed TGV from Paris. There are 160km of marked bike routes in the area and ultimately an 800km trail will link Cuffy near Sancerre to St-Brévin-les-Pins on the Atlantic. In turn, this will form part of the highly ambitious European rivers cycle route scheme, which will connect the Atlantic to Budapest and later the Black Sea, a 2,400km-long journey. Loire-a-velo.fr has information on accommodation and bike hire.

photo: shutterstock/mountainpix

*Sunlight on vinyards,
Chamoson, Switzerland*

MORZINE, FRANCE

Morzine has become to mountain biking what Chamonix once was to climbing – the place in the French Alps to flock to in summer. The streets echo to the clack of cleats and the mode du jour is skintight lycra. It has a wealth of terrain for all abilities (but particularly for gnarly riders), and there's a well-marked trail system, so you can travel huge distances without worrying about getting lost or stuck somewhere too tough (or easy) for you. Above all, many of the Portes du Soleil ski lifts stay open in the summer, and are equipped for bike carriage, so a lot of the pesky uphilling is removed.

Seven nights for £204, with B&B and transfers from Geneva, or £323pp, half-board. Bike hire £40 per day. Extra activities include everything from whitewater sports and zip-wiring to donkey trekking (01932 837 639, summermorzine.com).

GREEN COAST, SPAIN

Sandwiched between the Picos de Europa and the coast, España Verde is one of the most unspoilt and varied areas in Spain. An eight-day itinerary with Freewheel Holidays takes in medieval villages such as Santillana del Mar and the elegant town of San Vicente de la Barquera, climbing (or catching the local train) to Colombres before freewheeling down through the foothills to Llanes. You are then transported to the top of the San Roque pass for a leisurely ride down the valley of the River Miera and back to the coast and Santander. The 20-hour ferry ride from Plymouth to Santander (08705 360 360, brittanyferries.co.uk) costs from £80 return (includes reclining seat) for a foot passenger with a bike.

Tour from £549 including all transfers (optional lift up steep ascents), cycle hire, host support and B&B in family-run hotels (travel from the UK not included), (0845 3720 315, freewheelholidays.com).

CORDOBA, SPAIN

The hills around Cordoba offer some incredibly varied mountain biking terrain – from exciting descents down scree slopes to rolling paths across the scrublands; from speed plunges in rocky gorges to gentle meanders across farmers' terraces in the woods; and from leaps across mountain streams, to freewheeling to a halt on the beach by Lake Iznajar. Joyriders runs mountain bike holidays in Cerro Macho, between Cordoba and Granada, with guided rides for most levels. Accommodation is in an attractive farmhouse, which was a winery 300 years ago. It has a pool and a kitchen for self-catering.

From £399pp for six nights' B&B and free bar, including transfer from Malaga, Seville or Granada. Bike hire available from £99 a week (+34 957 723363, joy-riders.com).

RHONE VALLEY, SWITZERLAND

Here's a break from adrenaline-fuelled descents and heart-pumping climbs. Freewheel Holidays has designed cycling routes with a minimum of climbing that still allow you to enjoy the drama of the Alps. The Best of Switzerland route takes you through the Rhone valley (Switzerland's wine region) and pretty villages, allowing detours to the dramatic Aletsch glacier, with its ice grotto, to Zermatt, at the foot of the Matterhorn, and to the St Bernard Pass. With clever route planning, plus judicious use of railways and cable cars, all this comes while you barely raise a sweat.

From £769, including transfers, B&B, guiding and bike hire. Not including flights or train to Geneva (08453 720315, freewheelholidays.co.uk).

ON THE LEVEL, HOLLAND

They say there are more bicycles than residents in Holland. It is certainly one of the most cycle-friendly countries in the world, perfect for riders of all ages and abilities. Cycle off the Harwich-Hook of Holland ferry (stenaline.co.uk, from £29 one way for a bicycle and rider) and take your pick from the hundreds of cycle routes (15,000km of them in all) around the country. Meander along the canals of Rotterdam or Amsterdam or follow the Flower Bulb Route from Haarlem to Sassenheim, or Windmill Route where you'll come across 14 windmills in a row.

For details of routes, local tourist offices, accommodation and to order maps, visit holland.com (click special interests/cycling). 2 Wheel Treks (2wheeltreks.co.uk) offers a range of organised tours, from four to eight days throughout the Netherlands.

Gavin McOwan

TRAILBLAZER

Vélib', Paris

What?   A brilliantly simple self-service bike scheme, launched by the city authorities in July 2007.

Where?   The specially designed bikes can be picked up and dropped off 24/7 at any of the 1,450 terminals across town – that's one every 300m. Operators JC Decaux also run schemes in 16 other European cities including Lyon, Marseille, Toulouse and Seville.

What's their big idea?   To encourage cheap, clean and healthy transport for residents and visitors alike. As most journeys in the city take under 30 minutes, the first half hour of any ride is free, with subsequent half-hour units costing €1, €2 and €5. Participants take out a daily (€1), weekly (€5) or annual (€29) subscription, stump up a €150 deposit and then use as many bikes as they like during that period. According to Paris mayor Bertrand Delanoë, the nominal cost "enables everyone to take advantage of a practical, inexpensive and ecological means of transport".

Track record: Vélib' is the largest self-service bike initiative in the world. In its first year, the number of bikes available doubled to over 20,000 and some 40 million hire journeys were made, saving an estimated 10 million km in car trips. The bikes themselves are 99% recyclable and are cleaned with rainwater. The maintenance fleet is made up of electric and natural gas vehicles and a river barge.

The long view: The success of Vélib' has inspired successive London mayors Ken Livingstone and Boris Johnson to look at introducing a similar self-service scheme in the UK.

Awards and schemes: A host of environmental and engineering awards, plus the *Guardian*, *Observer* and guardian.co.uk Ethical Travel Award 2008.

More information: en.velib.paris.fr

ON FOOT

Little can beat a walking holiday for total escapism. Exploring cities, mountains and national parks on foot guarantees a degree of immersion in your surroundings sure to occupy a restless mind. And as a zero-carbon, zero-cost mode of transport, walking is an accessible, low-impact option to consider. Of course, the standard rules apply about behaving respectfully towards local wildlife and cultures, particularly if your trek takes you into fragile habitats. In this section we hope to inspire you with classic long-distance treks such as the GR5 in France, as well as less taxing walking festivals across the UK.

Why I love ... walking holidays

My idea of paradise is a sandy beach, a suitcase full of novels and easy access to cheap, delicious, local red wine. My second most overused four letter word is "taxi". So to say that I was dreading a proposed 180-kilometre walking holiday along the legendary pilgrims' way in northern Spain would be an understatement.

My mother was convinced I'd be injured. Two Spanish colleagues literally fell about laughing whenever I mentioned it. Friends were appalled. "At least the weather will be nice." "No, we're going to Galicia – they get two metres of rain a year. It's wetter than Ireland." "At least your driver will take your luggage each day." "No, we're going independently – we'll be carrying everything, including water." Long pause. "You haven't gone all religious on us, have you?" "No, I just thought it would make a change." Longer pause. "So, doing anything nice at the weekend?" "Walking 20 miles to get fit."

You might imagine that with all this fuss we were pioneers, the very first people to walk the final 250km of the Camino de Santiago de Compostela which, in its entirety, runs over 750km from the south of France through to the western tip of Spain. In fact, it is the world's earliest venture into mass tourism. Ever since the body of St James was said to have pitched up in a stone boat and been buried on the site of the cathedral in Santiago, millions of pilgrims have walked the ancient route. Most have done it for religious reasons, some as a penance, some to bring their village luck.

Day one was rather good fun. I didn't actually start crying until the morning of day two. It might have been the rain (it poured for most of day one - great fat rods of water which hadn't cleared by the second morning). It might have been dinner the night before (tasteless soup, indefinable fish, flan from a packet). It might have been breakfast (we couldn't find any). It might have been the realisation that I was already weary from the first day and I was going to have to do it all over again. In the same pair of trousers . Call this a holiday? Anyway, I blubbed.

Then suddenly, without warning, the sun came out. The yellow broom glowed, the wet oak leaves glistened. The soft, watery light was the kind Van Morrison likes to sing about. Once I'd stopped crying and actually got going the endorphins kicked in and I stopped obsessing about how far we had to go or what the weather was like. One moment it's 20C sunshine, the next dark clouds gather, (the week before it had snowed.) I began to appreciate the narrow paths between the dry stone walls. I started to enjoy the thump thump of my boots and the clack clack of my walking sticks on paths which so many people had walked before me. (A note here on walking sticks: they help propel you along, pulling you up hills like cross country ski sticks. Also very useful for pointing at things and thwacking nettles.)

We'd worried that the trek would be more like a sponsored walk with queues of pilgrims shuffling along in long, penitent rows. In fact, there were far fewer people than we had imagined and after the breakfast rush hour you naturally start to spread out (although it does get busier later in the summer when the devout try to get to Santiago for 25 July, one of the holiest days in the year) The days took on a similar timetable. We'd set off at 10am (despite best intentions, we found it impossible to get up any earlier) after eating as much breakfast as possible; walk for several hours, stopping for a break along the way. On shorter stints we'd get to our destination in time for a late lunch, other times we'd swing by a restaurant or cafe en route.

I'd hoped I might have some blinding epiphany, or a sudden notion of what the universe is all about. Instead I realised the running commentary in my head went something like this: "Right stick, left stick, right stick, left stick; will I have red wine when I get there? Or white wine? Red wine, white wine, red wine, white wine; oh, look a lovely black thingamajig bird, must look that up, must look that up; right stick, left stick." What was more meaningful was the fact that I stopped worrying how everyone at work was getting on for possibly the first time in my life. I subsequently discover that it's a proven medical fact that prolonged walking quietens the left side of the brain – the admin department – freeing you up to relax and think.

By the time we reached Santiago I felt partly ecstatic (not least because I was convinced I'd dropped two dress sizes: this subsequently turned out to be fanciful) and exhausted (the last stretch is uphill along unforgiving Tarmac and then you drop down into town, negotiating road works and the first fumes you've encountered for a week). Until we saw the beautiful old town with its towering, mossy cathedral, the official end of the journey is a strange anticlimax. I expected people to be showering us with ticker tape but the locals are inured to the silent stream of walkers and barely gave us a second glance. Presumably if you are a religious pilgrim there is a moment of pure joy when you go into the cathedral and kiss the Virgin's feet. If you're not religious you find a bar instead.

Whereas most pilgrims hang up their walking boots in Santiago, a day later we headed towards Finisterre on the west coast. By this point we were so gung ho about our new-found fitness we left all but the bare essentials behind and strode out like Janet Street-Porter. If anything, the countryside was even more beautiful than before. We ran up the hills and marvelled at the fact that we weren't out of breath. We calculated that the holiday had amounted to eight hours in the gym. Every day. I'd found my own vocation – I'd write to the Prime Minister and urge him to beat obesity by getting children to walk to school every day. Walking, I ranted, was the answer to all life's problems.

Louise France

Camino de Santiago footpath, Navarra, Spain

photo: shutterstock/Sybille Yates

Long-distance walking holidays

GR5, FRANCE

One of the best-known of Europe's sentiers de grande randonnée, or long-distance paths, the GR5 runs from the North Sea to the Mediterranean via the Alps. The southern third, a month's trek from Lake Geneva to Nice, is the most spectacular. David May, author of the informative grfive.com guide, claims the mix of Alpine pastures, snow-tipped peaks and charming inns, such as Les Gentianettes in La Chapelle d'Abondance (gentianettes.fr), along this section puts it on a par with Nepal's Annapurna circuit. There are numerous hostel-style refuges and gîtes d'étape along the way.

London-Geneva via Paris on Eurostar and TGV takes about eight hours, from around £64 one way; Nice to London by TGV and Eurostar via Lille takes around nine hours, from £63 one way (seat61.com).

KERRY WAY, IRELAND

You don't have to cross Europe to find a decent hike. A circular route around the Iveragh peninsula, the Kerry Way takes in 215km of rugged lakes, mountains, woodlands and coast as well as historic houses, ruined abbeys and standing stones. To do it independently takes 10 days (see kerryway.net) or see the highlights – including lakeside Muckross House (muckross-house.ie) and Black Valley (so-called because all its inhabitants died during the great famine) in seven nights' B&B with Contours (017684 80451, contours.co.uk) and have your luggage carried for you.

To book through train travel from the UK to Killarney, the start and finish point, plus the Fishguard-Rosslare ferry, contact SailRail (08450 755 755, sailrail.co.uk).

SENTIERO FRANCESCANO DELLA PACE, ITALY

At just 40km, Umbria's Sentiero Francescano della Pace (sentierofrancescano. provincia.perugia.it) is ideal for a long weekend. The pilgrimage path from Assisi to Gubbio retraces the route St Francis is said to have taken in 1206 after relinquishing his fortune in favour of a more humble life. You can even follow the saint's lead and break your journey at Vallingegno Abbey (00 39 075 920 158), now a comfortable agriturismo hotel, doubles from €91.

The nearest station to Assisi and Gubbio is Perugia, around two hours from Florence (from €8.75 each way; trenitalia.com). To get to Florence, take the Eurostar to Paris, and then an overnight sleeper (around £115 return, raileurope.co.uk).

CAMINO DE SANTIAGO, SPAIN

This month-long pilgrimage trail ends at Santiago de Compostela, Galicia, where St James' remains are supposedly buried. Routes abound, but the most popular, the "Camino Francés", runs for around 780km east to west crossing the French-Spanish border from St Jean Pied de Port. Don't expect a walk in the park: some still attempt it as penance (caminodesantiago.me.uk). Less hardcore is the final section from Burgos, taking two to three weeks. You can stay cheaply or for free in the pilgrimage huts and hostels along the route.

Plymouth-Santander from £59pp return (01752 227941, brittany-ferries.co.uk); Santander to Burgos is around two and a half hours by bus; Santiago de Compostela back to Santander from six hours (see alsa.es, the Spanish bus service).

LYCIAN WAY, TURKEY

You'll need both swimsuit and hiking boots to make the most of this 509km trek. Following Turkey's southern coast from Fethiye to Antalya, it passes white sand beaches, unspoilt villages, and sites such as the ancient Lycian city of Myra. Leave a month for the full thing (lycianway.com), although most people break it down into week-long sections, camping or sleeping in rustic guesthouses, such as the Watermill in Faralya (natur-reisen.de, €43pp).

Getting there is part of the fun, if you take the three-day train ride London-Istanbul (from £273pp return with a "10 days in 22" InterRail pass, an overnight train Istanbul-Denizli (£9 one way); see seat61.com for details, and a five-hour bus to Antalya or Fetiyhe (around £2.50 each way).

Rhiannon Batten

photo: shutterstock/K.Jakubowska

Lycian rock tombs in Myra, Turkey

British coastal walks

PITTENWEEM TO ELIE, FIFE

It is worth visiting Pittenweem just because of the name, and the Fife Coastal Path is a good additional reason. The section between the town and Elie includes two ruined castles plus good rockpools whose investigation for mini marine beasts may well distract you from going all the way. If you do make the distance, other rewards are the finely restored windmill and associated saltpans at St Monans and of course "Pittenweem, Pittenweem, Every fisher laddies' dream ..." You have go to find out why.

Six miles one way. Buses hourly. fifecoastalpath.co.uk.

CRASTER TO DUNSTANBURGH, NORTHUMBERLAND

Craster has the country's best kippers, so this could be a good post-breakfast hike. The seacliffs are excellent and the ruins of Dunstanburgh castle summon up every possible image of Macbeth, Richard the Lionheart and all those other mighty chaps. Find particularly interesting birdlife on the cliffs and at Newton beach and Newton Pool nature reserve. Lots of interesting plants and geology too, helpfully described by the National Trust which owns most of the land.

Six-mile circuit. Bus to Craster. walkingbritain.co.uk.

BOGGLE HOLE TO ROBIN HOOD'S BAY, NORTH YORKSHIRE

Boggle Hole is a lovely and often amazingly unfrequented cove compared with always bustling Baytown just up the coast. There's a youth hostel in the narrow ravine and the cliff or beach walks south to Ravenscar are a great alternative. It is essential to know tide times if using the beach, which makes the most fascinating of three ways of getting to Robin Hood's Bay. This is one of the UK's premier 'fossil coasts' and splitting loose chunks of rock will often reveal an ammonite. The clifftop path is clear if a little over-fenced but the disused railway half a mile inland is lovely for a round trip.

Three miles one way. Parking above Boggle Hole, bus to RHB. clevelandway.co.uk.

BURNHAM OVERY STAITHE TO WELLS-NEXT-THE-SEA, NORFOLK

If the sands of Holkham beach are good enough for the Royal family, picnicking from nearby Sandringham, then the rest of us should be OK. This walk begins from the lovely old windmill at Burnham which curiously used to stand at the end, in Wells. They moved it in the early 1800s. The big beach is almost seven miles of sand with sea lavender, dark green fritillary butterflies, peregrine falcons and just inland are the glories of Holkham Hall. Remember Gwynneth Paltrow all alone by the breakers at the end of Shakespeare in Love? It wasn't Hawaii — it was here.

Eight miles. CoastHopper bus. nationaltrail.co.uk/PeddarsWay.

SEVEN SISTERS AND BEACHY HEAD, EAST SUSSEX

The classic white-cliffs walk with lots of variations, going either way from Birling Gap which lies between the Sisters and the Head. Best start for buses or parking is the Seven Sisters country park at Exceat, then past the Golden Galleon pub (a pleasant start and/or finish) along a footpath across downland to the stunning cliffs. Turn right for a bathe at Cuckmere Haven, as sweet as its name, or left for the Gap and then up to the old lighthouse on Beachy Head. Peep, extremely carefully, at the modern one on the rocks far below. The keepers only get French terrestrial TV because the British signal beams from the clifftop way above their aerial.

Eight miles. Buses and parking. sevensisters.org.uk.

DURDLE DOOR & WHITE NOTHE CIRCULAR, DORSET

This walk starts and finishes at Lulworth Cove which is well-organized for transport and tourism, with cafes and a castle when you've finished with the coast. Don't expect to rush though. The switchback takes in the romantic arch of Durdle Door, where dropping to the beach means a climb back up the same way, but it's worth it. Next stop is well-named Scratchy Bottom and then more rollercoastering to Swyre Head, Batis Head and the obelisk navigation beacon and coastguard cottages at White Nothe (which really does mean 'white nose' – someone ancient must have lisped). You can circle back inland through gentle countryside at Dagger's Gate and Newlands Farm.

Seven miles. Bus and parking. southwestcoastpath.com.

HARTLAND QUAY TO HARTLAND POINT, DEVON

Very fine rocky shores are the target on this wild stretch of coast, where vile weather can actually make the whole experience more romantic. The quay is a pretty little spot, with Hartland Abbey behind dating back to 1157 and noisy with peacocks. Then it's all up and down along a three-mile switchback to the lighthouse at Hartland Point. The big grey lump out to sea is Lundy Island. You can wend back inland via Titchberry, Hartland village and other sources of cream-teas.

Six-mile circular walk. Bus at Hartland, parking near quay. southwestcoastpath.com.

photo: britainonview

Durdle Door, Dorset

STACKPOLE HEAD, PEMBROKESHIRE

One of the finest stretches of the Pembrokeshire Coastal Path, this takes in spectacular eroded limestone cliffs and the peaceful loveliness of Barafundle Bay. Bosherston Lily ponds – best in June – are an unexpected extra and the wild flora and fauna en route are terrific throughout. Start at Stackpole Quay, once a limestone harbour, now National Trust, and simply follow the cliffs south to the Head. It's back the way you came but who minds another dip at Barafundle?

Six-mile circular walk. Coastal Cruiser bus, parking. pcnpa.org.uk.

HILBRE ISLAND, WIRRAL

An exciting venture into the world of migrating birds and grey seals, with strict adherence to waymarking and tidal times essential. Hilbre is the biggest of three islets at the tip of the Wirral peninsular, reached from Dee Lane slipway in West Kirby when the tide is out. Times are clearly posted here with details of when you must leave Hilbre to get back safe and dry. You can stay on the island over high water, but that means being marooned for five hours with little shelter. Apart from abundant birdlife, the Hilbre Telegraph lookout station has been renovated by the Friends of Hilbre and is open on selected dates – which are good to choose, to benefit from the volunteers' knowledge and enthusiasm. Always keep to the marked route via Little Eye and Little Hilbre.

Three-mile circular walk. Train, bus, parking. hilbreisland.org.uk.

ELGOL TO LOCH CORUISK, ISLE OF SKYE

This is a long walk in the heart of the Cuillin mountains, craggy scenery of great grandeur surrounding a lonely sea loch. The distance is twice as long if you attempt a round trip, putting it in the Iron Man class. The best course is to get a boat in from Elgol and then walk back via Camasunary. Check weather conditions because the stream at Camasunary can rise too high to ford, forcing a long detour. The "bad step", a slanting slab above Loch Coruisk, is intimidating to some and other stretches of the walk are rough underfoot. Not for novices who can take the boat back while you march to rejoin them overland. 15 miles. Parking, bus, boat. walking.visitscotland.com.

Martin Wainwright

Walking festivals

England

ISLE OF WIGHT WALKING FESTIVAL

Drawing a crowd of 15,000 in May each year, the Isle of Wight has a themed walk for every taste – from ghost walks, pub walks and pram walks to tea party walks. And in case you prefer something even more niche, you can join the "romantic walk for single dog owners" or the Speed Dating Walk (isleofwightwalkingfestival.co.uk).

SOUTH AND HEART OF SUFFOLK WALKING FESTIVAL

The first festival in May 2008 offered more than 40 guided walks for a variety of fitness levels. Nearly half were accessible for prams and wheelchairs, with the vast majority either free, or less than a fiver (the more expensive walks usually include admission to an attraction). Highlights include a Constable-themed walk (southandheartofsuffolk.org.uk).

ULLSWATER WALKING FESTIVAL, LAKE DISTRICT

A popular walking destination year-round, but the annual Ullswater walking festival in May pulls together a range of varied and challenging guided walks for all levels. There are also a number of mountain biking training sessions for beginners, with bikes provided free of charge, practical map-reading and compass skills courses, and a photography walk (ullswater.com).

Wales

PRESTATYN WALKING FESTIVAL, DENBIGHSHIRE

Many festivals have one-off themed walks, but in 2008 Prestatyn went one better, having a giant theme for the whole thing: The Romans in north-east Wales. Under this heading, treks included A Saint, a Goblin Stone and a Sacred Hill and The Lost Roman City Varae. Annually in May (prestatynwalkingfestival.co.uk).

BARMOUTH FESTIVAL OF WALKING, GWYNEDD

If it's a challenge you're after, head to Barmouth in September and take on the nine-mile Rhinog Fach and Y Llethr walk – so hardcore they had to invent a new category of difficulty classification for it (A+ rather than the now tame sounding A). The walk takes in the most impressive peaks of the Rhinogydd mountains as you climb to Bwlch Drws Ardudwy, then a further steep climb to the summit of Rhinog Fach, a slight dip to Llyn Hywel and a final descent to Y Llethr, the highest peak of the range at a height of 756m (barmouthwalkingfestival.co.uk).

Scotland

NEWTON STEWART WALKING FESTIVAL, DUMFRIES AND GALLOWAY

Newton Stewart's annual event (the biggest walking festival in the south of Scotland) offers 26 routes. Choose a coastal or historic theme, such as a guided tour of the route taken by the English Army prior to the Battle of Trool in 1307. The festival, held in May, is also a great way to discover the largely unspoilt, 2,000ft-plus peaks of the region, with names like the Awful Hand and the Dungeon Range (newtonstewartwalkfest.co.uk).

CRIEFF AND STRATHEARN'S DROVERS' TRYST

Time to party like it's 1699 – this annual October event (slogan: "Let's Tryst Again") in Perthshire celebrates the lives of "the people who made Crieff the crossroads of Scotland in the 1700s". Now in its eighth year, the festival (which aims to be carbon neutral) "seeks to recreate the atmosphere of the droving days – without the inconvenience of 30,000 cattle", and offers walks, fly fishing, bushcraft skills, navigation classes, photographic walks, bagging Munros and rambling through the glens, plus the opportunity to kick up your heels at a ceilidh. The main event is the "Hairy Coo" – actually a mountain biking challenge covering many of the drove roads – followed by a huge barn dance (Crieff tourist information 01764 652578, droverstryst.co.uk).

Ireland

WEST CORK WALKING FESTIVAL, CO CORK

A small but enticing event in May, in the beautiful surrounds of West Cork, the festival is based in the areas of Bantry, Sheep's Head Way and Whiddy Island. On a variety of walks, you might discover anything from the ruins of a 16th-century church, to pre-famine burial grounds, to relics of the early Bronze Age (westcork.ie).

Northern Ireland

MOURNE INTERNATIONAL WALKING FESTIVAL, NEWCASTLE, CO DOWN

Takes place in June. Each evening walkers return from a variety of 10-40km routes in the Mourne mountains, and enjoy a few pints and a knees-up of traditional Irish music (mournewalking.co.uk).

Jersey

SPRING AND AUTUMN WALKING WEEKS

Foodies will find themselves in heaven when joining a spring walking week food trail outing. A celebration of Jersey's range of delicacies, the walks focus on oyster fishing, hens, Jersey Royal potatoes, wine estates and cheese production. More active participants can take the full five-day Around Island challenge, exploring beaches, headlands, castles and ancient burial chambers (jersey.com).

Sarah Bourn

photo: Tourism Ireland/Holger Leue

The Beara peninsula, Cork

TRAILBLAZER

Village Ways

What? Guided walking holidays hosted by Indian villagers in foothills of the Himalayas.

Where? In and around the wooded Binsar wildlife sanctuary, a day's drive north-east of Delhi, and just south of Tibetan border. A second project is under way in the Saryu valley, closer to the mountains.

What's their big idea? Bringing tourists to an area of outstanding natural beauty while training and encouraging local people to take over the management of the holidays. So far five guest houses have been constructed by local craftsmen using traditional materials. These are part-granted and part-loaned to the villagers who should own them outright in five to six years.

Track record: The projects are regenerating life in the villages and providing a way for local communities to derive an income from the wildlife reserve. "The national park was in conflict with local livelihoods," explains Village Ways' Linda Hearn. "Now they work together to protect crops." People are now leaving the city and are coming back to the villages, she says. "They can see a future." In addition, a charitable trust allows guests to make voluntary donations to village projects.

The long view: Similar schemes are being considered for Ethiopia and Thailand. "It's a fantastic formula, which can be replicated wherever there's a rural need," says Hearn.

Awards and schemes: Best Overseas Tourism Project 2007, British Guild of Travel Writers; Runner-up for the *Guardian*, *Observer* and guardian.co.uk Ethical Travel Award 2007. Best place to stay (worldwide), Times Green Spaces 2008

More information: villageways.com; UK +44 (0) 1223 750049; India +91 (0) 1164 623175 or +91 (0) 94 111 05450

UNDER CANVAS

Camping is by nature a lower-impact choice of accommodation because campsites use far less energy and water resources than hotels and resorts. They also have fewer communal buildings which means less cement - a carbon hungry material whose production is responsible for 5% of manmade Co2 emissions worldwide. It's still worth checking up on environmental policies however, as wildlife will often have been cleared to make place for pitches. The better campsites are installing solar-powered hot water, rainwater harvesting, strict policies on rubbish and conservation projects. In this section we list the best green campsites and how to go about wild camping, if you really want to leave nothing but footprints.

 **Why I love ...** wild camping

I can remember the first time I stayed up past midnight. It was still light outside, a sort of dream-like, pearly light, and so quiet that our voices echoed in the emptiness. I was 11 years old and in the Highlands of Scotland with Glenn Ford – not the actor; the one who's now a teacher in Derbyshire.

Days last forever in the Highlands in summer. At midnight we felt pleasantly sleepy but there was no way we were going to bed. We were in the hills, miles from anywhere and anyone, and we were staying up all night. Eventually – probably about 10 minutes later – we crawled into our little tent, and fell into a sleep frequently interrupted by the imagined scratching of wild animals on canvas. In the morning, I poked my head through the flap and felt afresh the shock of looking out into nothing. Nothing but dew-damp rocks and mountains beyond the little grass bowl we were camping in; above, the biggest blue sky I had ever seen.

It may sound criminally crackpot to dump two kids in the wilds of the Cairngorms, a place where serious weather can steal in like a ghost, but I am indebted to the scout group which took us out of our week-long base camp near Aviemore, split us into groups of two and dropped us into this no-man's land for a night's survival course. This was my first taste of freedom, feral freedom (we only learned later that an adult was quietly snuggled down in a bivvy over the next hillock from us), and from that moment, I loved everything about wild camping.

I loved the kit that was bought especially for that trip: the Trangia stove with pots that fitted inside each other like a Russian doll, the Spanish felt walking boots, even my first down-filled sleeping bag that left a trail of feathers for me to sweep up each morning.

Most of all, I loved waking up in the great outdoors rather than a smelly tent shared with 11 other boys, taking water from a mountain stream rather than negotiating the stagnant lake that always forms around a campsite's standpipe, and not having to endure interminable campfire singalongs.

Since then there have been wild-ish nights at festivals, tents half-pitched in the gardens of remote pubs, and the handy convenience of campsites up and down these isles. But there's always a compromise: the queue to the shower block or Portaloos or, the slightly suburban feel of waking up in a paddock next to a fleet of caravans.

Nothing beats striking out for the back of beyond. The watch comes off as soon as the tent goes up, and weekends unwind at a snail's pace. I've added fishing gear to the kit these days, but the home on my back is as light as can be. Provisions are simple, spartan even: porridge oats, couscous and dried tomatoes, biscuits, drinking water and a hip flask of whisky. Occasionally I'll throw in a few pieces of bacon to go with the trout I hope to catch.

I've played Huckleberry Finn on an island in the middle of Lough Corrib on the west coast of Ireland, cooking the trout I've caught in damp newspaper over a campfire. In Sutherland, I've been slapped in the face all night by a wind-battered tent only to wake in the morning to a gloriously calm mountain scene that New Zealand would be hard-pressed to rival. And I've gone to bed on an idyllic little grass ledge on a river in the Peak District and floated away in the night.

This year I'm planning on taking the family, including my two-year-old daughter, to Ram's Island in County Antrim for a high summer camp. Wild camping can be as challenging or easy as you choose – an amenable farmer's field will do the trick – but it's certainly not beyond anyone who enjoys getting back to nature and letting days stretch lazily out before them.

Andy Pietrasik

*Camping in the Andes -
Huarez, Peru*

Where you can pitch, and the rules you should follow

In England, Wales and Ireland, the letter of the law says you can't just pitch a tent anywhere that takes your fancy, no matter how remote. Someone, or some organisation, owns that land (every last inch of it), so you should seek permission before you wild camp.

In Scotland, the Land Reform (Scotland) Act 2003 makes wild camping legal in most cases when practised well away from dwellings and roads. For details of the Scottish Outdoor Access Code see outdooraccess-scotland.com. The Mountaineering Council of Scotland has some very helpful guidelines at mountaineering-scotland.org.uk/leaflets/wildcamp.html.

The whole point of wild camping is to get as close to nature as possible, so it would be rubbish if you then spoilt it for others. Bear in mind these basic principles:

- Pitch late, leave early. Stay for one night only
- Do not pitch within sight of dwellings and livestock
- Do not build open fires
- Do not wash with soap, shampoo or detergent, or urinate in streams, rivers or lakes. Any toilet duties should be done far away from water sources and well buried with a trowel
- Leave no trace: remove all litter (including sanitary towels, as animals will dig these up)
- Travel light – tinned food heavy, dry food light
- Stay high and dry. Pitch in a low area and rain could turn it to custard
- Good open view? Forget it, the wind and the cold will have you weeping for home. Find a natural windbreak, like a huge rock
- Don't camp by water (midges, damp, flooding, tides) or under a tree (lightning/falling branches)

Best places

Anywhere remote with no light and noise pollution or other people – for example, Highlands of Scotland (no permission required), Dartmoor, Exmoor, Snowdonia, the Pennines …

More information: v-g.me.uk/WildCamp/WildCamp.htm.

10 Family friendly campsites

BRITCHCOMBE COUNTRYSIDE HOLIDAYS, OXFORDHSIRE

With beautiful views, this is a relaxed and quiet site that makes an excellent starting point for walking and rambling (the Lambourn Downs and the historic Ridgeway path are on your doorstep). You are free to camp where you like and can have campfires in well-positioned fire pits (firewood is delivered to your tent). No of pitches: 30. Open all year round.

£4 per person per night, under 5s are free, 5-14 yr olds are £2, showers 50p, gazebos £4. Campfires allowed. Dogs allowed. 01367 820667, marcella@seymour8227freeserve.co.uk.

CLIPPESBY HALL, NORFOLK

Based within the broadlands area of Norfolk, Clippesby is a delightful safe-haven for families, perfectly placed to visit anything and everything "boaty," with seal-spotting boat tours available nearby. Clippesby is part of the Broads Cycle Network and there are route maps for trails from 5-15 miles long. Bicycles (with free helmets, locks trailers and tag-alongs) are available for hire. There's a large play area with swings and a climbing frame, plus a field for sports, and a brilliant outdoor swimming pool. No of Pitches: 100. Open April to October.

£14-£21 for two adults, a tent and a car. Extra adults are £5 per night, children (aged 3+ and students) are £2. No campfires but raised barbecues allowed. Dogs allowed on lead, £3.50 per night. 01493 367800, clippesby.com.

DENNIS COVE, CORNWALL

A lovely laid-back site, ideal for both families and smaller groups with breathtaking views across the Camel Estuary. With Padstow a ten minute stroll away and plenty of space for larger tents, this is a great spot for a family break. Particular highlights include bike riding along the Camel Trail (bikes for all ages can be hired from Padstow), sailing with the Camel Sailing School, windsurfing and waterskiing with the Camel Ski School on the Estuary (these activities are actually in Rock – across the river from Padstow and a short boat ride away) and the Lobster Hatchery. No of pitches: 42 with an overspill field. Open Easter to September.

£12.10-£15.90 for two adults, a tent and a car. Extra adults are £3.70-£4.90 per night, children are £1.60-£2.30. Special concession for hikers. Showers 40p. No campfires. Dogs allowed, £1.30-£2. 01841 532 349, denniscove@freeuk.com.

DOWNSHAY FARM, DORSET

"In-a-field" camping on a working dairy farm with spectacular views across the Purbeck Hills. The Swanage Steam Railway is a delight and the easiest way to visit both Corfe Castle and Swanage. Good walks across the Vale of Purbeck run right by the campsite and Studland Bay has a lovely, sandy beach. No of pitches: 60. Open Whitsun/Summer months.

£4 per adult, children aged 11+ are £2, children aged 4+ are £1. £3 per large tent, £2 per small tent or campervan. Cars/boats are £1. No campfires but barbecues allowed. Dogs allowed. 01929 480316, downshayfarm.co.uk.

GRANGE FARM, ISLE OF WIGHT

Peaceful and rural, a small, simple site with level, clean pitches and plenty of space for each tent. Highly suitable for children, with a well-stocked playground and lots of animals (such as rabbits, goats, donkey, horses, llamas and even water buffalo). The sandy beach is accessible via a short, steep path from the campsite – great for sea life observation, paddling, fossil hunting etc. NB Grange Farm is on a cliff top with no fence, so pitch as far away from the edge of the cliff as possible and make sure the door faces away from the cliff, to avoid prevailing winds. No of pitches: 60. Open beginning of March to end of October.

£11.50 per low season standard pitch, 2 people and vehicle. £20.50 per high season maxi pitch, 2 people and vehicle. Children are £2-£2.50. Free hot showers. No campfires but barbecues allowed. Dogs allowed on a lead, £1.50. 01983 740296, brighstonebay.fsnet.co.uk.

HODDOM CASTLE, DUMFRIES AND GALLOWAY

Extremely friendly, clean and well-run site with a great family atmosphere and an ideal location for a days golfing, walking, mountain biking or fishing. For the nature-lover, the campsite employs its own countryside ranger who organises nature trails where you can help with checking bird boxes, tree planting and animal spotting. For kids there's a playground and a games room with a pool table plus grassy areas to play games in or have a kick around. Pony trekking also available locally at Powfoot. No of pitches: 160. Open end of March to end of October.

£7.50 per standard pitch for 2 people in March, April and October; £10 with electricity. £10.50 in May, June and September; £13.00 with electricity. £14 in July and August plus bank holidays; £17 with electricity. Reductions for single people. £2 per extra adult per night. Children aged 7-16 are £1 per night, under 7s are free. No campfires but bricks provided for raised barbecues. Dogs allowed, £1.50. 01576 300251, hoddomcastle.co.uk.

NORTH MORTE FARM, NORTH DEVON

Slap-bang in the middle of beautiful coastal countryside, North Morte is that very rare thing: a popular seaside campsite for families which is quiet and peaceful at night. Five hundred yards away, Rockham Beach is pretty, secluded and perfect for rockpooling, paddling and barbecues. Play area on site. No of pitches: 150. Open Easter to end of September.

£6-£8 per adult depending on season, children to aged 15 are £2-£3. Gazebos £5 per night in high season. No campfires but barbecues allowed on concrete blocks. Dogs allowed, £1.50 in low season, £2 in high season. 01271 870381, northmortefarm.co.uk.

SPIERS HOUSE, NORTH YORKSHIRE

Lying in a forest clearing, this campsite is a great starting point for walking. Don't forget your binoculars – the forest is host to a great diversity of bird life and on a clear night, star-gazing here is second to none. Harry Potter fans check out nearby Goathland aka Hogsmead station on the nearby North Yorkshire Moors steam railway. There is a playground on site and which children will love, and lots of space for cycling. There is pony trekking available locally. No of pitches: 150. Open March to January.

£8.70-£13.50 per pitch per night for members, non members pay £3 extra. No campfires. Dogs allowed, up to 3 per party at £1 each. 01751 417 591, forest-holidays.com.

STOWFORD MANOR FARM, WILTSHIRE

This family-run farm promises a delightfully laid-back approach. The surrounding river Frome offers the shallow waters of an old ford where children can paddle and play. Kids may also be lucky enough to find piglets and free-range chickens running amongst them. Fairleigh Castle (medieval-themed events) is a two-fields walk from the site, and the acclaimed Longleat Safari Park is a short drive away. No of pitches: 10. Open Easter to October.

£10 per person per night. No campfires but raised barbecues allowed. Dogs on leads allowed. 01225 752253, stowford1@supanet.com, stowfordmanorfarm.co.uk.

TOM'S FIELD, DORSET

The site is eminently child-friendly, and offers something for kids of all ages, namely freedom. But the whole family can leave Tom's Field near the entrance, tiptoe through the rabbits and enter a beautiful sloping field. Walk to the top, then down the steep, daisy-strewn path to the fossil-rich coast. Back on site, the space, wind, views and lack of impediments at the top of the adjoining field make this a king of kiting spots. No of pitches: 120. Open mid-March to end of October.

£10 per two person tent and car, £13 per family tent. Extra adults are £4.50 and children are £2.50. Showers 25p. No campfires but raised barbecues allowed. Dogs on leads allowed. 01929 427110, tomsfield@hotmail.com, tomsfieldcamping.co.uk.

Eco/organic campsites

ABBEY HOME FARM, CIRENCESTER

Although the main attraction here is the food - with the farm shop stocking superb quality meats, amazing cheeses and gorgeous greens, all from the farm - this site really offers the chance to taste the simple life. Away from the hustle and bustle, here everything happens at a slower pace. As well as the main Green Field camp site, the four yurt eco-camp offers stunning alternative accommodation for groups. NB Toilets are very basic composting loos. Other facilities include cold tap, wood fuelled hot water system and gas ring at yurt site. No of pitches: approx 24. Green Field camping open all year round, Yurts Easter to October.

£4 per person per night in Green Field. £975 per week in 4-yurt eco-camp. Campfires in designated areas only. No dogs. 01285 640441, theorganicfarmshop.co.uk, info@theorganicfarmshop.co.uk.

CAERFAI FARM, PEMBROKESHIRE

Poised on the Pembrokeshire coastal path, this site is ideally situated for walkers but you may also wish to try your hand at snorkelling or fishing in nearby Caerfai Bay. While everything you could want is within striking distance, the farm also uses renewable sources – solar, geothermal, wind and biomass energy – to make delicious Caerfai cheddar and Caerphilly cheese on site (sold in site shop). All pitches are large and may accommodate two tents. No of pitches: 70. Open Whitsun to late September.

£6.50 per adult, children aged 3-16 are £3. £1.50 per night reduction for walkers and cyclists. No campfires but raised barbecues allowed. Dogs on leads allowed. 01437 720548, cawscaerfai.co.uk, chrismevans69@hotmail.com.

EWELEAZE FARM, DORSET

This isn't just a campsite. This is a campsite on a working organic farm with its own half a mile of private beach and Jurassic cliff. Not only can you fish for your supper here, you can then cook it on a campfire on the beach. And if all this toasting marshmallows to the sound of breaking waves with the smell of wood smoke and the sea breeze isn't enough for you, it's just a bracing three-mile cliff walk (via the pub) over to Weymouth. There is a fabulously well-stocked camp shop selling organic produce including Aberdeen Angus beef. No of pitches: 140. Open late July to late August only.

£5 per adult on weekday nights, £7.50 for weekend nights. Children are £2.50. 20% discount offered to all campers arriving with no form of motorized transport. Free indoor showers/ outdoor solar-powered shower, free firewood. Campfires allowed. Dogs allowed. 01305 833690, eweleaze.co.uk.

photo: shutterstock/Chris Mole

Pembrokeshire coastal path near Caerfai Bay, Wales

FORESTSIDE FARM, STAFFORDSHIRE

The site is set on an organic dairy farm in 156 acres of beautiful, undulating Staffordshire countryside with panoramic views of the Weaver Hills and Dove Valley. If you want peace and tranquility, this is the place to be. Pitches are well spaced enough to provide plenty of privacy. There is access to coarse fishing on site and the farm hosts the British Eventing Horse Trials in late June. Locally, there are plenty of country pubs and eating places to suit all tastes. No of pitches: up to 6. Open all year round.

£6 per person per night. Under 5s are free. Campfires not allowed. Dogs allowed. 01283 820353, forestsidefarm.co.uk, stay@forestsidefarm.co.uk.

TRELOAN COASTAL FARM HOLIDAYS, CORNWALL

Formerly known as Arthur's Field, this tranquil site has a history of natural farming methods. Working shire horses still pull the plough across a hillside that looks out over the spectacular Gerrans Bay. The south-west coastal path runs through the end of the site and can lead you to a variety of secret coves including the delightfully named Peter's Slosh, which is great for rock pooling and fishing. Swimming, scuba diving, sunbathing and surfing are all catered for on nearby beaches. You may also ride or work the shire horses, depending on the season. No of pitches: 49. Open all year round.

£9.50-£19.50 per pitch (two adults) per night. Campfires allowed by special arrangement. Dogs allowed (for a small charge in peak season). 01872 580989, coastalfarmholidays.co.uk, enquiries@coastalfarmholidays.co.uk.

TRAILBLAZER

Kelling Heath Holiday Camp

What? A family-owned and family-friendly holiday park offering holiday homes, woodland lodges, camping pitches and caravan breaks with a range of environmental activities.

Where? Two hundred and fifty acres of woodland, heathland and wetland with views of the north Norfolk coast

What's their big idea? The park, which has a repeat customer rate of 83%, runs a series of conservation schemes and wildlife activities including a long-standing red squirrel breeding programme. It aims to act as "an interface between suburban areas and the countryside" offering "learning in a soft way while relaxing on holiday". Children from four to 12 can learn about bushcraft, pond dipping and how to make nest boxes.

Track record: Kelling Heath has a strong commitment to environmental stewardship and the management of the rare habitats on its site. It has planted a Norfolk orchard, using records dating back to 1290. It has just invested £100,000 in a new shower block with rainwater harvesting, solar water heating, and a ground source air exchange. This should save 119,600 litres of water and 5739kg of CO_2 per year.

The long view: They are writing their second 10-year plan and hope ultimately to be the UK's first carbon neutral park.

Awards and schemes: David Bellamy Gold Conservation Award for 11 years; Visit Britain Quality in Tourism ratings score of 93.2% in 2007; Excellence in England park of the year 2002; and British Airways Tourism for tomorrow award in 1999.

More information: 01263 588181, kellingheath.co.uk.

ACTIVE

Ask many adventure sports enthusiasts what drives them and they answer that it's as much the desire to be at one with nature as the adrenalin rush of the activity itself. The skier's silent view from an uncrowded summit, the surfer's surrender to the swell of the waves and the diver's wide-eyed encounter with marine life should – and can – serve to heighten awareness of the fragility of the natural resources they journey to see.

These activities, as well as wildlife-viewing holidays can serve to awaken support for conservation projects as well as placing a market value on preserving natural resources in destinations. The income generated by diving, snorkelling and coral tourism can far outstrip revenue from commercial fishing in reef areas – with the Great Barrier Reef Marine Park Authority alone recording A$5.1bn generated by tourism in 2006–7, compared to A$139m from commercial fishing.

Yet the stakes are higher too. These activities typically take place in delicate natural habitats which can rarely sustain mass tourism and where a momentary careless move by one visitor – on to a coral reef for instance – can inflict years' worth of damage. So it pays to be aware of some simple steps you can take to safeguard the future of these resources and how you can influence the travel and hospitality industries to green up their acts.

SKIING

Why I love ... ski touring

Ski touring, or cross-country skiing from cabin to cabin, is one of the best ways to explore a winter wilderness. It's less about being the fastest dude down the slope and more about slowly enjoying a nature trip with your partner, family or friends. You spend the night at cosy chalets without needing to book in advance, then push on to another cabin the next day. The atmosphere is usually more relaxed and intimate than at a big downhill resort, with little chance of finding skiers boozed up to the small hours. You can use normal downhill poles, but you'll need a pair of cross-country skis, which keep your heels free to help you "walk" on the snow. A tour starts right outside your chalet door: you put on your skis and head to the nearest mountainside. Most people scale it by skis, which is exhausting but infinitely more satisfying than using a lift.

Ski touring often takes place in national parks, so no one has bulldozed the landscape to build a five-star hotel, and no lifts are blighting the mountainside. As most start and end points are reachable by train and bus, you won't need a car. Accommodation tends to be cosy wooden lodges rather than mega hotel complexes.

Norway's dramatic landscape of mountains and fjords is one great destination for ski tourers. The Norwegian Trekking Association (+47 40 00 18 68, turistforeningen.no/ English,) manages more than 440 cabins across the country and organises ski touring tours. A top spot is Haukeliseter, on the southern end of the Hardanger plateau and national park, in south central Norway. From Haugesund or Oslo, take the four-hour Haukeli express bus to Haukeliseter (nor-way.no).

Rooms at Haukeliseter (haukeliseter.no) start from £80 for a single room, breakfast included. A bed in the dormitory is £23. Visitors who don't have equipment can rent cross-country skis, poles, ski shoes and ski adhesive bands to climb up slopes, for £34 per day.

Another great option is Finse, on the northern end of the Hardanger plateau. It is reachable by train (nsb.no) from Bergen (two and a half hours) and Oslo (under five hours). Even easier, and also great fun, is to get to Oslo and then jump on the tube for about 20 minutes. You will arrive in Nordmarka, the Norwegian capital's green belt, a paradise of rolling hills covered in pine and birch trees. You can ski a whole day, stay over night at an NTA cabin before heading back the next day (tube line 1 to Frognerseter or tube line 3 to Sognsvann).

A word of caution: make sure to be fit and well prepared before heading off on a ski tour and get familiar with the mountain rules. Always let someone know where you are heading, be mindful of the weather, don't go alone, have a map and compass and don't hesitate to turn back. If you don't, you can get into serious trouble.

Gwladys Fouché

Ski touring, Valle d'Aosta, Italy

photo: shutterstock/Roca

CAN YOU BE A GREEN SKIIER?

NO

Leo Hickman, journalist and ethical living adviser

When you jump off that chair lift for the first time every season, fill your lungs with frigid air and glance at that mountain vista ahead, it's hard not to feel a connection with nature. Immersing yourself in this environment is arguably one of skiing's key attractions.

But strip away the glamour and the thrills and you are left with a list of environmental woes. And that"s not taking into account the fact that the busiest slope in any ski region is the line of aircraft descending to the airport. You cannot talk about skiing without mentioning climate change. Skiers, of all people, should be aware of the rapid changes occurring on the world's mountain ranges. Glaciers are in speedy retreat and snow lines are rising quickly.

Skiers are not directly causing these problems, other than by being members of the human race. But the skiing industry is frantically, forlornly, trying to stave off the deleterious effects of climate change with a series of measures that will only exacerbate the problem in the long run. The arrival of snow cannons at virtually every major resort over the past decade is the most worrying of trends. Working through the night as the skiers' attention turns to the delights of schnapps and fondue, these spray particles of water mixed with nucleating agents into the freezing air to create a blanket of artificial snow. A lack of the real stuff has forced the industry to rely on these machines, but their environmental impact is considerable.

Mountain Wilderness, a French conservation group that described skiing as "the cancer of the Alps", says that 4,000 cubic metres of water are needed to cover one hectare of piste for a season – whereas a hectare of corn needs only 1,700. Across the Alps, it is estimated that artificial snow consumes the same amount of water each year as 1.5 million people.

Incredibly, in some regions, tap water is used, but elsewhere river water is extracted from the valleys below and pumped back up the mountain.

This causes two problems. First, there is the energy expenditure: Mountain Wilderness says that it requires about 25,000 kilowatt-hours, costing about €150,000, to cover just one hectare of piste with snow for a season (that's largely why the cost of ski passes has risen so much in recent years). Second, dumping river water at high altitude disrupts biodiversity because it introduces nutrients in the water into an area where they wouldn't otherwise be.

Using artificial snow also means that the pistes now take up to a month longer than normal to melt in the summer, preventing many plant species lying dormant underneath from germinating and flowering, leading to huge muddy scars in the summer meadows where the pistes once lay. Just take a look on Google Earth at satellite images of, say, the Chamonix valley or Aspen during the summer months.

"Artificial snow is not the root of all evil, but it is very close," says Sergio Savoia, the programme director of WWF Switzerland. "One of the biggest problems is psychological: snow cannons give tourists the idea that it is business as usual. But we don't actually have much snow."

Some low-lying resorts are experiencing winter nights that are too warm even to use snow cannons. There are reports that helicopters are being used to ferry snow to threadbare pistes in order to keep these resorts in business. In 2002, Italian police set up a task force to investigate the "theft" of snow from glaciers by the truck load in order to serve nearby resorts. The alternative is to abandon such resorts and chase the snow, by building new lifts and hotels further up the mountain. This is already being seen in some places.

But, despite the promises of resort owners, how environmentally sensitive can a concrete mixer really be when taken high up into a wilderness area and put to work?

YES

Veronica Tonge, responsible travel consultant

Many people take the view that the downhill ski industry ruins the environment, consumes vast amounts of energy and cannot possibly be in harmony with the principles of responsible or sustainable tourism. However, it has been the saviour of many mountain communities and traditions, halting the depopulation and poverty that occurred at the end of the 19th century.

It requires positive action, however, for a sport such as skiing, with its requirement for lifts, pistes and artificial snow, to operate on a green basis.

Ski lifts and artificial snow-making do require power for the ski season but they are increasingly efficient and clean since they no longer run on diesel and the electricity can come from renewable sources. Many resorts in Europe derive nearly all their power from hydroelectricity and, in America, Vail Resorts became one of the world's largest corporate users of renewable energy when it switched its five resorts and offices to use wind power.

Lech in Austria has reduced its CO_2 emissions further and improved air quality by building a biomass plant to provide heat and hot water to the resort and by providing a free public bus service to remove the need for cars. Therefore, staying for a week could result in negligible emissions.

So what about the chemicals in the artificial snow and the vast quantities of water it requires? Resorts have used proteins to help the artificial snow freeze at higher temperatures; however, studies have been inconclusive on the impacts. Nonetheless, some resorts have never used them, such as those in the Austrian Tyrol where the artificial snow is made from pure water – evidenced by the certified organic pastures underneath. The water is either taken from rivers or reservoirs built to store rainwater up the mountain. In Austria, the reservoirs have to undergo environmental impact assessments before construction and often end up blending so harmoniously that summer walks are routed to them. The rivers are assessed to work out the exact amount of water that can be safely taken out without damage to the wildlife and this water is even filtered to ensure that it is pure.

And what about the delayed snowmelt? We have all seen mountains where the only snow remaining is that of the piste of artificial snow. Repeated scientific studies have found no negative impacts of artificial snow or delayed snowmelt on vegetation and, in the same way a plastic bag protects your favourite garden plants from spring frosts, artificial snow has been found to operate in the same way for the Alpine vegetation.

Pistes are the other requirement for skiing. Although some have been created by bulldozing the mountain, there is a new technique called the "soil push" method, whereby the topsoil and vegetation is removed as "turf", the land is machine-graded underneath and then the topsoil is re-laid, which effectively keeps all the plant and insect diversity intact as before. Some resorts are reducing the need for prepared pistes altogether by reclassifying advanced runs as 'itinerary' routes which are not prepared or groomed, providing exciting challenges for experienced skiers.

So can you ski and keep your green conscience clear? Yes, but only if you select your resort carefully. Check websites such as the Ski Club of Great Britain (skiclub.co.uk) and Save our Snow (saveoursnow.com) for lists of resorts that are taking positive environmental steps, but do your own research, too, by checking out the resort's own websites. They are increasingly realising that green credentials can win them more visitors. Choose the right resort and your conscience can be as clear as the mountain air.

Méribel ski resort, France
photo: shutterstock/Dmitry Naumov

Purpose-built ski resorts pose serious environmental problems due to the way they are constructed and the vast amounts of energy and water needed to power lifts and artificial snow-making machines. Wildlife-friendly forested mountainsides are typically levelled in order to make way for long, flat pistes, while snow cannons drain local water supplies. Yet most skiers will tell you they love the mountains and consider skiing a way of tuning in to nature.

It's an irony not lost on ski journalist Patrick Thorne, who has been to more than 200 resorts in the past 20 years. He has set up a website (saveoursnow.com) to raise awareness of green issues in skiing, in particular the effect of climate change on ski areas and what skiers can do to limit the damage their holidays cause.

Travelling by train is top of Thorne's recommendations. "It's the travelling to the resort rather than the resort itself which has the biggest carbon footprint," he says, recommending skiers going to the Trois Vallées in the French Alps – the world's largest ski area – use Eurostar's dedicated services to Bourg St Maurice or Moutiers (eurostar.com/ski). He also advises skiers to try cross-country skiing, snow-shoeing and ski-touring, which aren't dependent on large, groomed slopes and ski lifts.

The most environmentally friendly resorts are listed on the Ski Club of Great Britain's Green Resort Guide (skiclub.co.uk/skiclub/resorts/greenresorts), which rates more than 200 ski resorts on their environmental credentials. North American ski resorts lead the way, particularly Aspen and Jackson Hole in the US, and Sun Peaks in British Columbia, while in Europe, Lech in Austria scores highly.

Richard Hammond

 # Destinations for greener skiing

GRAND VALIRA, ANDORRA

Although Andorra isn't a massively popular destination with most European skiers, the Grand Valira resorts of Soldeu and Pas de la Casa are beating many of the more famous resorts on environmental practices. Both have the ISO certification and host an environmental festival to raise awareness, as well as educational campaigns. Woodland has been preserved as much as possible, so skiers will enjoy many runs through the trees, ski slopes are sown with grass in the summer to protect soil, bird nesting areas are sign-posted and cordoned off and it is working on a scheme to compost all organic waste. All the oils used in slope machinery are biodegradable.

To get there by train: Eurostar to Paris, overnight sleeper from Gare d'Austerlitz to l'Hospitalet près l'Andorre, and a bus into Andorra – there is no rail station (sncf.com; andorrabus.com).

KAPRUN, AUSTRIA

Home to the first lift company in Austria to receive official recognition for its environmental standards, Kaprun uses renewable energy to operate all its cableway systems and offers a free bus service from resort to the ski areas to cut down on car use. The Kitzsteinhorn lift is connected via a long pipe to the sewage system, which helps prevent pollution on the mountain. Kaprun Tourism: +43 6542 770, zellamsee-kaprun.com.

LECH, AUSTRIA

A leading European resort in terms of environmental activities, Lech boasts a biomass communal heating plant that heats hundreds of hotels, homes and businesses. Some of the ski lifts are solar-powered, and solar roof panels heat water for works in resort buildings. To get there by train: Eurostar to Brussels, Thalys high-speed link to Aachen, overnight on weekly Bergland Express (berglandexpress.com) to St Anton am Arlberg then a short taxi transfer (booked with the train ticket). Or take the Eurostar to Paris, overnight train to Munich (with new en suite sleeper carriages) then local trains to St Anton, for post bus that takes around 40 minutes to the resort (020 7619 1083, europeanrail.com), Lech Tourism: +43 5583 2245; lech-zuers.at

GÎTE DU MONT-ALBERT, QUÉBEC, CANADA

Québec province is great for cross-country skiing and other low-impact outdoor activities, with over 2,500 miles of trails. One of the best places to stay is the four-star Gîte du Mont-Albert in the Gaspésie national park, the highest part of the Appalachians in the province. It has 60 rooms in a huge 1950s complex as well as a dozen lodges and 25 woodstove-fired cabins dotted around the grounds. At the nearby visitor centre, you can book nature tours to see caribou, white-tailed deer and moose, and organise snowshoeing, cross-country skiing and ski-touring across the Chic Chocs mountain range (+1 418 890 6527, sepaq.com/pq/gas/en/gite.html).

From C$268 per night for two people on a dinner, bed and breakfast basis. Daily coaches link Québec City and Gaspé to Sainte-Anne-des-Monts, a 30-minute drive from the Gîte. Trains also run from Québec City and Montréal to Sainte-Anne-des-Monts.(sepaq.com/pq/gas/en/gite.html; +1 418 763-2288; gitmtalb@sepaq.com)

CHAMONIX, FRANCE

The resort launched a green website (chamonixgoesgreen.org) this year, giving information on the town's green initiatives, including replacing local buses with ones that have 80 % lower emissions, recommending eco-friendly hotels and measuring and maintaining air quality. The Mont Blanc Eco Tourism Association has been set up to develop sustainable tourism projects. Chamonix Tourism: +33 450 53 00 24, chamonix.com.

MEGÈVE, FRANCE

As one of the ski resorts that developed around a pre-existing village, Megève is a better option than a rambling, purpose-built resort, and has retained its traditional character by remaining small-scale. It was also the first French resort to receive the ISO certification. The tourist office uses hybrid vehicles, and many of the local hotels have good environmental practices.

To get there by train: Eurostar to Paris, Rail Europe "Snow Train" overnight to Albertville, bus transfer to Megeve (eurostar.com; raileurope.com).

BELVEDERE B&B, CHAMBONS, ITALY

At the Belvedere B&B, a restored 16th-century Alpine "casa" in Chambons in the heart of Val Chisone, you'll be cracking open a bottle of Beba local ale before you think twice about the crowded pistes of the Trois Vallées. There are three double rooms, basic but each has a private bathroom and two have mountain views. It's in the Piedmont region – so expect organic "slow food" – and many of the facilities are eco-friendly, such as a wood-fired heater, recycling and low-impact activities, including a cross-country ski circuit, which starts from right outside the front door. There's also snowshoeing nearby in the Troncea valley. Or, if downhill slopes are just too tempting, the resorts of Sestriere and Puri (home of the last winter Olympics) are a 30-minute drive away (owners can provide transfer). +39 0121 884701, belvederebedandbreakfast.com.

From €60 per night for a double room. To get there by train: take a morning Eurostar to Paris and a TGV from Gare de Lyon to arrive in Turin that evening. From Turin's Porto

Nuovo station take a train to Pinerolo, then a bus towards Fenestrelle or Sestriere and walk from the Depot village stop.

SAAS FEE, SWITZERLAND

Ensuring that tourism is sustainable is a top priority here and the local community showed it was keen for green as far back as 1950, when the first road to the resort was built, and it was decided to keep the village car-free. The policy lives on, and today tourists are ferried around in electric taxis. Building restrictions are very tight, so only typical Valais chalet-style structures can be built; one third of each building's facade must be wood and all must have gabled roofs. It won "energy town" status in 2002, a Swiss clean energy award, and, since 1996, has been part of a network of 150 communities of the Alliance in the Alps project, which follows the Alpine convention's aim to protect the environment and promote sustainable tourism. Green places to stay include Hotel Ferienech Hohnegg's Biochalets (hohnegg.ch).

Get there by train: take the Eurostar to Paris and walk the few metres across to Gare de l'Est. Take an overnight train to Zurich and connect on to Brig, then it's an hour's bus ride to the resort, (0844 848 4070, raileurope.co.uk).

ASPEN, COLORADO, US

Flying to the US doesn't make for a super-green skiing holiday, but Aspen, famous as a playground for the rich and famous, is an unlikely pioneer of green ski practices and policies. It was the first American resort to get the ISO 14001 accreditation, the first to launch a climate change education campaign in the industry, and its own climate policy. Its lifts are operated on wind power, piste bashers are run on bio diesel and the highland patrol headquarters have a solar power system. It has also donated more than $1m to the Environment Foundation and more than 50% of its employees are members.

Gemma Bowes and Richard Hammond

photo: shutterstock/Helmut Konrad Watson

Lech, Austria

# Low-impact ways to enjoy the snow

SNOWSHOEING, FRENCH PYRENEES

Ditch the skis and explore the mountains on a pair of snowshoes – just strap the light frames to some waterproof boots and away you go. And off the crowded pistes, you're more likely to spot wildlife. Mountainbug runs trips from an 18th-century stone chalet in the village of Barèges. From there it's just a few minutes' shuffle into the Pyrenees where you can follow the tracks of chamois, hare and ermine (+33 5 62 92 16 39, mountainbug.com).

GREEN CHALET, FRANCE

Base yourself at this eco-chalet just outside Bourg St Maurice and ski the three mountain areas of Les Arcs, Sainte Foy and La Rosiere. As well as the usual in-chalet entertainment – sauna, Nintendo console, table football and bar – the power is bought from wind and solar farms in northern France, all the food waste is composted and the owners are installing a solar roof and wood-pellet fired hot tub.It's 5km from Bourg and you can go bar-hopping in the other resorts courtesy of a minibus taxi service run on restaurant waste oil. Reductions available for guests who arrive by the Snow Train, which runs from the UK to the French Alps (0033 479 0842 06, green-rides.com).

CROSS COUNTRY SKIING, GOMS VALLEY, SWITZERLAND

Learn to cross-country ski at Blitzingen in the Goms valley where there's access to some of Switzerland's best cross-country trails. You'll be given two lessons at the start of the week to learn the basics, then you'll be free to practise your skills at your own pace before a final review lesson at the end of the week. A week's half board at the four-star Hotel Castle includes train travel, equipment, lessons, ski pass and a travel pass for the upper valley. Packages with flights are also available (01653 617906, inntravel.co.uk).

TAKE THE COACH

Coach travel to the Alps is a schlep, but a cheap one. National Express's Eurolines service runs from London Victoria to 12 resorts in France and Switzerland, including Val d'Isere, Bourg-St-Maurice, Tignes and Chamonix. You can take skis or snowboard for free and your UK National Express connection will cost only £15 (nationalexpress.com/eurolines).

Snowcoach runs package ski holidays by coach from various points in the UK to St Gervais, Valmeinier and Val Cenis in France and Mayrhofen and Kirchdorf in Austria. It works with the Travel Foundation, Friends of Conservation and Climate Care to minimise environmental impacts (01727 866177, snowcoach.co.uk).

SKI AT HOME

Closer to home, and providing there's a decent snowfall, the Slochd, near Inverness, offers cross-country skiing and low-level ski touring in the forested trails of the Spey Valley, part of the Cairngorms National Park (01479 841666, slochd.co.uk).

Richard Hammond

photo: shutterstock/Brendan Howard

Cairngorms National Park, Scotland

Mark Smith, seat61.com

Train services to the slopes

From the UK, the French Alps is the simplest area to reach by train, with three different options to choose from. The weekly Saturday Eurostar ski trains run direct from London St Pancras to Bourg St Maurice, Aime La Plagne and Moutiers, giving access to 14 resorts including Tignes, Val d'Isere, Les Arcs, La Plagne, Courchevel and Val Thorens (eurostar.com/ski).

The Snow Train is another weekly service, easy to pick up from the Eurostar and running from Paris Gare du Nord to six French stations serving Les Trois Vallées, Paradiski, Mont Blanc and Espace Killy (snowtrain.co.uk, or Rail Europe on 0844 848 8885)

Take the Eurostar and connect to regular scheduled SNCF trains to Chamonix, via Chambéry, Moutiers, Aime La Plagne, Bourg St Maurice and Annecy. These run day or night and not just during the ski season.

SAFARI HOLIDAYS

Why I love ... green safari holidays

Going to Tanzania and not seeking out its animal life might seem heretical, but if you are an independent traveller, on the move in remoter areas, the cost of "going on safari" might just be too high. Getting up close to Africa's finest mammals usually comes as part of a luxury package. But there are a growing number of alternatives – reasonably priced, and with a sustainable approach to tourism.

Take the Ruaha National Park. It's Tanzania's second largest and one of its least known – which makes for great empty spaces and few tourists. The nearest town, Iringa, is 110km away so most visitors fly to the luxury lodges inside the park. But outside the park are several locally owned and managed lodges. Ruaha Hilltop Lodge is one of them. Perched on the slopes of Ideremle mountain, it commands an extraordinary view – watch both sunrise and sunset over a bronzed or green (depending on the season) bush.

Alban Lutambi is Hilltop's owner and manager. He's a former road-building contractor who has poured his own money into creating this delightful spot, with eight cottages (all with that same unforgettable view). Like other locally owned places, Hilltop battles to compete with the tourism establishment's well-oiled marketing connections. Yet Lutambi does not forgo the details: a glass of fresh mango juice on arrival; a cool face towel to wipe off the red dust after a day on safari. And Lutambi's ties with nearby communities give visitors a look at local life that you don't see in a remote lodge in the park.

If staying outside the park boundaries precludes dawn and dusk animal sightings, daytime drives and walks make up for that. This rolling wilderness, studded with the great angular-branched baobab trees, and intersected by the Ruaha river, is known for its magnificent elephant population as well as for other mammals and, in particular, its bird life.

A driving safari can cover the ground and will deliver you to concentrations of animals – anxious zebras, shifty buffaloes, distinguished elephants – but walking safaris take you closer, both physically and mentally, to the soil. A walk with a park ranger beside the river brought sightings of distant crocodiles and giraffes, but just as intriguing was being shown the four-square track of a hippopotamus or the bizarre, sprawling nest of the hammerkop, a large stork-like bird that buries its eggs in a three-roomed nest, decorated with old bones, and the pink flowers of shrubs snaffled for their moisture by giraffes. A slow safari sometimes has the edge over slicker four-wheel drive versions.

Tanzania is a very big place and getting anywhere takes time, but that can be factored in as a positive part of the trip. For example, the journey to Ruaha from Dar-Es-Salaam: go by train (from the magnificent, Chinese-built Tazara railway station) to Mbeya – that leg of the trip will take nearly 24 hours. The train is clean, well-supplied with food and beer, and the world outside, of villages and landscape, is endlessly diverting. From Mbeya, get the bus to Iringa, a town with jacaranda-lined streets, a cool climate and eclectic architecture. It has an intriguing history (see the war cemetery) as a former German stronghold and a centre of local resistance by the local Hehe people and their chief Mkwawa, who killed himself rather than submit to the Germans in 1898.

From Iringa, Hilltop Lodge (which has an office in the town) will arrange transport to the lodge – a two-hour journey along a sun-baked ochre road, and an opportunity to observe the routine of village life – bicycles and cattle, women carrying firewood, children dawdling home from school, and, because Tanzania also lives in the modern world, a herdsman with a mobile phone.

Full board, US$80, per person. Drive safaris from Hilltop Lodge: US$100 per day per vehicle, with driver/guide. (+255 26 270 1806/+255 784 726709, ruahahilltoplodge @yahoo.com).

Polly Pattullo

photo: Wilderness Safaris/Mike Myers

Elephants leaving the water, South Luangwa National Park, Zambia

Green safari holidays

THE MAASAI AND BIG FIVE IN KENYA

Porini safari camps offer tented safaris at four bush camps. Limited to 10 guests apiece, the camps are run on environmentally sound principles in low-impact, non-permanent accommodation. Solar power provides electricity, while sustainable charcoal briquettes are used to heat water. Depending on which camp you stay in, there are opportunities to see elephants in the shadow of Kilimanjaro, watch rhino in the largest rhino conservancy in East Africa, walk with Maasai warriors, view the annual Maasai Mara wilderbeest migration and tick off the "big five". Two of the conservancies in which camps are located, Amboseli and Mara, are owned by Maasai communities and are run with the aim of creating income for local people. Porini Camps/Gamewatchers Safaris won Best for conservation of endangered species or protected area in the 2008 Virgin Holidays Responsible Tourism Awards.

Trips cost from around £540 per person for a two-night safari to £3,300 per person for an eight-night safari (porini.com; +44 (0)207 100 4595).

TRACKING A BENGAL TIGER IN NEPAL

The lowlands of Nepal are home to the Bengal tiger as well as leopards, deer, Asian one-horned rhino, Langur monkeys and the rare Gangetic dolphin. Tribes Travel offers a wildlife-watching itinerary that takes in Badia National Park in the west, Chitwan National Park and Koshi Tappu Wildlife Reserve in the east. The trip includes several elephant-back safaris on which it may be possible to track a Bengal tiger. Accommodation includes the Nepali-owned Gaida Wildlife Camp, located on the boundary of Chitwan National Park. Each of the 32 bungalows are fitted with solar-powered showers, with greywater collected for use in the gardens. While there is a generator to supply electricity, lighting is by candles and lamps. Several of the staff are from the local village and food for the camp is sourced from local markets. Organic waste is composted.

A 14-night trip costs £2,035 per person, based on two passengers sharing a double/twin room (not including international flights). Tribes.co.uk; +44 (0)1728 685971.

photo: Wilderness Safaris/Mike Myers

A cheetah in the grass, Kafue National Park, Zambia

TAKING A SAFARI ON FOOT IN ZAMBIA

Zambian Horizons is a collective of camps in Zambia operating responsible safaris. They offer traditional vehicle-based trips to see leopard, lion, and elephant from permanent lodges, but the country is famed for its lower-impact walking safaris. The camps contribute to community development, conservation and educational projects.

For example, Robin Pope Safaris sources its staff primarily from the local Kunda tribal community and for 15 years has supported Kawaza school in Nsefu village. Visitors can choose to spend a day or night at the village. Norman Carr Safaris also supports local education and as part of this has instigated a tree-planting programme for carbon offsetting at Yosefe School, with 100% of donations going to the scheme.

A seven-night safari with Robin Pope Safaris costs between £1,840 and £4,300 depending on the season Contact individual camps for their latest prices. For contact details of all Zambian Horizon camps, see zambianhorizons.com/operators.html.

COAST AND COMMUNITY IN TANZANIA

Located in Eastern Tanzania, Kisampa is a private conservation area adjoining the coastal Saadani National Park. It is not a "big five" safari, but its open grasslands, forests and rivers offer the chance to see primates and many bird species. Guests stay in bungalows or tents constructed by local craftspeople from renewable materials. There are no flushing toilets; instead rooms have composting toilets flushed by adding a scoopful of dead leaves. The camp has a strong community focus, with people from five villages involved in its operation. It pays a concession fee for each bed filled, employs local people and raises money for local community improvements. Its efforts have resulted in building of the area's first secondary school for some 200 students, 30 of which have full-time scholarships. Kisampa also acts as collection and buying hub for local beekeepers.

Prices start at £110 per person per night, +255 754 927694 | +255 746 316815 | +255 753 005442 (sanctuary-tz.com).

CONSERVING A LAKESIDE WILDERNESS IN MOZAMBIQUE

Nkwichi Lodge sits beside Africa's third largest lake, Niassa. The lodge is part of the Manda Wilderness Conservation Project, which seeks to balance community development with conservation. It is working with local communities to conserve 250,000 hectares of wilderness. In the 600 square km game reserve, visitors can spot elephant, sable, reedbuck, leopard and 300 species of birds. Guests can also volunteer on longer-term conservation projects. The lodge was built with the aim that the environment would return to its natural state in two years if it was removed. Grey water from sinks runs into a pit to be filtered through fine sand, while toilets drain into eco-composting pits. It is run entirely on solar energy and thanks to a sustainable agricultural project working with 58 local farmers, 20% of the lodge's food comes from within a 25km radius.

A 10-night stay combining bush and beach safaris in Zambia and Mozambique costs around £2,900 (mandawilderness.org/home.html; info@mandawilderness.org).

STAYING IN A RHINO HAVEN IN KENYA

Lewa Wildlife Conservancy in Kenya is a non-profit organisation that works to conserve wildlife and habitats with assistance from local communities. Once a cattle ranch and later a rhino sanctuary, this 65,000-acre reserve is home to a fifth of the world's Grevy's zebra, black and white rhinos, plus 70 other species of mammals and 350 species of birds. It conducts research into endangered species, rescues threatened animals and translocates animals to improve their chances of survival. Lewa's community work aims to support conservation by reducing poverty. Projects include supporting eight primary schools, running micro-credit programmes for women, helping set up irrigation schemes and building healthcare facilities. It derives its money from tourism: all profits from Lewa Safari Camp go to Lewa Wildlife Conservancy.

Bush and Beyond offers an eight-night safari that includes two nights at Lewa Safari Camp from £2,280 (lewasafaricamp.com; lewa.org; bush-and-beyond.com).

HELPING SAVE CHEETAHS IN NAMIBIA

The world's last surviving cheetah population lives in Namibia. It is possible to contribute to conserving the species during a stay at Elandsvreugde (Eland's Joy), a working farm that is also the headquarters of the Cheetah Conservation Fund. The farm is also home to kudus, hartebeest, warthogs, jackals, leopards and brown hyenas. Volunteers stay in two-person rondavels. The camp is powered by solar energy and water use is limited to preserve supplies. A typical day might involve gathering data for a wildlife survey, feeding captive cheetahs and helping educate local farmers and children about the importance of conserving the cheetah, which is often seen as a problem animal.

Earthwatch offers a 15-day visit for around £2,765, +44 (0)1865 318838 cheetah.org (earthwatch.org/exped/marker.html).

SAVING ENDANGERED TIGERS IN CENTRAL INDIA

Opening in October 2009, Banjaar Tola is a tented camp overlooking the river Banjaar at Kanha National Park, Madhya Pradesh, where a 2007 census showed that tiger populations had dropped by 65%. Apart from small quantities of canvas and steel, the camp has been constructed using local materials and labour. Although air-conditioning units are installed, these are energy-efficient units that deliver both cooling and heating. The tents also have double layers of canvas and insulation to help keep them cool in summer. Meanwhile, in winter, water destined for the bathrooms is pumped under the floor to provide extra heat. Low-energy light bulbs are used inside the tents and outside lights are solar-powered. The camp is a joint venture between Taj Hotels Resorts and Palaces and andBEYOND (formerly CC Africa). One of Taj Safaris' main aims is to demonstrate to neighbouring communities that tigers are more valuable alive than dead because of the money that can be derived from responsible ecotourism. The company is a member of the Travel Operators for Tigers Campaign (TOFT), a travel-industry initiative aimed at promoting sustainable tourism in India's wildlife reserves.

TransIndus offers a 10-day package with three nights at Banjaar Tola from £2,884pp sharing, including full board accommodation at Banjaar Tola, B&B accommodation elsewhere, return international flights, transfers and internal travel, +44 (0)208 566 2729 (transindus.co.uk; toftigers.org; tajsafaris.com).

Carlolyn Fry

TRAILBLAZERS

Wilderness Safaris, Botswana

What? A safari company that sees itself primarily as a tool for conservation, with 6.5m acres in Southern Africa under protection.

Where? More than 50 lodges and camps in Botswana, Namibia, Malawi, South Africa, Zambia, Zimbabwe and the Seychelles.

What's their big idea? Protecting Africa's wild resources by making tourism pay with fair returns for local communities. "The resources belong to the planet but the local people are the custodians," explains Chris Roche, an ecologist with the company.

Track record: Set up in the early 1980s, by game rangers disillusioned by the largely South-African owned safari industry in Botswana. Like-minded rangers then expanded into neighbouring countries and bought concessions around the fringes of national parks as land use was revised in the 1990s. They introduced photographic safaris on land previously used for hunting or under threat from mining companies. Partnerships with the Save the Rhino Trust among others have tripled the numbers of endangered black rhino in Namibia.

The long view: "We see our business as a carbon offset, though we don't market it as such," says Roche. "Our model is to protect the carbon sinks and not let them be farmed or deforested." Next up are projects to reintroduce freshwater terrapins and indigenous bird species to their island in the Seychelles and look at creating savannah corridors between parks in Angola, Zambia, Namibia and Zimbabwe to promote genetic diversity.

Awards and schemes: Their Damaraland Camp in Namibia was awarded the Tourism for Tomorrow Conservation award in 2005. The camp is run in partnership with the local Torra community and has significantly boosted numbers of desert-adapted elephant and black rhino. Rocktail Bay Lodge in KwaZulu-Natal won the Tourism for Tomorrow award in 1999.

More information: wilderness-safaris.com.

*A lion and an approaching storm,
Zambia*

photo: Wilderness Safaris/Mike Myers

SCUBA DIVING

Each year, thousands of British travellers visit coral reefs all over the world, from the Red Sea to Indonesia and the Great Barrier Reef. Yet the world's coral reefs – the "rainforests of the sea" – are under imminent threat. According to the World Wildlife Fund, 27 have been destroyed and, if present trends continue, 60% will be lost in the next 30 years.

While the most significant threat to coral comes from pollution, over-fishing and climate change, bad scuba diving practices can cause significant damage to these fragile ecosystems. The key to all good diving is buoyancy control – the more in control you are the less likely your fins, hands, knees and scuba equipment will bump against the coral and damage it. On average, it takes 25 years for coral to recover from a diver's single clumsy brush against it. Too many divers at a site can also cause disturbance to fish and the coral, so check that your dive operator avoids the busiest dive sites.

Responsible dive operators should also have a policy of anchoring only to permanent buoys (attached by concrete to the sea floor) rather than dropping anchors on or near reefs. Padi (padi.com) runs a course on protecting the marine environment and a peak performance buoyancy course, which both count as "speciality" courses required for the master scuba diver certification. It also partners with Project Awaare Foundation (projectaware.org), a non-profit organisation originally started by PADI, and dedicated to underwater conservation, which organises activities in partnership with dive volunteers. You can also put your dive holiday to good use by contributing your underwater observations to the global dive log (earthdive.com).

Project Aware's top tips for greener diving include:

- Do not touch or stand on fragile habitats
- Never feed or collect aquatic life
- Control buoyancy at all times
- Secure dive equipment
- Choose Project AWARE environmental tour operators
- Get involved in conservation initiatives and monitoring
- Eat sustainable seafood.

For a copy of Project Aware's Ten Ways a Diver Can Protect the Underwater Environment, or for other Aware diver tips, visit the global initiates section of projectaware.org.

Ricahrd Hammond

TRAILBLAZER

Blue O2

What? A UK tour operator specialising in Red Sea diving holidays, with a holistic attitude to responsible tourism.

Where? The company has its own fleet of liveaboard boats at Hurghada, Egypt, and also runs trips to the Maldives. It hopes to introduce trips to Thailand, Malta and the US Virgin Islands.

What's their big idea? Lowering the company's environmental impact and that of its guests. Initiatives include subsidised reef clean-up safari holidays which do not return a profit and sponsorship of Bite-Back, a UK marine conservation organisation.

Track record: Divers are invited to donate to Bite-Back and become actively involved with preservation work. Guests are also educated in best practice diving and the importance of buoyancy control. On-board waste is minimised and boats are being fitted with bin separators, can crushers and sealed storage for biodegradable waste. All crew staff are local and receive environmental awareness training. Local food and diving supplies are preferred to imports.

The long view: The company is seeking to spread best practice by lobbying for a plastic bag ban in Hurghada. It is also supporting marine biologist Elke Bojanowski in a study of the Longimanus shark in the Red Sea.

Awards and schemes: Best in a Marine Environment, Virgin Holidays Responsible Tourism Award 2007

More information: blueotwo.com

Green diving holidays

VOLCANIC LANDSCAPES IN DOMINICA

Dominica's underwater volcanic landscape, which includes hot-water fumaroles, provides an unusual backdrop for a rich diversity of marine life. Rare seahorses, flying gurnards, yellowtail snappers and barracuda are a few of the creatures that divers can get up close and personal with. Scuba Diving Magazine rated Dominica first for Macro Life in 2008. Rosalie Forest Eco Lodge, on Dominica's east coast, hosts visitors in tree houses and jungle cabins and offers professional PADI diving courses at all levels. It has a strong sustainable-living policy. As well as composting waste and using dry toilets, it relies on solar energy, a microhydro system and a wind turbine. These provide green electricity, pump water from the river and heat water.

Per-night prices range from £8.50 for a hammock space to £60 for a wooden cottage that sleeps two. Diving packages are available with full-board, all courses and equipment included +1 767 446 1886; 3riversdominica.com.

CONSERVING CORAL REEFS IN MADAGASCAR

Blue Ventures runs research and conservation projects from a permanent field station in southwest Madagascar. Diving volunteers work alongside Malagasy and international field scientists to conduct research underpinning local management plans for the 4th largest coral reef in the world, the Grand Récif de Tuléar. The company works with host villages to find ways to protect biodiversity, reduce poverty and improve the quality of life for local communities. Accommodation is in wooden eco-cabins. Blue Ventures limits its impact on the terrestrial environment by minimising freshwater use, restricting electricity to a few hours each day and promoting renewable sources where possible. The company was highly commended in the Best Volunteering category of the Virgin Holiday Responsible Tourism Awards in 2008.

Prices vary according to a participant's current diving qualifications. Expedition periods range from three to 12 weeks. A six-week trip ranges from £2,100 for a person with no diving certification to £1,900 for someone with a PADI Advanced Open Water Certificate. +44 (0)20 3176 0548; blueventures.org.

CAVES AND TUNNELS IN SARDINIA

Argonautica Diving Club is located in the coastal village of Cala Gonone, overlooking the Gulf of Orosei. This forms part of the Gennargentu National Park. A treat for divers is the park's 40km stretch of limestone cliffs, which provide submarine caves, tunnels and gorges to explore. The centre runs PADI courses for beginners and speciality courses such as 'cavern diver', for more experienced visitors.

The centre reduces its impact in the water by using low-emission engines, anchoring in the sand and encouraging guests to take courses to improve their buoyancy. Guests are also asked to sign a 'conduct code' covering responsible diving behaviour such as not touching corals or marine creatures, leaving litter or blowing bubbles under rocks. It recommends locally run apartments and hotels for visitors; its own apartments are powered by solar energy.

Diving package prices start from £360 per person for two people. This includes six dives with tanks and weights, self-catering accommodation and a shiatsu massage. Cavern dives are around £9 extra per dive, while diving kit costs around £13.50 per dive to hire, (argonauta.it/uk/act_a.htm).

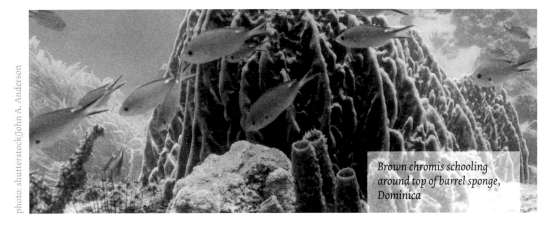

photo: shutterstock/John A. Anderson

Brown chromis schooling around top of barrel sponge, Dominica

WRECKS AND SHARKS AT NUSA ISLAND RETREAT, PAPUA NEW GUINEA

The Retreat is located on sandy Nusa Island, off the coast of Kavieng, New Ireland Province. The waters encircling Nusa Island hide a bounty of WWII ship and aeroplane wrecks, including an American bomber, Japanese submarine and Catalina Flying Boat. Larger creatures, such as eagle rays, manta, tuna, and whitetip sharks patrol the region's current-swept channels. Divers stay in traditional bungalows, looking out across the water. The retreat has been designed to have a low-impact on the environment; the toilets are of the dry-composting variety and showers use groundwater. Drinking water comes from harvesting rainwater.

Ten dives with tanks and weights, including flights, transfers and meals costs from £865pp. Book with Dive Worldwide: 0845 130 6980, diveworldwide.com or nusaislandretreat.com.pg.

PRISTINE CORAL AT MALUANE, NORTHERN MOZAMBIQUE

The Maluane Project is a science-based conservation project and sustainable low-impact tourism initiative run by private investors in partnership with the Zoological Society of London. The project site, chosen specifically for its potential for combining conservation with luxury tourism, encompasses three islands, a coastal strip and an inland area. One of the project's lodges, Vamizi Island Lodge, offers diving and snorkeling on pristine coral reefs. Surveys of the area have revealed rare seagrass beds, 30 genera of unbleached corals, 75 reef fish species not previously recorded in Mozambique, five species of turtle, calving hump-back whales, and basking whale sharks. Accommodation is in luxury beach houses, built using local materials.

Mid-season prices per person per night are around £375. tribes.co.uk; +44 (0)1728 685 971, maluane.com; vamizi.com.

WATCHING WHALE SHARKS IN THAILAND

The waters around the Similan islands are home to whale sharks, the largest living fish species. The fish, which are filter feeders and harmless to humans, can grow to 40 feet long. Wicked Diving, a collective of scuba diving instructors operating around Khao Lak, offers day trips, liveaboards and places on research expeditions to see and monitor the whale sharks. Wicked Diving runs its liveaboard boat on biofuel. Detergents and soaps used on board are biodegradable, while sheets and towels are made from fairtrade organic cotton. Visitors can opt to stay at Golden Buddha Beach Resort on the island of Koh Phra Thong, which minimizes water use, has no hot water or air conditioning and limits electricity from its diesel generator to between 6pm and 11pm. The resort is run along community friendly lines and has sponsored a turtle conservation programme for the past decade.

Beachfront bungalows at Golden Buddha Island start from £65 per night. (Closed from June 1 to September 1 2009.) For diving package prices contact Wicked Diving directly. +66 8 4333 152; wickeddiving.com, goldenbuddharesort.com.

Carolyn Fry

SURFING

Most surfers of any vintage are aware of the environmental issues of sewage and chemical discharge into the world's oceans and seas, but how many are also concerned about the chemical makeup of their own equipment or the emissions they generate to pursue their global lifestyle?

Of all adventure sports enthusiasts, surfers are perhaps the most likely to come face to face with environmental hazards as they are directly exposed to the best and worst of the marine environment. "The centre of a surfer's existence is the ocean, the cleanliness of the water and the beach," says Michael Fordham, author of The Book of Surfing. "We are more attuned to it than any other group of people." Yet for a potentially super-green, carbon-free sport, surfing still has several eco-issues to overcome.

The main issue remains the transport emissions, but, says Fordham: "There's no need if you're a beginner surfer to fly to the Caribbean or hit the Pacific – you won't be as good as the waves you encounter." Instead, why not go local, pool petrol money with friends and fill a van with people and boards for an old-school surfing trip?

Most stages in the manufacture of wetsuits, boards and surf wax have traditionally used petrochemicals and highly toxic substances. Wetsuits are made from petroleum-based neoprene, while surfboard production involves a cocktail of nasties, including toluene di-isocyanate during production of the foam "blank" and carcinogenic fibreglass dust from the sanding process – not forgetting all the resins in the coating. In 2005, the abrupt closure of California-based Clark Foam in the face of multimillion-dollar lawsuits and fines for breaking environmental regulations caused a period of eco-introspection in the

Preparing for the waves at
Newquay, Corwall

surfing community. The company had supplied about 90% of the world's polyurethane foam blanks and had admitted emitting more than 1,814kg of styrene fumes annually.

Some innovations have since appeared on the horizon, with sportswear company Patagonia trialling limestone-based neoprene in wetsuits, and the Eden Project researching hemp-based surf board blanks. Plant-based resins and foams are already used in other technologies and could perhaps be adapted. Surfers Against Sewage (sas.org.uk) has funded research into greener boards by Ocean Green (oceangreen.org), which has developed a "2/3rds greener" balsa wood and hemp cloth board but still using polyester resin. "Any solution has to be market driven: you as a water user must demand that your toys don't harm the environment you love," urges SAS.

Then there is the issue of the impact of the growing popularity of surfing on the local environment, with litter, beach fires and overcrowding the key concerns. Some popular destinations are even considering building artificial reefs to attract surfers and potentially encourage domestic surf tourism – Bournemouth began constructing Europe's first such reef in the summer of 2008.

Fordham remains optimistic about the future course of surfing, believing that the more people who go surfing, the more they will be exposed to the environment and will be inclined to look after it. "The ambition for many surfers has been that we can become custodians of the coastlines. As in all things there will be a core vanguard of surfers who will push things forward with the masses trailing in their wake."

Surfing at Trevaunance Cove, St. Agnes, Cornwall

Liane Katz

photo: shutterstock/Stephen Aaron Rees

Green surf breaks

GLOBALBOARDERS, CORNWALL

"GlobalBoarders are pioneering sustainable surf tourism", says Sam Bleakley, two times European longboard champion and a man who's surfing ethos is very much focussed on keeping it green. One look at the company's website makes this clear – a whole rash of green awards and a responsible tourism policy featuring everything from staple-less office staplers to bio-diesel fuelled transport to the beach.From £305 pp (two nights) to £705 pp (seven nights). Train London – Penzance from £75 return, globalboarders.com.

ALGARVE SURF & YOGA RETREAT

Live the natural way in a tipi in the Costa Vicentina National Park on Portugal's Algarve coast which has great waves in winter, whilst the nearby Atlantic coast is the place to head for in summer. Surf and yoga lessons are also available. From the surf camp you can actually paddle a canoe down to the beach, surf all day, catch your dinner and cook it back at the camp as night falls – about as close to nature as you'll get on a surf holiday.From €130 pp per week shared tipi accommodation. Yoga lessons €26, surf lessons €28. Train London – Faro from £207 return, surfalgarve.com.

SURF ATLANTICO, NORTHERN SPAIN

Surf Atlantico can show surfers of all abilities the wide range of wave riding options available along the coast of northern Spain. The company is green through and through, from being carbon neutral to working with local businesses to supply goods and services, as well as encouraging guests to learn about the regional culture and even offering Spanish lessons alongside surf lessons.From £439 pp for seven days plus flights. Brittany Ferries Portsmouth – Santander. Foot passengers from £224 return (plus free whale spotting en route), responsibletravel.com.

TYF ADVENTURE, PEMBROKESHIRE

TYF Adventure is one of Wales' best established outdoor centres and according to founder, managing director and surfer Andy Middleton has long had an eco-friendly approach to its activities, from being carbon neutral to recycling 95% of waste and offering local organic food in the bar of the converted windmill where the company is based. And you don't need to burn large amounts of fossil fuels accessing the waves since TYF's base in St. David's is within easy access of several good surf beaches. From £165 pp per weekend (group of four). Train London – Haverfordwest from £71 return (note that this service is renowned for its unreliability), tyf.com.

ERRANT SURF HOLIDAYS

Errant offer a worldwide wide range of surfing and surfing-related holidays, and all of them are carbon neutral – the emissions resulting from your travels are offset, and this is built into the cost of your holiday. Errant also work with the Carbon Neutral Company to minimise the impact of their activities on the environment, including involvement with a number of green forestry projects around the globe. Prices vary, errantsurf.com.

Where to find greener surf kit

PATAGONIA

Not only does Patagonia make a range of cool, environmentally friendly surf gear, they are also founder members of One Percent for the Planet (onepercentfortheplanet.org), which since 2002 has encouraged members of the business community around the world to contribute one per cent of their sales to various environmental groups. One Percent say their aim is to get companies to recognise that industry and ecology are inherently connected and that positive results come about from connecting businesses, consumers and nonprofits through philanthropy, (patagonia.com).

FINISTERRE

Cornwall-based Finisterre are a 2008 *Observer* Ethical Awards Winner, producing a range of technical apparel for surfers designed to have minimal environmental impact. Company co-founder Tom Kay says "We focus on high quality products made from recycled or natural materials – some produced in the UK, others made at the Miquelina Foundation in Colombia which is run by nuns for 'at risk' women". All four members of this small, committed company are enthusiastic surfers, (finisterre.com).

Alf Anderson

FAIRTRADE AND ETHICAL

Planning a responsible holiday is about far more than your carbon footprint. Checking out where your tourist dollars will actually go and how local people are treated are important steps which can make a huge difference to host communities. If offered a slice of the tourism cake, local people and businesses can benefit fairly from your stay and enrich your experience as a visitor. If excluded, tensions can often surface. From "voluntourism" to conservation trips and charity fundraisers, trips that "give something back" have never been more popular. In this chapter we explain how to make sure that your good intentions will translate into a solid and long-lasting benefit to those you leave behind.

 **Why I love ... volunteering holidays**

The day before I took my daughter to the Sunderbans in north-east India, the Times of India reported: "A 21-year-old resident of Patharpratima was killed and partly eaten by a tiger in the Sunderbans ... Buno Bhakta was part of a five-member group that had gone into the Chulkati forest to look for crabs. The tiger attacked when they were returning with their catch later in the day."

I discreetly tore the article out of the paper and hid it. Imogen, who is 11, was already alarmed enough about going to an area where the wildlife regarded mankind as supper. I was more worried about getting Delhi belly and whether Imogen would be overwhelmed by the poverty she would probably see.

We were going on a volunteering and wildlife holiday in the Sunderbans to test whether children and conservation work mix. Very few travel companies allow children to do volunteering work: most children don't have the strength, skills or patience to do practical jobs and a lot of the places where volunteering help is needed are physically challenging.

Hands Up Holidays, which aims to blend sightseeing with "meaningful volunteering experiences", can tailor trips to suit the traveller, so children can be included in the plan. I had been lured by the picture of a gorgeous tiger walking out of a forest towards water on the Hands Up website, although it stressed that seeing this elusive animal was pretty unlikely. Even so, Imogen still had concerns after reading about the Sunderbans in Lonely Planet: "Thanks to strategic perimeter fences near villages, the number of human deaths attributed to tigers has dropped from an estimated 200 a year to about 34.' 'Hmmm – nearly three a month," she said.

The Sunderbans form the biggest area of tidal mangrove forest in the world, spreading from West Bengal in India to Bangladesh. The Indian part of the Sunderbans covers 4,262 sq km, with 2,585 sq km given over to a national park and tiger reserve. It is only about 90km from Calcutta, where we had spent the first three days of our holiday taking in markets, temples and exhaust fumes. But the journey to the Sunderbans Jungle Camp on Bali Island where we were staying takes five hours – two-and-a-half by car through dusty villages and endless salt water pans to Sonakhali and another two-and-a-half by boat.

Bali Island has some 25,000 people, but no mains water, electricity, roads or cars. People live in homes built from sticks, mud and straw, they burn dried-out cow pats on their fires, and the cows, goats and chickens live in the front yard. After Calcutta, it's heaven. The Sunderbans Jungle Camp is one of 20 run by Help Tourism, a Calcutta-based organisation that channels at least 75% of its profits to the local people, who share ownership and help run its projects in the north-east and east of India.

Although small – it has six basic, but clean cabins sleeping a maximum of 20 people – the Bali Island camp employs 19 people, provides a water pump for people who previously had to walk a couple of kilometres to collect clean water, helps fund the local school and supplies a medical service. Solar electricity is supplemented by a generator in the evening, and if you want a bath, you ask for two buckets of hot water instead of one. But the food is amazing. Huge vats of vegetable and fish curries, chapatis, rice, and chutneys are made fresh every day.

The camp faces Gomdi Khal, part of the Saznerkhali Wild Life Sanctuary – an area of reserved forest. Our guide, Tanmoy Ghosh, took us there on a small rowing boat, along the river separating the two islands. The river looked about 1km in width, yet Tanmoy told us that a tiger had swum from Gomdi Khal to Bali just a few months earlier. The 2.5m fence that runs along the bank, dipping down into the water where creeks led into the island, acts more as a psychological barrier than a physical one to the tigers, which can easily scale the wire.

The next day we were on the water by 6am. We passed six kinds of kingfishers, fish eagles, egrets elegantly stalking along in the mud, monkeys, a lesser adjutant stork, a mangrove whistler, the occasional wild boar and spotted Chittal deer, immense saltwater crocodiles and water monitors. After dinner Tanmoy offered to take us on a night walk. "Hold the torch up at your eye level and shine it along the edge of the field," he said. We did, and were rewarded with myriad luminous green jewels twinkling in the undergrowth. Spiders' eyes, he explained. En route he pointed out a spot where a tiger had prowled a few weeks ago; Imogen slipped her hand into mine and we edged a bit closer to Tanmoy.

The next day, just after we had started out, the captain of the boat peered through the mist at a beach about 500m away and said "Tiger!" Everyone jumped up and started arguing in ferocious whispers about whether it was a tiger or a wild boar. 'It's too fat and dark to be a tiger,' said one of the boat hands. By the time we had reached the beach, the wild boar-like tiger had melted back into the forest, but left clear tracks in the mud. It was definitely a tiger.

That evening villagers staged a folk musical celebrating the forest goddess Bonobibi and the tiger god Dakshin Roy. Afterwards one of the actors told how he had been fishing at night with two friends. He had been sitting in the middle of the boat, and when he looked round, the friend who had been behind him had disappeared. There had been no noise, no struggle. It seems every family has been touched by such a loss.

Our volunteering days were fabulous, too. We "taught" English in the primary school – about 20 four- to eight-year-olds now roughly know the words to "Heads, shoulders, knees and toes" and the "Hokey Cokey". I wish we had come better prepared. We also planted mangrove saplings in the mud on the river side as a defence against cyclones. The planting bit is easy – you grab a sapling and plunge it into the mud – and you can plant about 200 trees in 20 minutes. Actually walking in the mud, which is knee high and has the consistency of a crème caramel, is something else. As we floundered, about 30 locals collected to watch us. What we lacked in teaching skills we made up for in entertainment value.

While Imogen and I felt we could have contributed more to the island – we should have spent more time planting and less birdwatching – and we got a lot more out of India than we gave back, the low-impact, sustainable tourist practised by Help Tourism and Hands Up Holidays is vital. We are both desperate to return, especially if we can repeat the experience of staying in and becoming part of a small community.

So if your kids like playing in mud, meeting other kids, fishing and watching wildlife – with the odd shiver-inducing night walk thrown in – this is the holiday for them.

The Hands Up Holidays Sunderbans Smiles trip costs £1,050, excluding flights but including two nights' half board at the three-star Fairlawns Hotel in Calcutta, and seven nights' full board at the Sunderbans Jungle Camp. Visit handsupholidays.com or call 0800 783 3554. Flights cost from £400 return to Calcutta but book well in advance, especially if planning to travel over the Christmas period.

Jill Insley

Who best to volunteer for...

The best organisations offer genuine environmental and developmental benefits to the world, rather than a glorified holiday in the sun. You can get a sense of an organisation's commitment to the work it supports by checking whether it tries to match your particular skills to its programmes. Find out exactly what work you will be expected to do; whether the organisation has built up a good relationship with a local NGO or charity and if there is long-term commitment to their projects.

Make sure you ask where all the money goes – how much does the organisation spend on internal administration costs, staff wages, your food and accommodation and training, and how much actually goes on the projects? Be wary if you are quoted more than 15% for "agency admin".

VOLUNTEERING IN THE UK

BTCV
The charity runs more than 120 practical conservation holidays each year in the UK. A wide range of activities are on offer, from dry-stone walling in Lincolnshire to beach sweeping in Devon, or picking up woodland management or hedge-laying skills. Prices range from £60 to £260 including accommodation and food. Volunteers have to find their own way to a local pick-up point (01302 388 883, btcv.org).

The Hebridean Whale and Dolphin Trust
The trust welcomes volunteers to help with education and conservation projects year round. No background knowledge of cetaceans is required but you will need to be enthusiastic and willing to learn about the marine mammals and their environment and lend your skills to a busy charity. Work may include gathering scientific data, creating educational resources, giving talks, helping with beach cleans and running workshops (whaledolphintrust.co.uk).

National Trust
The trust runs around 450 working holidays every year in England, Wales and Northern Ireland, ranging from two to seven days and costing from £60 a week including food and hostel-type accommodation. Cottage accommodation is also available on their "premium" holidays with groups of volunteers sharing domestic duties. Choose from habitat maintenance in the Brecon Beacons to volunteering at an event in the grounds of a stately home. Check out "working holidays" at nationaltrust.org.uk.

The National Trust for Scotland
The Trust's Thistle camps for volunteers were a sell-out in 2008, offered in locations as diverse as Fair Isle in Shetland and Grey Mare's Tail by Loch Skeen. Activities include

archaeology, crofting, wood-working and surveying, carrying out a bat survey and helping a small island community make hay for the winter (thistlecamps.org.uk).

Trees for Life
Help with the award-winning charity's work to restore the Caledonian Forest to 600 square miles of the Highlands to the west of Inverness. Only 1% of the original forest remains and overgrazing by sheep and deer prevents most natural regeneration. To date more than 650,000 trees have been planted. Volunteer-work weeks are open to groups of 10 aged over 18 and with reasonable levels of fitness. No conservation experience is necessary. Transport to and from Inverness, accommodation and vegetarian or vegan food is provided. See treesforlife.org for details and booking, and tflvolunteer.org for independent reports from volunteers themselves.

The Wildlife Trusts
With 765,000 members, the Wildlife Trusts is the largest UK voluntary organisation dedicated to conserving the UK's habitats and species and manages 2,200 nature reserves. More than 36,000 volunteers a year work in locations such as the Fens, the Peak District and Pembrokeshire. Vacancies for 2009, for example include volunteer assistant wardens on Skomer Island off the Pembrokeshire coast. If you want a little more comfort, consider taking a guided natural history holiday with Wildlife Travel (wildlife-travel.co.uk) – all profits are donated to the Wildlife Trusts (01636 677711, wildlifetrusts.org).

photo: The Wildlife Trusts/Doug Walsh

Puffin on Skomer Island, Pembrokeshire

VOLUNTEERING OVERSEAS

People and Places (see Trailblazer, page 196) works with local partners in Pakistan, Madagascar and South Africa (travel-peopleandplaces.co.uk).

Quest Overseas, with policies for "responsible volunteering", has worked on 14 projects across Africa and South America over the past 10 years (questoverseas.com).

Blue Ventures, a not-for-profit organisation and one of the most credible marine organisations, has responded to a request from the government of Madagascar to bring volunteers over to work on marine conservation projects alongside local scientists (blueventures.org).

Raleigh International, the youth development organisation has long-established connections with local community groups and conservation organisations (raleigh.org.uk).

2 Way Development (2way.org.uk) and **World Service Enquiry** (wse.org.uk) provide long-term placements.

Student Partnerships Worldwide offers students under the age of 28 opportunities to work with local charities in India, Nepal, South Africa, Tanzania and Uganda (spw.org).

Liane Katz and Richard Hammond

Questions to ask before you volunteer

- What does the work involve?
- Will your skills be individually matched to the community's needs
- Who decides what I'll be doing?
- What is the involvement of the community project during and beyond my stay?
- Who runs the projects?
- Is there any continuity?
- Is there support for volunteers?
- How is my money spent?
- How are volunteers vetted, and how long does this take?
- Can I talk to previous volunteers?
- Can I talk to local people before I travel?

For more information, download the free ethical volunteering guide from ethicalvolunteering.org

10 Fairtrade holidays

CHILOÉ ISLAND, CHILE

Join a small-group community tour to the remote Chiloé Island, just offshore from Chile's lake district. Stay in family-run rural lodges where you'll go fishing with a Chilote, help prepare local Atacameño dishes, and try your hand at spinning and weaving. See the salt pans and lakes of the Atacama desert, too, and hike among the lakes and glaciers of the dramatic Torres del Paine. A 14-night trip costs from £1,428 per person, not including flights (020 8747 8315, journeylatinamerica.com).

ALBERGUE CERRO ESCONDIDO, COSTA RICA

Costa Rica is famous for its ecotourism, but this lodge deep in the forest on the Nicoya Peninsula has a strong social as well as environmental agenda. It is one of a network of community-based lodges that give all their profits to local villagers. Unlike the country's many eco lodges aimed at the well-heeled, this is cheap and cheerful – just four teak cabinas with shared verandas – but there's good, home-made food cooked in wood-fired ovens, and lots of trips to the jungle, including treks to waterfalls, guided birdwatching and boat trips out to the islands. A room costs £18, or £5 for volunteers (+506 650 0607, asepaleco.com).

TRAIDCRAFT TOUR, CUBA

See fair trade in action on a Traidcraft two-week tour of the island. You'll go hiking in the Topes de Collantes mountains, swim in waterfalls in the Viñales National Park while stopping off in Ciego de Avila to stay at one of the cooperatives that supply Traidcraft's fair trade juice. Traidcraft runs similar fair trade holidays in India, Thailand and Peru, and in 2009 will be offering trips to Vietnam, Ghana, Costa Rica and Nicaragua. A 15-day trip costs £1,325 including most meals but not flights (+44 191 265 1110, traidcraft-tours.co.uk).

NAPO WILDLIFE CENTRE, ECUADOR

You'll get a local's view of the Amazon rainforest at this pioneering eco lodge fully owned by the Anangua Quichua community. Local guides take you to explore jungle lakes and creeks by dug-out canoe, to see tropical birds and monkeys including monk saki, spider monkeys, and golden-mantled tamarins. You can also help the indigenous community harvest bananas and prepare chichi, a beer-like drink made from manioc. An 11-day tour of Ecuador, including four nights at Napo costs £1,155 per person, not including flights (01728 685971, tribes.co.uk).

HIMALAYAN HOMESTAYS, INDIA
A traditional working farm 5,000m up in the breathtaking scenery of Ladakh. The homestay accommodation is as basic but authentic as they come – a mattress on the floor and long drop for the loo. You're invited to eat meals in the kitchen with the family who make curries from local ingredients and the majestic Himalayas are on your doorstep. Ten per cent of the income is given to the Snow Leopard Conservancy and the rest is distributed among the community. Costs £5 a night half-board (+91 3592 228211, himalayan-homestays.com).

ABA-HUAB CAMPSITE, NAMIBIA
One of several community-run campsites in the Twyfelfontein-Uibasen Conservancy in the country's north-west from where you can go on locally guided tours of the spectacular Twyfelfontein ancient rock carvings. Desert elephants are also regular visitors to the region and you can learn about the life of the bushman. A two-week trip including two nights at Aba-Huab and other campsites in the sand dunes of the Namib Desert, Damaraland and Etosha National Park, costs from £1,275 per person, including some meals, return flights from Gatwick to Windhoek and 4x4 car hire (020 8232 9777, expertafrica.com).

FINCA ESPERANCA VERDE ECOLODGE, NICARAGUA
On an organic coffee farm, more than 1,200m up in the mountains of Nicaragua, this 26-bed eco-lodge is situated in a nature reserve. While local people run the coffee operation, the travel side is run by volunteers from North Carolina with the aim of helping the local owners earn an alternative income to coffee. Nearby are jungle treks, waterfalls and a butterfly farm. Ten per cent of the lodge's income is invested in rural water projects and local schools. A five-day coffee and campesino cultural tour costs £176 per person based on two people sharing a room, including all meals, accommodation and guided walks (+505 772 5003, fincaesperanzaverde.org).

BULUNGULA, SOUTH AFRICA
The daily dilemma at this backpacker's lodge on the Wild Coast, in the Eastern Cape, is whether to chill out on a hammock or go canoeing up the beautiful Xhora river. Local fishermen will show you how to catch fish with throw nets, and land crayfish and octopus by hand. The solar-powered lodge, certified by Fair Trade in Tourism South Africa, is a joint venture between a South African and the Xhosa-speaking Nqileni community who also organise horse-riding, canoeing and guiding trips. Double room costs £14 a night, a bed in a dorm costs £6 (+ 27 47 577 8900, bulungula.com).

KAHAWA SHAMBA, TANZANIA

A coffee cooperative in the beautiful foothills of Kilimanjaro that was set up with help from Britain's Department for International Development, development charity Twin, Cafédirect and Tribes Travel. You stay in basic traditional huts made out of vines from the nearby forest and thatched with dried banana leaves, and there are guided walks and horse-riding trips along the nearby river valley. Costs £56 pp full board (01728 685971, tribes.co.uk).

HACIENDA BUKARE, VENEZUELA

Expect chocolate treats prepared by the local cooks with every meal when you stay at this small cacao farm in the hills above the Paria peninsula on the Caribbean coast. The owner is a local guide who runs a guesthouse at his hacienda where you'll learn how he turns fine organic cacao beans into high-quality chocolate used in bars and truffles. Nearby are hot springs, sandy beaches at Paria and walks in the cloud forest of Cerro Humo national park. Five nights' full-board costs £630, including transfers and return flights from Caracas to Carúpano (020 7281 7788, geodyssey.co.uk).

photo: shutterstock/vera bogaerts

Palafitos (stilt houses) in Chiloé, Chile

TRAILBLAZER

Tribes Travel

What? An award-winning independent operator with a strong focus on community involvement and fair trade in tourism. Offers tailor-made trips often with a wildlife theme.

Where? 18 countries in Africa, Asia and South America, the most popular being Tanzania, Ecuador, Botswana and Peru.

What's their big idea? Fair Trade Travel – a concept trademarked to the company. "When we started in 1998, our philosophy was always that we wanted a company that benefited local people as well as wildlife and environment," says co-founder Amanda Marks. "It's all about self-determination and ownership."

Track record: Tribes has helped set up two community-owned and run tourism initiatives – Kahawa Shamba (see page 248) in Tanzania and Incatambo in Peru. The company also rates its destinations with eco-ratings for sustainability, and fair trade ratings for their social responsibility. This extends to ground handlers who must prove that they operate on similar principles.

The long view: The company sends 1,000 customers away each year and intends to remain small and specialist. "It's possible to be a responsible tour operator if you're larger but it's very difficult," says Marks. The travel industry has a duty to behave responsibly. "We are all guardians of it," she says.

Awards and schemes: Best tour operator, Responsible Travel awards 2005, Best Tour operator, Tourism for Tomorrow awards 2002

More information: tribes.co.uk

Volunteering holidays

HANDS UP HOLIDAYS

Before I set up Hands Up Holidays I was working in the City in banking and head hunting. I was at a bit of a crossroads. I'd learnt some good business skills but was a bit disillusioned and looking for something else. Two travel experiences in 2002 led me to change direction. First I went to Guatemala to learn Spanish and ended up teaching the family English, before travelling round the country.

Then I went to South Africa and a friend who is a tour guide put me in touch with a house-building association and I helped with building work in a township outside of Cape Town, before exploring southern Africa. I loved the combination of cultural immersion with giving something back and the adventure of travelling. Slowly the idea for Hands Up Holidays began to form. I went back to the City until the end of the year, then took time out to study and work on my business plan.

My very first itinerary, prepared by my friend the tour guide, was in South Africa. I was close to launching when someone in the travel industry told me I should wait until I had more destinations to gain more credibility, so I ended up travelling a lot and building up relationships with volunteer projects and local tour operators. When we launched in 2006 we offered about 20 destinations. The idea is that a Hands Up Holiday is a starting point for people to dip their toes into volunteering, then hopefully go on to do something more substantial.

We also encourage people to volunteer back at home in their own communities, and become advocates or on-going sponsors for projects they've worked on. Projects range from being a reading partner in schools in countries where they speak English such as South Africa, to repair and renovation work or environmental conservation.

It's very rewarding for our clients, as well as the communities they're helping. There's no comparison to what I was doing before; setting up Hands Up Holidays satisfied my passion for travel and desire to make a difference and I wouldn't go back.'

Hands Up Holidays (0800 783 3554; handsupholidays.com).

Christopher Hill, founder Hands Up Holidays

SCHOOL EXCHANGE PROGRAMME

I went to Ghana with Explore on a two-week tour in December 2004 and loved the country. I didn't know anything about it before I went, I ended up there by default really (Thailand was where I'd planned to go) but it was such a fascinating experience, the people were so lovely and there was a real buzz about it.

When I found out that the tour guide's brother was a teacher, too, I started to think about how we might be able to work together. I work in a small private school in north Devon and the children aren't exposed much to other cultures so I thought it would be a great opportunity for them to learn about other children's lives in Ghana.

I applied for funding from the British Council and received a Reciprocal Visit Grant, which meant myself and a colleague were able to visit the school to set up the project and two teachers from Ghana were able to come to us.

It was eye-opening. The school is in a village called Boanim in the Ashanti region. It's very basic with open-sided classrooms, and the primary school just has corrugated tin roof huts with dirt floors. We brought as much educational equipment with us as we could and we were welcomed with a ceremonial pageant by the chief and the elders.

We started a correspondence programme between the pupils, and began fundraising for more books, educational games and stationery to take out. Last year, we took four girls from the sixth form to visit the school, staying in the family compound of one of the teachers. It was an incredible experience for the girls – they were shocked by the poverty and learnt a lot. It was wonderful to see how much they got out of it and the relationships they formed with the Ghanaian children.

We're now hoping to raise more funds to continue the project. It's been so interesting and rewarding; we want to plant 150 teak trees there to mark our school's 150th anniversary this year too.'

Deborah Sharman, head of food and nutrition, West Buckland School, Barnstaple, Devon

FAVELA PROJECT

It all started when I was travelling in Brazil. I met Teresa who was volunteering there, we were both looking to leave what we'd been doing in the UK (I was in media and she was a manager at Centrica) – and both wanted to learn to dance samba. Slowly an idea started to form.

People feel daunted by Rio and it's hard to get beyond the usual tourist traps. We built up relationships with locals and really got to know the city and felt we could offer an insider's guide and unique holiday experiences. We got involved with community work in the favelas (slums), painting people's houses, and found that visitors were really interested in joining in. So we started Jingando Holidays, which offers holidays in Rio combining dancing and community work and the chance to see Brazil from a local's point of view. The people are poor financially but culturally rich, it's good to give something back and people really do make a difference, even doing something in an afternoon or a day can have an impact.

We're involved with the Julio Otoni favela project helping fund a community centre and out-of-school activities to keep kids off the streets. We're also developing a footwear brand, Jingando shoes, bringing fashion and ethics together and making sure the money comes back to the locals. It's all been a fantastic experience – it's important to do something for reasons that aren't about making money and are environmentally and socially positive.'

Jingando Holidays (020 8877 1630; jingandoholidays.com).

Kate Nowakowski, co-founder Jingando Holidays

Richard Hammond

photo: shutterstock/Jose Miguel Hernandez Leon

Looking towards the Favela da Rocinha, Rio de Janiero

TRAILBLAZER

People and Places

What? Small specialist volunteer placement organisation working in partnership with organisations in host countries to develop long-term projects in education, health and social care, business and administration and conservation.

Where? The Gambia, South Africa, Swaziland, Nepal and Indonesia. "It's a fairly tight portfolio but we don't look for projects, we look for partners with close links to the community," explains programme director Sallie Grayson.

What's their big idea? "Truly accountable, ethical, responsible, sustainable volunteer travel". All profits after operating expenses used to serve host communities and the aim is to ensure projects become sustainable beyond the involvement of international volunteers.

Track record: 80% of each volunteer's fee is paid directly to the relevant local partner in the host community and all partners have committed to financial transparency and accountability. Applicants are strictly vetted (including criminal record and medical checks) and matched to placements, a process which can take several months. They are then fully briefed and put in touch with previous volunteers. The project itself must approve all applicants before they pay a penny for their placement.

The long view: "We shouldn't let the fear of not doing enough stop us doing a small amount." says Grayson. "It's a question of checking that the projects are responsibly managed, that they are community driven."

Awards and schemes: Highly commended in the 2007 Responsible Tourism Awards.

More information: 08700 460 479, travel-peopleandplaces.co.uk

 # Destinations where wildlife tourism makes a vital contribution to conservation

MADAGASCAR

An extremely poor country but incredibly rich in wildlife and plant species found nowhere else on the planet. However, the country's natural resources have been severely depleted and the country is now considered one of the world's top conservation priorities. Wildlife tourism at national parks and reserves is one key area providing the Malagasy people with sustainable income and employment.

BORNEO

Borneo is home to an ever-decreasing rainforest, threatened by the invasion of palm oil plantations and logging. Two of the world's most endangered species live within the scant remaining conservation areas – the orang-utan and the Sumatran rhinoceros. Both animals can be found within the conservation area of Danum Valley, though even this area itself has a selective logging programme. More tourists could help the protection of these and other pockets of rainforest and help with funding for corridors between the rainforest areas.

BRAZIL

Home to one of the world's largest rainforests, Brazil holds a segment of the key to the world's future in terms of climate change. But the rate of deforestation in the country is alarming. Visitors to the Amazon can stay at the excellent award-winning Cristalino Jungle Lodge whose Cristalino Ecological Foundation (CEF) is dedicated to the conservation and development of sustainable practices in this region. Employment through ecotourism as opposed to farming is paramount for sustainability here.

ZAMBIA

Zambia is one of the poorest countries in Africa. The country is heavily reliant on tourism and has recognised this economic crutch by setting aside almost one third of the country to national parks. The wildlife here is superb and tourists can choose operators and lodges with community projects that support local schools and conservation projects.

COSTA RICA

Costa Rica has attained a star status for ecotourism. The authorities have set aside a third of the country as protected areas and, with such a diverse range of habitats, landscapes and flora and fauna, it is a wildlife lover's dream. The country is now heavily reliant on tourism and is home to a vast range of species, many of which are endangered.

Mel Kinder,
Wildlife Worldwide

A zebu cattle cart in an avenue of baobab trees, Madagascar

photo: shutterstock/Muriel Lasure

FAMILY FRIENDLY

Speak to most parents about slow travel with kids and a "you must be joking" look eclipses their faces. Why should we trade in a short budget flight for an overland odyssey of indeterminate length and marriage-breaking stress? Why should we forgo lazy Mediterranean sun for the weather-beaten home front? Even the greenest of us would admit that low-carbon travel is a far greater challenge when kids are in tow.

But equally, many parents find the experience of having children leads them to reassess their own environmental footprint – after all, it highlights the kind of world our children will inherit if we don't change our way of life. Combine climate-change awareness with an increasingly fraught and expensive airport experience, and greener family travel even becomes appealing.

In this chapter we offer suggestions for the best family and eco-friendly breaks at home and abroad, plus vital tips on keeping children entertained as you wind down from frenetic flying holidays.

 **green family holidays**

"The water isn't salty, Mum," my five-year-old son shouts joyfully as we swim back to the deserted white soft sands of Kiani Akti. He is right: the water that flows into this section of Souda Bay, on the north-west corner of Crete, is from a mountain river that gushes past hillside olive and orange groves and culminates in a tumultuous surge at this tiny beach. This mixture of currents, temperature and taste provides the perfect metaphor for our first trip to Crete, which I had always resisted for fears of the ravages of mass tourism. But then we found our little village in the mountains, Megala Chorafia, where traditional Cretan life fights successfully for a place among the rapids and dangerous undercurrents of concrete and plastic tourism found elsewhere on the island.

We stayed at a villa owned by a local, Stelios Botonakis. He rents it out through British firm Pure Crete, which as well as offering accommodation in locally owned Cretan villas, arranges a range of activities for guests which are designed to support the traditional lifestyles of the island's mountain villagers. Stelios, whose smile is as big as his generous spirit, built this house himself. Beautifully crafted in white stone, it overlooks the snow-capped White Mountains and endless olive groves, and is elegantly and simply furnished.

The Botonakis family lives next door and quickly makes us feel at home, while giving us plenty of holiday "space". We aren't really "space" people, however, and when Stelios arrives with a gift of his homemade wine, we invite the family in that night to help us drink it. It is May Day, so the whole family is around to take us up on our invitation, each arriving with a gift: wine, cake, cheese or a traditional May Day flower garland.

We light a fire in the vast stone fireplace and swap life stories, our new friends putting us to shame with their good English. Our children are in their element as they are passed from lap to lap. The evening reaches a touching finale when Stelios gives a rendition of a traditional Cretan song, raising the hairs on the back of my neck. We will never forget the beaches, ancient monuments, sunshine, tavernas and mountain gorges. But evenings like that are not in the guidebooks.

Our other top trip is to Taverna Lemonia, a 20-minute drive along twisting roads into the White Mountains. This taverna has not only stunning views, but is also home to Leonidas, one of a handful of olive farmers still using traditional olive presses. We take a tour of the small mill where he uses a donkey to turn the massive stone wheels that crush the olives. This is cold-pressed olive oil, now a rarity in Crete, as heating olives allows for faster pressing, but as our bottle proved, a less intense flavour. Leonidas is also a master craftsman, and shows us his workshop, full of traditional stringed instruments that he makes, bespoke, for local musicians. We are invited into the family house for coffee and cheese pies, made from their own mizithra (a soft goat's cheese) and horta (wild greens). As we tuck in, Leonidas picks up a lyre and plays for us.

There should be more companies like this, which aim to both support the local economy and to preserve Cretan culture. Not in a way that enshrines it, but by simply keeping it alive.

Pure Crete offers a week in a villa in Crete including flights and a discount for children. It also offers activity holidays covering walking, history and conservation, (0845 070 1571, purecrete.com).

Catherine Mack

 **Family days out in the UK**

BEWILDERWOOD, WROXHAM, NORWICH, NORFOLK

A treetop adventure, complete with treehouses and jungle bridges for young eco-activists(01603 783900, bewilderwood.co.uk).

CENTRE FOR ALTERNATIVE TECHNOLOGY, MACHYNLLETH, POWYS

Explore this incredible eco-adventure playground complete with organic cafe and hands on activities for all ages. Enjoy a 50% discount if you arrive by train (01654 705950, cat.org.uk).

CENTRE FOR ECOLOGY, KINGHORN, FIFE, SCOTLAND

Take a tour of Scotland's first carbon neutral dwelling, the Earthship, and enjoy the surrounding grounds buzzing with insect life, well-stocked vegetable gardens and a network of coastal walking trails to take you further afield (01592 891567, cfec.org.uk).

CREAM OGALLOWAY, CASTLE DOUGLAS, SCOTLAND

A day out at this family-run organic dairy farm wouldn't be complete without sampling some of the delicious ice cream produced on site. Take a farm tour and hang out in the natural adventure playground designed for adults and kids (01557 814040, creamogalloway.co.uk).

ECOS MILLENNIUM ENVIRONMENTAL CENTRE, BALLYMENA, ANTRIM, NORTHERN IRELAND

Learn about the major challenges facing our planet through interactive displays and an impressive array of alternative technologies at this visitor centre set in 150 acres of land, complete with sand pit, play park, willow tunnel and duck-feeding opportunities! (028 2566 4400, ballymena.gov.uk/ecos).

photo: BeWILDerwood

The BeWILDerwood adventure tree house park in Norfolk

EDEN PROJECT, BOLDELVA, ST AUSTELL, CORNWALL

A sensory family adventure that teaches about self-sufficiency alongside the plant kingdom. And who can resist a visit to the steamy tropics biome? (01726 811911, edenproject.com).

GARDEN ORGANIC, RYTON-ON-DUNSMORE, COVENTRY, WARWICKSHIRE

Promoting organic gardening, this visitor attraction offers something for all the family. Discover the Vegetable Kingdom, an interactive exhibition on the history and role of vegetables. Also offers an organic restaurant and shop (024 7630 3517, gardenorganic.org.uk).

GO APE, NATIONWIDE

Get kitted out with a safety harness and enjoy swinging in the treetops at one of 17 family-fun adventure centres round the UK (0845 643 9215, goape.co.uk).

GOODLEAF, ISLE OF WIGHT, HAMPSHIRE

Recreational tree climbing with qualified instructor. Swing from the treetops and enjoy a homemade picnic under the boughs to round it all off (01983 563573, goodleaf.co.uk).

GREENWOOD FOREST PARK, SNOWDONIA

Go wild in the forest at this woodland-themed adventure park where young visitors build dens and much more (01248 671493, greenwoodforestpark.co.uk).

KEW GARDENS, RICHMOND, SURREY

Plenty to do within 300 acres of botanical gardens. Explore Climbers and Creepers adventure playground and learn about bees, plant pollination and much more (020 8332 5655, kew.org).

LIVING RAINFOREST, HAMPSTEAD NORREYS, BERKSHIRE

Explore the incredible ecosystem and learn about banana and coffee production as well as discovering more about the rich wildlife of rainforest regions (01635 202444, livingrainforest.org).

LONDON WETLAND CENTRE, BARNES, LONDON

One of the best features of this extensive wildfowl reserve is the bird airport, a viewing observatory where visitors can enjoy watching birds coming into land. Also home to Explore, a fabulous play area complete with giant water vole tunnels (020 8409 4400, wwt.org.uk/London).

NATURES WORLD, ACKLAM, MIDDLESBROUGH

Activity centre based on nature and science. The Earth Ship building invites visitors to experience life without fossil fuels in 2020 and there's lots for children to do and explore (01642 594895, naturesworld.org.uk).

WEALD AND DOWNLAND MUSEUM, NEAR CHICHESTER, EAST SUSSEX

This is a fascinating open-air museum demonstrating rural life over the last 500 years. Plenty of children's activities take place during summer holidays offering opportunities to learn traditional crafts such as making natural dyes, baking bread and more (01243 811363, wealddown.co.uk).

Melissa Corkhill

photo: Go Ape

Go Ape runs high-wire forest adventures in 17 UK locations

Family-friendly green trips around the world

PATAGONIA ECOCAMP, CHILE

Teenagers will be wowed by this end-of-the-world adventure. EcoCamp Patagonia, in the Torres del Paine National Park, is made up of a circle of geodesic domes reminiscent of the local Kawesqar people's huts. Accommodation is in snug insulated eco-pods with fleece sheets and sheepskin covers to keep out the cold. Trekking in the Patagonian wonderland of mountains, fjords, pampas, ice fields and volcanoes holds an exciting choice of soft or hard adventure. Kayaking and horse riding are also on the menu with expert Patagonian guides, taking in the exceptional flora and fauna of the area.

Three-day Ice trekking costs from US$790 per person including full board and guiding. A five-day trek costs from US$1,578 including full board and guiding. Book through Cascada Expediciones (+56 2 232 9878, info@cascada.travel, ecocamp-patagonia.com). Nearby El Calafate has an international airport and a train station.

RIVER CRUISE, BRITTANY, FRANCE

Soak up the Celtic charm of the cruising region of Brittany and visit the medieval towns and chateaux that line your route. The temperate climate, and numerous parks offering leisure and water sports amenities make this a perfect place to visit, whatever the time of year. Le Boat's week-long Capital Cruise travels 127km from Messac along the peaceful River Vilaine to Dinan, stopping to visit the regional capital, Rennes. Dinan is a perfect example of a medieval town on the banks of the River Rance. There are plenty of opportunities for on-shore fun; tennis and horse-riding at Betton, swimming at Lehon's open-air swimming pool and picnics on the lake at Combourg.

Prices start at £610 for a two-berth boat sleeping up to five people (leboat.co.uk). Take the ferry from Portsmouth to St Malo and drive on to Rennes or Messac, or take the train to Messac, Rennes or Nantes. Flights also available to Nantes or Rennes.

SPICE ISLAND BEACH RESORT, GRENADA

Grenada inspires adventure seekers of all ages with kayaking, snorkelling, hiking through the rainforest at Grand Etang, exploring indigenous plants, scouting the wildlife at Levera national park, bird-watching at La Sagesse Nature Centre, and getting up close and personal with mona monkeys. In between island exploration, stay at the eco-trendsetter Spice Island Beach Resort, where the Nutmeg Pod children's centre is open daily for kids ages three to 12. A solar-rooftop heater warms all the water, there is an onsite desalination plant for the dry season, the swimming pool is saltwater and fruit and veg is local and organic.

Triple suites from $1,065pp per night full board. Discounts for children; supplements for high season (spiceislandbeachresort.com, spiceisl@spiceisle.com).

YOGA BREAKS, LE MARCHE, ITALY

Set on a 100-acre wooded hill around a farmhouse, close to the renaissance gem of Urbino in central Italy, The Hill That Breathes is a holistic centre running family yoga weeks in the summer holidays. It feels more like renting a large house (complete with Italian chef) for you and your friends than a hotel, with the perfect mix of hanging out by the salt-water pool, followed by a peaceful yoga class. The children do yoga or other activities separately. Sustaining the local wildlife (including deer, boar, badger, fox and red squirrel) is second nature to all who work there. Destination visits with environmental benefits are available, including walks in the mountains led by a local guide, an expert on the flora and fauna of the area, who naturally imparts his love of this environment and his desire to maintain and nurture it.

Take Eurostar to Paris and overnight train to Bologna, then intercity train to Ancona. Driving takes around 16 hours from London. A week costs £695 per adult with discounts for children comprising full board and all yoga/activity sessions. Massages and treatments are also available, at £45 a session (thehillthatbreathes.com; behappy @thehillthatbreathes.com).

HELL BAY HOTEL, SCILLY ISLES, UK

To holiday here is like returning to a charming adventure from times past while for children it offers a car-free, this century Swallows and Amazons existence. Bryher's Hell Bay hotel's success lies in its ability to encourage low-impact tourism while maintaining a traditional daily life, which means the 60-strong community is thriving. Puffins, hoopoes and bald sea eagles abound.

Take a train or drive to Penzance then or 20-minute scheduled helicopter to the Scilly Isles. You can buy a combined rail and helicopter ticket from First Great Western on 0845 601 0573. Double rooms cost from £130 per person per day, half board. Interconnecting rooms are available and there is a Royal Yachting Association recognised sailing school (01720 422947, hellbay.co.uk).

AQUACITY RESORT, PROPAD, SLOVAKIA

Billed as the "world's leading green resort", Slovakia's AquaCity is both eminently affordable and fun. This waterpark and spa is virtually self-powered using geothermal water and solar energy. Situated under one giant roof and open year-round, the pools, restaurants and choice of three- or four-star hotel are within a few minutes walk. AquaCity has 14 naturally heated warm indoor and outdoor swimming areas and massage pools; ball parks and playgrounds; a 20m high Mayan pyramid of chutes; waterfalls and toboggans; a sauna and permanent snow cave; and a spa centre with 11 salt, menthol, herb and steam inhalation rooms. Outdoor activities in the surrounding parks and mountains include walking, biking, golf, summer tubing and "adult scootering" (wheeling down the lower slopes of the High Tatras on a large-sized kid's scooter), or there's the nearby Tatra Bob for those who like the thrill of sliding down steep chrome rails on a small plastic sledge.

Czech Travel (0845 270 3800) offers a three-night stay at AquaCity from £299 per person, including flights and half-board accommodation in the three-star AquaCity Seasons hotel and free access to the waterpark and spa (aquacityresort.com) Fly direct to Propad or drive, in around 18 hours from London.

HORSE RIDING IN THE TRIGLAV NATIONAL PARK, SLOVENIA

photo: The Riding Company/Kat Tiefenthal

A horse and chalets at the Pristava Lepena

If your children think nature is boring and they get "stiff legs" even at the suggestion of a walk in the countryside, then head to the Pristava Lepena. This is a small cluster of environmentally friendly wooden chalets in pure Robin-Hood-and-Indiana-Jones territory. There's free archery (with or without the home-made bows), a pool, and some Lipizzaner ponies. Budding cowboys can have lessons in the "corral" while experienced riders can head off on some spectacular adventures into the surrounding national park. You can also raft the river rapids, abseil down waterfalls or take to the skies under a paraglider.

The Riding Company offers seven nights' half-board at the four-star Pristava Lepena from £578 per person. Discounts for children and supplements for high season apply. Adrenaline sports cost around £56 per person per day with professional guide and all equipment. Mountain bike hire £10 per hour. (theridingcompany.com, info@theridingcompany.com).

Fly to Trieste, Klagenfurt or Ljubljana, take the train via Paris and Munich, or drive.

VIL UYANA, SRI LANKA

For many, Sri Lanka's coastline is its main asset but the spectacular inland rock fortress of Sigiriya is where the island's true heart lies. Conveniently, the area is also home to Vil Uyana, an eco-haven for wildlife and families alike. Wetlands, lakes and reed beds surround comfortable residences perfect for young adventurers. There's excitement on your doorstep – where the swimming pool melts into a lake of snoozing crocodiles. Beyond that you can go pond dipping, partake in nature quizzes, walk with the resident naturalist, or explore the vertiginous Sigiriya.

Vil Uyana is 153 km from Colombo International airport. A double room at Vil Uyana costs from US$400 per night. Tailor-made nature tours for children are available on request (viluyana.com, +94 11 5545711).

ANGAVALLEN FARM, SWEDEN

In 2008, Ängavallen Farm won a prize for being Sweden's best ecological restaurant. While this is something that children might not always appreciate, they generally do appreciate a guided tour of the farm, while their parents linger over a gourmet meal in peace. Kids also tend to enjoy practical exercises on offer, like stuffing sausages in the kitchen or having fun in the bakery. Should you fancy a change, Ängavallen is just 15 minutes away from one of Sweden's best beaches.

A stay costs 650 Swedish Kroner per person based on four guests per room, and includes a the Ängavallens ecological breakfast buffet. It's 350 Swedeish Kronor for children under five and 500 SEK for children aged 5-12. All children's activities are free. Travel by overnight ferry from Harwich to Esbjerg and then onwards by train or car, or take the Eurostar to Brussels and connecting trains via Cologne or Hamburg and Copenhagen (angavallen.se).

AGER FOUNDATION, MALTA

Malta's AGER Foundation is run by volunteers who are passionate about promoting sustainable rural development, predominantly on the island of Gozo. It has harvested a selection of farmers and the like to introduce traditional family orientated activities to visitors, who can opt to stay in farmhouses or visit for the day from the mainland. Spend a day tending and herding sheep and goats with the chance of shearing in the spring or making delicious Gozitan cheese. Other trips include fishing in a traditional "dghajsa", herb picking and salt collecting.

Activities (for which they will collect you by horse and trap from the ferry terminal or from your farmhouse) generally cost less than €10 for children and €20 for adults. (agerfoundation.com). Flying to Malta is by far the quickest option with kids – then it's a boat transfer to Gozo.

Sarah Siese

Keeping them entertained: slow green journeys with kids

Station anagrams

Take the name of the last station you passed through and write it down. Everyone has to get as many words as possible from the letters available before the next station – when you add up scores. With younger children it's best to do this in big letters and rip the page up so they can be physically rearranged. York will present problems but you could ignore it and keep working on Doncaster until you pass Northallerton. Naturally you let the kids win. Ages 5-6+

Speed-plating

As cars overtake on the motorway, spot the last three letters of their number plate and instantly give the full version of the acronym. For example: CFW might be Crazy French Wombats. With children this game almost always degenerates into a scatological nightmare. I will never forget when my eight-year-old son spotted DWF and immediately came up with Dad's Wednesday Fart. It changed the atmosphere of the journey. Ages: 5-6+

A to Z of ...

Going around the group, think of animals (or countries, fruits, vegetables, parts of the ship if you are on a ferry, etc) in alphabetical order. More demanding is to make an unending sentence with consecutive letters, and remember what went before, for example: Actually, before cool dinosaurs exterminated five great ... Ages: 4-5+

Pub cricket

One person is 'in' and they acrue runs according to the names of the pubs passed and the number of legs in that name. For example: if it's the Red Lion, they've struck a four. If it's the Farmer's Rest, then that's just two. If there are no legs in the name – the Punchbowl – then they are out and the next batsman comes in. English rules do not allow more than six runs per pub, whatever the name, but Australian do. With antipodean rules, the Five Horsemen would be 30 runs. No good on motorways or trains, unfortunately. Even three- to four-year-olds can play this one, as long as you shout out the names of the pubs for them.

Book titles

An old chestnut. "Have you read...?" followed by a ridiculous but appropriate name for the author. Our old favourites have been, Empty Tanks by Phil Errup, and the classic Caribbean-Geordie Cookbook by Wendy Boatcomesin. A variation, which I have known seven-year-olds manage, is the village names game. In this you have to come up with a suitably bizarre explanation for the name. Fearby, for example, was named after a dreadful attack by killer insects. Points are awarded, and points mean prizes. The advanced version, only really suitable for teenagers plus, is the vicar game. As you pass a village sign, you have to say who the vicar is. It's usually very rude, but what can you expect with English place names like Sexhow and Staines? Children under seven don't usually get the idea.

Kevin Rushby; photo: shutterstock/Maria Pavlova

TRAILBLAZER

Higher Lank Farm, Cornwall, UK

What? A 500-year old working farm dedicated to welcoming young families – visitors can only stay with a child under five in tow.

Where? St Breward, near Bodmin in Cornwall.

What's their big idea? To promote green living and relaxed farmyard fun for kids and their carers.

Track record: Baby gear and babysitting, is provided, meaning parents need not bring more than a few favourite toys. Guests can even try out reusable nappies and take advantage of a free nappy laundry service. Accommodation in the nursery rhyme barns is efficiently insulated and heated by wood-burning stove using the farm's own timber, while the home-made food is organic and local wherever possible. Those arriving by train can get picked up from Bodmin Parkway and cycle hire is available.

More information: 01208 850716, higherlankfarm.co.uk

Pisac market, Peru
photo Guy Marks, Tribes Travel

SECTION THREE

DIRECTORY

DIRECTORY

in association with greentraveller.co.uk

The properties listed here were judged on a range of criteria including their policies on minimising the use of energy, waste and water, how they source food and supplies, conservation of local habitat and biodiversity, employment practices and contributions to community projects. The vast majority were inspected personally.

Most of the following reviews were written by Richard Hammond, founder of greentraveller.co.uk and editor of Alastair Sawday's *Green Places to Stay*.

Find and share more green travel tips with Guardian readers at ivebeenthere.co.uk/tips/green.

OUR RATINGS EXPLAINED

🍃 A rating of 1 leaf indicates first steps taken towards environmental sustainability and/or socially responsible tourism.

🍃🍃 A rating of 2 leaves indicates a deeper commitment towards environmental sustainability and/or socially responsible tourism.

🍃🍃🍃 A rating of 3 leaves indicates an outstanding commitment towards environmental sustainability and/or socially responsible tourism.

FULL CIRCLE YURT, LAKE DISTRICT
RATING:

Yurt camps are fast becoming the preferred pad for luxury campers – they're stylish, waterproof and big enough to house a four-poster bed as well as a wood stove to keep you snug. Full Circle camp lies in the grounds of Rydal Hall, a historic house owned by the Diocese of Carlisle between Grasmere and Ambleside. The three yurts – including the 'red' honeymoon yurt are the genuine article, fashioned out of wood, canvas, cotton and wool in Ulan Bator. The site does not use electricity and offers wind-up torches and radios. A discount is available if you arrive via public transport.

A 3-day weekend or Monday-Friday stay at Full Circle costs from £250, a week from £340.

lake-district-yurts.co.uk, 07975 671 928

ROSE HILL LODGES, TURF-ROOFED CABINS, CORNWALL
RATING:

A development of turf-roofed cabins that attempt to strike a balance between "green" and "luxury", but lean towards the latter. To balance the hot tub on the veranda, the lodges have efficient recycling systems insulation that slashes heating requirements.

Two-bed self-catering cabin at Rose Hill Lodges that sleeps up to four from £290 for three nights, £540 for a week. Get there with BioTravel Taxis, which run on chip-fat. 01637 880006, biotravel.co.uk. Further information: Green Tourism Business Scheme, green-business.co.uk; CoaST, cstn.org.uk.

rosehilllodges.com, 0845 0731088

LA ROSA VINTAGE CARAVANS, NORTH YORKSHIRE MOORS
RATING: 🀄

La Rosa Campsite, near Whitby, North Yorkshire is a 20-acre site in the North York Moors National Park with eight vintage caravans, showers in a converted byre, a compost loo in a shepherd's hut and a big top. Try the Victorian roll-top bath in the orchard, with views down onto the valley.

Adults cost £27 a night, including bedding, candles and firewood. An evening meal costs £8. Tea parties held for £5. Small children stay free of charge.
larosa.co.uk, 07786 072866

NATURAL RETREATS, AISLABECK, YORKSHIRE DALES
RATING: 🀄

A mile from the market town of Richmond, these green-build single-storey houses are tucked beneath a wooded hillside. The upmarket cottages have sloping roofs planted with grasses and their south-facing floor-to-ceiling double-glazed windows allow light to flood in. All water comes from a natural spring, you are given an organic hamper including wine on arrival and there is a wood burner to cosy up to after your day out. Further Natural Retreats are planned in the Lake District, Snowdonia and the North York Moors and the company plans to open at each of the UK's 14 national parks by 2011.

In 2009 a cottage for six cost from £360 for two nights and from £770 for a week in low season and from £1,210 in high season.
naturalretreats.com, 0161 242 2970

MESMEAR, CORNWALL
RATING: 🀄 🀄

The stone-and-slate facade of this stylish 18th-century mill conversion near Polzeath on the north Cornish coast is typical of the region's farm buildings, yet the interior is another world. The rooms have been designed to create a sense of "loft-style living" while the decor is eclectic eco-chic: rattan chairs, bean bags and wooden tables. Underfloor heating is provided by geothermal energy, which saves the property 12 tonnes of carbon dioxide emissions a year, and a wood-burning stove will top up the heat. An underground spring provides drinking water and fills the solar-heated outdoor swimming pool.

The Mill (sleeps 10) costs from £4,300 a week full board, including housekeeper/cook; the barn (sleeps four) costs from £900 self-catering. mcsmear.co.uk, 01208 869731

ECO-CABIN, SHROPSHIRE
RATING:

This single-storey wooden lodge in the Shropshire Hills may look like it has been plucked from Scandinavia but it is the vision of the local owner. The cabin is built out of wood, wool, reeds, lime and clay, and most of the furnishings are from a community recycling scheme or have been plucked from a local junk shop. The lodge has solar power and a wood-pellet stove to heat the snug living room. You can also order a delivery of local organic food and rented bikes can be delivered to the cabin by Wheelywonderfulcycling.co.uk.

From £420 a week or £95 a night (minimum two nights) for four people. Take the train to Craven Arms from where you can arrange to be collected by the owner.
ecocabin.co.uk, 01547 530183

STRATTONS HOTEL, NORFOLK
RATING:

This family-run country house near the market town of Swaffham in the Brecks sets the standard for eco-friendly boutique hotels. The owners have turned a grade II-listed building into a swirl of colour. Choose between 10 themed rooms, including the "theatrical red room" with a four-poster bed and fireplace, and the 'boudoir' with wallpaper splashed with renaissance art print. The food in the restaurant is from Norfolk and all the hotel's waste is recycled. You will receive a 10 per cent discount if you arrive by public transport.

Take the train to King's Lynn then hop on the local X-1 bus from Peterborough which stops right outside the door. Double Rooms cost from £150; suites from £200.
strattonshotel.com, 01760 723845

LANGDON BECK, NORTH PENNINES
RATING: 🔘🔘🔘

In the heart of Teesdale, Langdon Beck is the YHA's greenest hostel. A wind turbine and photo-voltaic panels generate more than 60% of the 31-bed hostel's power, while solar panels heat the water. Sheep's wool and recycled newspapers provide the insulation and rainwater is harvested from the roof. From the dining room/lounge there are superb views over the moors and you are close to the 70ft High Force – England's highest waterfall. Evening meals are served in the hostel, which also has a range of local real ales and organic wines.

A bed costs from £13.95. Take the train to Darlington, Arriva 75/76 bus to Middleton-in Teesdale then Upper Teesdale bus link 73 (traveline.org.uk).
yha.org.uk, 01629 592708

HIGHER LANK FARM, CORNWALL
RATING: 🔘🔘🔘

This one is for kids. In fact, you can go there only if you have one child under five (older children are welcome to join them). It is a 500-year-old working farm near Bodmin Parkway train station offering B&B in the farmhouse or self-catering in a barn. Everything is provided – books, games and jigsaw puzzles, hundreds of videos, cots, baby carriers and spare buggies and babysitters in the evening; even reusable nappies are lent free of charge and cleaned (or your own reusable nappies are laundered by them free of charge). Get the train and arrange a pick-up, or rent bikes from Go By Cycle (gobycycle.co.uk). The extended Camel trail now starts right outside the farm.

A double room with two cots (or single beds) costs from £291 per family for four nights. Dinner is £16 per person, nursery tea £4.50 per child. The two self-catering barns, the largest sleeping up to four adults and five children, cost from £650 a week.
higherlankfarm.co.uk, 01208 850716

THE ECO LODGE, LINCOLNSHIRE
RATING:

A small, innovative self-catering lodge in eight acres of woodland in Old Leake, Lincolnshire. The lodge was built using local wood and is powered by a large wind generator and solar panels. Cook on a wood-burning range in the kitchen or outside on the BBQ – fuelled by the owner's homemade charcoal. Wash using a filtered rain-water system. The lodge, which looks out over a poplar-lined meadow, is close to Route 1 of the National Cycle Network.

A week at the lodge (which has two bedrooms each with two beds) costs £340 plus a one-off £5 supplement per person. Shorter breaks from Friday to Monday cost £170 plus a £5 supplement per person Travel by train to Boston from where you can arrange to be picked up by the owner or get a taxi.

ecolodge.me.uk, 01205 871396

SOUTHWAITE GREEN, CUMBRIA
RATING:

These four four- and five-star farm cottages at the western edge of the Lake District boast slate and oak floors and an innovative underfloor heating system using heat from the ground or the air. Sheets and towels are organic cotton, eco-paints adorn the interior and local Cumbrian craftsmen have supplied some of the furnishings – made from sustainable timber. Solar panels heat the water and sewage and waste water is treated via a bio-digester and reed bed. Loweswater and Crummock lakes are within a 20-minutecycle.

A cottage costs from £410 for seven nights and a three-night break costs from £320. Ten percent of profits go to ActionAid and Third World Organics.

southwaitegreen.co.uk, 01900 821005

DEEPDALE FARM, NORFOLK
RATING:

A 1,300-acre working farm with an 80-pitch campsite, a basic backpackers hostel for up to 50 and a converted granary for groups of up to 18. The hostel and toilet blocks have solar-powered underfloor heating. The majority of the hot water comes from solar panels in fact. The farm is close to beaches and saltmarshes of the north Norfolk coast, including Blakeney Point for bird-watching and the chance to see common and grey seals. Sailing is just up the road. There also 4 teepees which can hold up to 4 people each.

Camping costs from £4.50 per adult, £2 per child; a dorm room in the hostel costs from £9.50 a night; teepees are £40 a night if just two people are staying, £72 if there are 3-6 people staying. Hire of the Granary is from £144 per night for a group stay. Take the train to King's Lynn then taken the Coasthopper bus (norfolkgreen.co.uk), which drops you off at the farm.
deepdalefarm.co.uk, 01485 210256

TRELOWARREN, CORNWALL
RATING:

Deep in woodland, a mile from any road on the south coast's Lizard peninsula, Trelowarren sits in one of Europe's top five botanical sites, offering 1,000 acres of woodland walks. Two 16th-century thatched cottages, an 18th-century house and a barn have been restored, while eight cottages have been built – with more on the way – mainly using locally sourced or recycled materials. All the properties and an outdoor pebble-lined pool are heated by a vast woodchip boiler fuelled by coppicing from the estate; most of the fish, game and herbs used in Trelowarren's restaurant come from with 10 miles of the estate.

A self-catering cottage for four at Trelowarren costs from £450 a week
trelowarren.co.uk, 01326 222105

OLD CHAPEL FORGE, CHICHESTER
RATING:

This 17th-century former chapel has been remodelled with all the usual green credentials you'd expect from a winner of the gold award of the Green Tourism Business Scheme. There's solar thermal heating and waste water recycling. The owners have also included some subtle eco features, such as a sun pipe that funnels natural light into the bathroom and recycled iron drainpipes for water harvesting. The owners organise bike hire so you can cycle the 18km Salterns Way from the centre of Chichester to the beach at East Head (conservancy.co.uk). Pagham nature reserve and Chichester harbour are nearby and the owners organise star-gazing weekends as well as breaks on the South Downs.

From £65pp B&B cycle hire is £12 a day.
oldchapelforge.co.uk, 01243 264380

COTTAGE LODGE, BROCKENHURST, NEW FOREST
RATING:

The green award-winning Cottage Lodge is a restored 17th-century B&B five minutes' walk from Brockenhurst train station in the heart of the national park. There's free tea and scones if you arrive by train and if you do come by car you're encouraged to leave it in the car park while you explore the forest on foot, by bike or on horseback. There's thick insulation throughout the rooms and kitchen waste is recycled, while packaging is returned to suppliers for re-use. Ingredients for their "New Forest breakfast" are all sourced from within 10 miles of the lodge and it won. Maps and detailed instructions are provided on the many circular walks from the lodge and there's cycle hire in the village from where you can explore over 100 miles of off-road cycle tracks.

Rooms from £25 B&B.
cottagelodge.co.uk, 01590 622296

THE HALL, MILDEN, SUFFOLK
RATING:

The Hall, Milden, in Lavenham, is a large 16th-century farmhouse and a typical energy black hole, yet there's much more to this green getaway than pulling on your wellies to see a few farmyard pigs. A huge wood burner heats the large hall, dining/living room and bedrooms, fuelled by coppiced wood from the farm's hedgerows; there's a comprehensive compost and recycling programme; and the breakfast is sourced either from the farm or local suppliers. Owner Juliet, an ecologist, has files of suggestions for how to keep the kids occupied, including nature trails, scavenge hunts and just plain messing around in the ponds. Bikes are free of charge and there are plenty of walks.

A room costs from £60, self-catering from £250 for 4 for a two-night weekend.

thehall-milden.co.uk, 01787 247235

POLLAUGHAN COTTAGES, CORNWALL
RATING:

These family-friendly cottages on the south coast of Cornwall have won awards both for sustainability and their high standard of self-catering accommodation. They were the first cottages in Cornwall to be assessed under the Green Tourism Business Scheme and have a Gold rating. Located on the direct line from Paddington, the owners can collect you from Truro. Unwind on a farmstead in the company of donkeys, sheep and buzzards, pick your own on the vegetable and flower patch or try the nearby cycle trail. Home cooked meals are also available as room service if you feel like a break from self-catering.

Cottages sleep 5-6 plus a cot, and cost from £390 per week in low season.

pollaughan.co.uk, 01872 580150

STAYINGCOOL DESIGN APARTMENTS,
MANCHESTER AND BIRMINGHAM
RATING:

These serviced design apartments aim to offer a more relaxed alternative to a city-centre hotel with a nod towards sustainability. Expect designer furniture, (unplugged) Apple Mac gadgets and a fridge full of local, organic or fairtrade produce. Energy and waste minimisation strategies are in place while laundry and bathroom toiletries are eco-friendly. Choose from 13 apartments in Manchester and four in Birmingham.

Apartments in Manchester cost from £115 per night and from £125 per night in Birmingham.

stayingcool.com; 0161 832 4060

CAMPING PODS, ESKDALE, LAKE DISTRICT
RATING:

Eskdale Camping and Caravanning Club Site sits in a valley just outside the village of Boot, a good drive away from the larger Lakeland towns, over the Hardknott Pass. In 2008 it opened 10 pods arranged in circular clusters of four and six in a copse set apart from the main camping lawn. Made of locally sourced timber and insulated with sheep's wool, each identical micro-lodge is designed to sleep four and simply offers a hard foam floor, a small window and an LED light on the ceiling. They are basic but quirky, alternative and affordable. Outside, each pod has its own raised wooden decking area and has access to impeccable onsite facilities.

The pods are available from 1 March–14 January for £35 per pod per night. The site is accessible via the West Coast main line.
campingandcaravanningclub.co.uk, 01946 723253

BEDRUTHAN STEPS HOTEL, CORNWALL
RATING:

A favourite with families, this large 4-star hotel in north Cornwall has a collection of eco awards and a full-time sustainability manager. Food (and more) is bought locally, solar panels and light sensors in the cloakrooms cut down on energy use and dual flush toilets save water. There is also a spa, though organic Voya and REN treatments area available.

Rates start at £78 pp per night for two people, half board and sharing a room.
bedruthan.com, 01637 860860

Scotland

WILD CAMPING, KNOYDART
RATING: 🟠🟠🟠

There are plenty of places to pitch in the wild in this remote stretch of Scotland's north-west coast. One of the best is a level area just behind the 'long beach', a short stroll round the bay from where the ferry drops you off at Inverie harbour. The Knoydart Foundation has an office in the village where you can arrange to hire a boat for fishing or to explore the sea lochs and bays around the islands before returning for a platter of freshly caught scallops at The Old Forge. They also run a bunkhouse sleeping up to 25 if you prefer a roof over your head.

Sleeper Euston-Mallaig via Glasgow from £155 return (scotrail.com, 0845 6015929), ferry Mallaig-Knoydart is £10 return, based on a group of more than six (bluebadgercruises.co.uk, 01687 462656). knoydart-foundation.com, 01687 462656

BLUE REEF COTTAGES, ISLE OF HARRIS
RATING: 🟠🟠

Overlooking a vast sandy beach, these two remote cottages (each sleeping two) are rated five-star by the Scottish Tourist Board. Open the door to find a hamper of local produce (black pudding, jam and shortcake) plus a bottle of champagne on ice. The cottage's turf roofs curve into the landscape and provide added insulation to keep in the heat from the cosy wood-burning stove. Everything is recycled and the owners have planted 4,000 native trees on the croft. It's a 10-minute walk to a great restaurant and there are boat trips out to the islands around Harris.

Costs from around £950 a week for two. Take the train to Mallaig (firstscotrail.com, 08457 550033), catch the ferry to Skye, the bus to Uig, then the ferry to Harris (calmac.co.uk). stay-hebrides.com, 01859 550370

LOCH OSSIAN HOSTEL, SCOTTISH HIGHLANDS
RATING: ☺ ☺ ☺

Those in London can catch the sleeper train from Euston just after 9pm and wake up the next morning in the heart of the Scottish Highlands. After breakfast at Corrour station it's just a mile to the spectacular Loch Ossian – just enough of a walk to wipe away the sleep from the journey and pinch yourself. The hostel is on Rannoch Moor in a clump of birch and rowan trees overlooking the loch. There are two dorms and a fully equipped kitchen that's powered by a combination of wind turbine and solar panels. Thanks to a green makeover in 2006 there are compost toilets and a reed-bed waste water filtration system. Climb up the 3,100ft Munro (Carn Dearg) and you are likely to see deer, red squirrels and pine martens.

A bed costs £15 per person for Scottish Youth Hostel Association members and £16 for non members. The entire hostel, sleeping up to 20 people, is also available to rent. The sleeper train from Euston to Corrour costs from £19 each way (firstscotrail.com, 08457 55 00 33).
syha.org.uk, 08701 553255

HUNTINGTOWER LODGE, FORT WILLIAM
RATING: ☺

Overlooking Loch Linnhe and just a few minutes from Fort William and the gateway to Ben Nevis, this lodge has been gold-rated in the Green Tourism Business Scheme under the previous management. Recently renovated with efficient insulation, it looks on to wildflower meadows at the front and back of the house. Free lifts are offered to and from Fort William station and into the town for evening excursions. Food is locally sourced wherever possible and materials recycled.

Rooms cost from £90, including breakfast. Take the sleeper from Euston to Fort William, from £112 return (firstscotrail.com).
huntingtowerlodge.com, 01397 700079

Wales

BRYN ELLTYD GUEST HOUSE, NORTH WALES
RATING:

At this lakeside B&B at the foot of the Moelwyn mountains range in the heart of the Snowdonia National Park, solar collectors heat the water and the wood burner is mostly fuelled from the grounds. The food is all local lamb and beef from Ty Isaf Ffestiniog and pork from Llanfrothen. The owner is a qualified mountain guide and canoe coach and offers guided walks. It's just a mile to the train station at Blaenau Ffestiniog and 100 yards to Tanygrisiau train station, from where you can catch the Ffestiniog narrow gauge railway through the mountains to the harbour at Porthmadog.

A night at Bryn Elltyd costs from £28 per person B&B. Dinner is from £14.

accommodation-snowdonia.com, 01766 831356

TRERICKET MILL VEGETARIAN GUESTHOUSE, POWYS
RATING:

Part guesthouse, part bunk house, part campsite – all Grade II listed. B&B guests, campers and bunkers pile in to the dining room for delicious and plentiful veggie food – fair-trade, wholefood and free-range – from a chalkboard menu. Stoves throw out the heat in the flagstoned living rooms; the bedrooms are simple pine affairs, well insulated and efficiently lit. On a Site of Special Scientific Interest – Skithwen brook runs through the property – the mill hosts a breeding colony of bats in the roof each summer, quite a sight at dusk. The owners draw water from a private borehole, serve eggs from their own ducks and hens and compost and recycle where possible.

Camping is £6 pp per night, the guest house costs between £58 and £73 per night and the bunkhouse is £12.50 pp per night.

trericket.co.uk, 01982 560312.

MAMAHEAVEN RETREATS, HEREFORDSHIRE
RATING:

Weekend breaks at an organic restaurant and manor farm in the Welsh borders, providing mothers with babies under 18 months with massage, organic food and yoga sessions. The restored manor farm dates from 1280 with a great medieval hall, Elizabethan wing and converted bedrooms in the threshing barn. Enjoy organic linens as well as food and wine served up by owner Daphne Lambert, co-author of the Organic Baby and Toddler Cookbook. Cleaning products are eco-friendly and cots, high chairs, home cooked baby food and bibs are provided. There are five retreats per year, Friday to Sunday.

A retreat costs £550 and is inclusive of food, board, yoga, massages, childcare and workshops. Pick-up can be arranged from Hereford station, which is just over three hours direct from Paddington. Look for the family-friendly carriage on board. Mamaheaven can also arrange car-pooling. mamaheaven.org; 01273 671762

UNDER THE THATCH GIPSY CARAVAN, SOUTH-WEST CEREDIGION
RATING:

Under The Thatch won the *Guardian*, *Observer* and guardian.co.uk's Ethical Travel Award for 2007. The caravan is run as a low-impact, eco-friendly concern. There are compost and recycling facilities and local wood for the fire. The cottages were restored using lime rather than cement, oil-based paint and sheep's wool insulation; some have solar panels, others reed-bed sewage systems, wood-chip boilers and recycled furnishings. Unlike many holiday homes, Under the Thatch properties are let all year round – at reduced prices if necessary.

Two nights at the Romany caravan cost from £99 midweek; a three-night weekend from £159 and a week from £209. underthethatch.co.uk. 01239 851 410

UNDER THE THATCH'S TREHILYN ISAF, PEMBROKESHIRE
RATING:

Griff Rhys Jones' old cottage on the Strumble Head peninsula in Pembrokeshire is the greenest of a growing number of properties let by Welsh social enterprise company Under the Thatch. The firm aims to restore derelict buildings as year-round holiday lets. Trehilyn Isaf has virtually carbon-neutral, wood-pellet fuelled central heating and sheep's wool insulation, but as manager Greg Stevenson says, there is "not a hippy sniff about it". All mod cons are found and the living room has a TV and DVD player. The wood-burner is fuelled by sustainably managed forests and the building is cement-free. There are two bedrooms and two bathrooms. Trehilyn Uchaf, next door can also be rented if you have a larger group.
Trehilyn Isaf costs from £230 for a 3-night weekend.
underthethatch.co.uk, 01239 851410

THE ROUNDHOUSE, PEMBROKESHIRE
RATING:

There are few walks in Britain that can beat Pembrokeshire's coastal footpath. En route is the Roundhouse, a small eco-cottage overlooking St Brides Bay near Haverfordwest. It's a former croquet pavilion that has been turned into a model environmental building by a local architect. There are solar panels and a wind generator (with a dial so you can read how much electricity they generate), a reed bed drainage system to ensure your waste water doesn't pollute the coastline, and a masonry stove that stores the heat in the walls overnight. Most of the insulation for the main building is made from sheep's wool and the restaurant for the accompanying hotel has a sustainable sourcing policy.
From £345 a week.
druidstone.co.uk/roundhouse, 01437 781221

BRECON BEACONS BUNKHOUSES
RATING:

A group of bunkhouses in the Brecon Beacons offers access to circular walking trails and cycle paths in the national park. Glynmeddig bunkhouse is a converted stone barn in the Cilieni Vally of the Upper Usk with underfloor heating, double beds and is graded four-star by the Wales Tourist Board. Recycling is encouraged on-site. Wain House Bunkbarn, Llantony, in the Black Mountains has a small dining area with a wood-burning stove and long wooden table, hot showers, and is yards from a cosy pub beneath the ruins of Llantony Priory.

A bed at the Wain House Bunkbarn cost £8pp per night on a group only basis. Glynmeddig costs £1,100 for a maximum of 20 for a weekend. glynmeddig.co.uk, 01874638949, bootsbikesbunkhouses.co.uk, llanthony.co.uk

TYF ECO HOTEL, PEMBROKESHIRE
RATING:

A converted 200-year-old windmill at the edge of St David's in the Pembrokeshire coast national park. The old mill stones lie at the front of the building and although the sails have gone, the original windmill tower still stands. The low sofas and corner bar in the front room are more hostel than hotel, but the restaurant and rooms are smarter and you can climb up to the tower lounge for an excellent view of St David's and the coast. Nearly all the food is organic, local and seasonal, and as well as veggie options there's organic wine, beer and cider. The hotel is 10 minutes from the beach and can arrange plenty of adventure activities.

From £30pp per night.
tyf.com, 01437 721678

EUROPE   Iceland

HOTEL HELLNAR, SNAEFELLSBAER
RATING: 🔆🔆

Hotel Hellnar is at the foot of the enormous ice-covered Snaefellsjökull glacier on the northwest coast, in an area of wilderness that brims with lava caves and geothermal pools, just over two hours from the capital. The Scandinavian-style hotel is a simple, single-storey building – you sleep in twin rooms, each with a view of the glacier on one side and the sea on the other, and there's also a small timber cottage for six. It's the first hotel in Iceland to be awarded the Green Globe eco-label – the hotel is made out of local materials, the breakfast is organic, and for dinner there's local fish, veggie options and organic wine.

A twin room costs from IKK14.850 B&B.

hellnar.is, +354 (0)4 35 6820

Ireland

THE MUSTARD SEED AT ECHO LODGE,
CO. LIMERICK
RATING: 🔆

A large kitchen garden supplies vegetables and herbs for the organic restaurant at this large country hotel in southwest Ireland. There is a strict recycling policy and cycling, angling, horseriding and walking tours of the Golden Vale are available close by. The award winning hotel and restaurant are set on seven acres of grounds including a herb garden and orchard.

A standard room is €95 per person, a superior room is €120 pp and dinner is €62 euro. Take the train from Euston to Holyhead and ferry across to Dublin with Sailrail (08450 755755, sailrail.co.uk). Then catch the train to Charleville from where it's a taxi ride to the lodge.

mustardseed.ie, +353 (0)69 68508

HAGAL HEALING FARM, CO. CORK
RATING:

Hagal is different. It always was: the farmhouse was built 150 years ago by one man in 40 days. You can take lemon-balm tea under the huge old vine in the conservatory among candles and Buddha chimes, retreat from the pressures of modern life into a secluded corner of the beautiful wild garden, eat subtly spiced organic vegetarian food – or learn to cook it yourself. Seating is low and ethnic; the yoga room at the top has views of Bantry Bay, as does the chill-out room with its white sofas and angel cards.

The detox delight, two days full board is €365.
hagalholistichealth.com, + 353 (0) 27 66179

Channel Islands

LA VALETTE CAMPSITE, ISLE OF SARK
RATING:

Camping just isn't camping without a decent view of the stars on a clear night and a slot-token shower unit. Which is what you can expect at La Valette campsite on the French-facing east side of the Isle of Sark – the smallest of the four main Channel Islands, about 80 miles off the English coast and about as far from city lights as you can get in the UK. The campground overlooks the sea, there's fresh produce available from the farm and the four minutes of hot water for the shower comes courtesy of a solar thermal unit and a £1 token. Cars aren't allowed on the island, but though it's only three miles long and a mile and a half wide, you need a bike to explore all the coves and bays over a long weekend – luckily, you can hire one up the road from the campsite.

A night at La Valette costs £7pp or £4 for the under 10s. Take the
Weymouth-Guernsey ferry (condorferries.co.uk) then a ferry to Sark
(sarkshipping.info).
sercq.com, 01481 832202

France

CANVAS CHIC, ARDÈCHE
RATING:

A luxury campsite in the south of France where you can sleep out in style from the comfort of a cosy four-poster bed in an oak-framed yurt-style domed tent. Of the 14 yurts, 10 are designed for families, with access to a conventional tent where there's a fully equipped kitchen, while four other yurts, intended for couples, are a short walk further into the leafy oak forest in a more secluded part of the camp. The site is at the edge of the stunning Ardèche Gorge, in a nature reserve that the owners hope to regenerate in partnership with the local forestry department. A trail from the camp leads down the side of the gorge to an opening in the forest and out on to an idyllic natural bathing area surrounded by towering limestone cliffs.

Three nights at Canvas Chic cost from £255 per tent including breakfast for two. In summer take a direct Eurostar from London to Avignon Then it's a bus from Avignon station to Vagnas (towards Aubenas) Arrange a pick up by hosts from Vagnas on booking.
canvaschic.com, + 33 (0)4 75 38 42 77

LOUBATAS ECO-GITES, PROVENCE
RATING:

All that summer sun is put to good use at the solar-powered 35-bed Loubatas, the first of a series of eco-gîtes. Green living classes are offered during the week or you can rent it at the weekend and learn for yourself thanks to the energy-preserving building design and gadgetry. Sensors switch off lights in unoccupied rooms, food and waste are recycled and the toilets are wood-flush and water-free.

Rent the whole place from €370 for up to 20 people; then it's €13 per person per night.
loubatas.org,+ 33 (0)4 42 67 06 70

L'HÔTEL LES ORANGERIES, LUSSAC LES CHÂTEAUX, VIENNE
RATING:

An environmentally sensitively restored 18th-century farmhouse in the village of Lussac-Les-Chateaux in the west of France. Natural materials have been used in the renovation of the property, which was the first hotel in France to win "Eco-Label Européen" accreditation based on 84 criteria from energy and water to waste and education. Their new restaurant will source local, mostly organic ingredients.

A room costs from €75 and an apartment for 4 or 5 people costs from €105. Take the Eurostar (eurostar.com) to Paris, then it's a 90 minute train ride from Paris Montparnasse to Poitiers (sncf.co.uk) and then a 30 minute local train to Lussac.
lesorangeries.fr, +33 (0)5 49 84 07 07

LE POUJASTOU, PYRENEES
RATING:

The Pyrenees may be less popular than the Alps but they're no less dramatic and are strong on low-impact mountain activities. Bagnères-de-Luchon is on the French side by the Vénasque and Céciré mountains – reached by a scenic two-hour train journey from Toulouse. The town has a geothermally heated spa dug into the mountain known as a 'Vaporarium', which the French have been using since Roman times. 3km out of town, in the small village of Juzet-de-Luchon, is Le Poujastou, a converted 18th-century inn with five rooms.

Double rooms from €49 per night bed and breakfast, dinner €18pp and a picnic basket is €8pp. Riverboarding and canyoning available from €28pp.
lepoujastou.com, +33 (0)5 61 94 32 88

THE ORION B&B, CÔTE D'AZUR
RATING:

Four treehouses in a wooded area 15 minutes inland from Cagnes-sur-Mer, just along from Nice on the Côte d'Azur. The treehouses are actually stand-alone, solid structures, made of red cedar and built between the trees rather than perched on their trunks. You climb up to them via an outer wooden staircase rather than swinging over on a vine with a monkey on your back. Rooms are furnished with the trappings you'd expect in this part of the world – a huge double bed and large fluffy pillows, wooden bath and open "massage shower" – even an internet cable connection. Back on terra firma, lounge by a swimming pond cleaned through a sophisticated natural system of gravel and aquatic plant filtration.

€700 for a long weekend for two B&B.
orionbb.com, 0033 6 7545 1864

COVERT CABIN, DORDOGNE
RATING:

These off-grid cabins sit on the banks of a lake in a private woodland within the Perigord Vert natural park in Dordogne, France. The owner claims guests won't have to "forgo any home comforts". There's a solar-powered shower and a normal flushing lav – water being supplied via a wind-pump – a gas oven and a gas fridge, oil lights and even a wind-up radio. A small supply of beer and wine is thrown in, and if you can't be bothered to cook for yourself, there's a chef on standby to serve dinner on your deck. He'll even do the washing up.

€450 per week May to September, the rest of year €325, for a cabin for two. By rail to Angouelme, by air to Limoges.
Covertcabin.com, bobcabin@wanadoo.fr

Greece

MILIA TRADITIONAL SETTLEMENT, CRETE
RATING: 🛶🛶🛶

Milia was an abandoned village above the Topolia gorge in the western foothills of Crete's White Mountains, now restored as a hikers' hostel and organic farm. The stone houses have simple bedrooms, bathrooms and a dining room. Spring water has been piped in, there are wood burning stoves, iron beds and solar panels for (some) electricity. Everything is bought locally in Chania or grown on site and served fresh. You can also hire bikes and there is sometimes a small spring-fed pool to dip into when you return from the mountains.

Rooms are from €60 a night. Bike hire is €10 a day.
Milia.gr/english, +30 2821 046774

IONIAN ECO VILLAGERS, ZAKYNTHOS
RATING: 🛶🛶

In green Zante, under pine-scented hills, a short stroll from miles of sand, this collection of brightly coloured villas, apartments and stone cottages splashes over ancient olive groves in gardens of citrus and bougainvillea. Comfortable homes, many solar-powered, have sea views, timbered ceilings, tiled floors, simple kitchens, and open showers. The Gerakas peninsula, now part of the marine park, is one of the last nesting sites of the loggerhead sea turtle and a rescue and rehabilitation centre for turtles is due to open to the public in 2009.

From £410 per week for two.
relaxing-holidays.com, 0871 7115065

Italy

LOCANDA DELLA VALLE NUOVA, NEAR URBINO
RATING:

There are plenty of rural places to stay in Italy that offer local, organic produce, but La Locanda near the hilltop town of Urbino in Le Marche goes the extra mile to do its bit for energy conservation. Surrounded by ancient, protected oaks, the 1920s farmhouse has been converted into a well-insulated modern, smart country house with five doubles and one twin room as well as a self-catering apartment for two. There's purified water, solar heating and a wood-fired stove fuelled by coppicing from the 185 acre farm woods where you can gather truffles in autumn. There's a riding school next door, a swimming pool and a gentle afternoon circular walk around the farm that will help work up an appetite.

Bed and buffet breakfast is €54 per person. Horseriding is €20 per hour. vallenuova.it, +39 0722 330303

BARBIALLA NUOVA , TUSCANY
RATING:

A converted 19th century villa and two farmhouses with apartments on a 500 hectare organic farm, 30 minutes from Florence and Siena. The buildings were renovated using original local materials. There's no air-conditioning and you can go searching for white truffles in the woods. Solar panels power heat the water and the owners hope to become self-sufficient thanks to a new photovoltaic plant. There are seven apartments and one villa to rent, all self-catering, though you'll be tempted to raid the garden for herbs, fruit and vegetables.

The Le Trosce villa sleeps 8-10 and costs from €1,250 for a week. The apartments sleep 2-6 and cost from €440 a week. barbiallanuova.it, +39 0571 677004

TENUTA LE SORGIVE, MANTUA
RATING:

A peaceful, low-impact organic farm, 10km from Lake Garda in Solferino. The heating is provided by a vegetable biomass system and you can buy the farm's organic produce. All waste water is filtered and re-used. There are eight en-suite rooms and two apartments sleeping four. Owners the Serenelli family have been farming since the 12th century and you can sample their jams, wine, honey and charcuterie in the dining room.

The apartments cost between €470-810 per week Rooms are €70-€90 per week
lesorgive.it, info@lesorgive.it, +39 0376 854252

BELVEDERE B&B, CHAMBONS,
PIEDMONT
RATING:

The English owners of Belvedere B&B will pick you up at Turin's Porta Susa train station and take you to their restored 16th-century Alpine "casa" in Chambons in the heart of Val Chisone. There are three double rooms, basic but each has a private bathroom and two have mountain views. It's in the Piedmont region – so expect organic "slow food" – and many of the facilities are eco-friendly, such as a wood-fired heater. A cross-country ski circuit starts from right outside the front door and there's snow-shoeing nearby in the Troncea or Orsiera natural parks.

A room costs €60 a night and a three-night snow shoeing package costs €290 half board.
belvederebedandbreakfast.com, +39 0121 884701

LAMA DI LUNA, PUGLIA
RATING:

Lama di Luna is the unlikeliest of green getaways: a huge, renovated 18th century working farm near Andria, 70km from Puglia. The computer controlled heating is powered by 48 solar panels that make use of all that blissful southern Italian sun. Nine of the estate's rooms have been converted into large, en suite guestrooms, each with a snug fireplace. There's one apartment for four. Sleep in unbleached cotton sheets, wash with pure olive soap and tuck into an organic breakfast on a terrace overlooking olive, cherry and almond groves and the coast.

April-December a double room at Lama di Luna costs between €140 to €150 B&B a night and an apartment for four is €200 B&B, including free use of bikes. Ryanair (ryanair.com) flies Stansted-Bari from £10 one-way, inc tax. From Bari, it is a 45-minute drive to Lama di Luna. lamadiluna.com, +39 0883 569 505

Norway

ONGAJOK MOUNTAIN FARM, ARCTIC LAPLAND
RATING:

If Santa had a bolthole, this would be it. Ongajok is a cosy, traditional Norwegian farm tucked away in the remote far north of Norway in Finnmark, the land of the Sami people. The farm has been converted into an eco-friendly centre for outdoor activities such as cross-country skiing, ice fishing, reindeer-sledding and snow rafting. The centre mainly caters for groups so the emphasis is on communal living and the pine rooms are comfortable but very basic. Spend a night in the wilderness in a lavoo tipi where you'll learn tips on how to keep warm, Sami-style.

Rooms are Nkr1,790pp half-board including all activities. ongajok.no, +47 7843 2600

WESTERAS, WEST COAST
RATING:

The Geiranger fjord on the west coast of Norway is a recent addition to the Unesco World Heritage list. The sheer size and isolation of this part of the country means that it's easy to escape the crowds and appreciate the deep blue waters of this awesome natural phenomenon. For a bird's-eye view, stay at Westeras, perched on the side of the lush green hills overlooking Geiranger at the head of the fjord. It's been a working farm in the same family since 1603, but the new generation is diversifying into tourism and has built five self-catering wooden cabins, each with a double room, bunk beds, and a basic kitchenette.

A cabin for five costs from NOK500 per night self-catering
geiranger.no/westeras +47 70 26 32 14

Portugal

CERRO DA FONTINHA, SAO TEOTONIO
RATING:

These self-catering cottages are made from locally sourced, natural materials. Showers have stone bases and terracotta surrounds, pebbles embedded in walls create coat and towel hooks, thick cuts of wood become mantelpieces, stone sofas are cosily cushioned. You have countryside on the doorstep, a eucalyptus wood for shade, good restaurants and Carvalhal beach nearby – hire mountain bikes to get there. There's also a little lake for swimming and fishing.

€55-€120 per night.
cerrodafontinha.com, +351 282 949 083

Spain

HOTEL CERRO DE HIJAR, ANDALUCIA
RATING:

The hotel is just an hour inland from Malaga in a remote part of Andalucía, yet to be touched by the sprawling development creeping up from the Costa del Sol. There are four suites and 14 large bright double rooms with the kind of mountain views you'd only expect to see after a day's hiking. Local Andalucían food served in the restaurant, and while it's a relatively large country hotel with an outdoor swimming pool, all the rubbish is recycled, and each year the three Spanish owners have introduced a new eco feature, such as solar heating for the water and a waste water irrigation system.

Rooms from €51.50, breakfast €8.80, dinner from €35. Bike hire is €10 a day, horse-riding €12 an hour.
cerrodehijar.com, +34 952 112 111

LOS CASTANOS, ANDALUCIA
RATING:

Explore Andalucia's pueblos blancos from Los Castanos, which trains local women in hotel management. Just 10km from Ronda, but a world apart, this small boutique hotel in the tiny village of Cartajima promises a taste of "authentic Andalucia" amid the mountain air. Explore the villages of the Alto Genal valley on foot, birdwatch, naturewatch or just relax. Painting weeks were introduced in 2008.

From 116 euros per night B&B.
loscastanos.com, +34 952 180 778

CAN MARTI AGRITURISMO, IBIZA
RATING:

Can Marti is a working organic farm in a tranquil wooded valley in the north of the island where the loudest noise is likely to come from a donkey's bray or the clanking of cattle bells and you can explore the wilder parts of the island away from the crowds and throbbing beats. There are three self-catering apartments in an old, lime-washed stone farmhouse and a separate stone cottage overlooking sloping terraces of almond, fig and olive trees. Solar panels supply all the electricity and waste water is re-used through filtering reed-beds. Breakfast is organic, with home-made breads, jams and fruit juice. Bikes are provided free of charge so you can cycle on signposted trails into the island's interior or to nearby sandy beaches.

An apartment for two costs from €130, the cottage for four from €190. Breakfast is €10. The owner donates 7% to African nongovernmental organisations.
canmarti.com, +34 971 333 500

L'AYALGA POUSADA ECOLOGICA, ASTURIAS
RATING:

L'Ayalga is in La Pandiella, a small hamlet in the Redes nature reserve in Asturias, conveniently located between the craggy limestone mountains of the Picos de Europa and the uncrowded beaches near Llanes on the rural north coast. The old farmhouse was restored using lime, and the wood is treated with natural oils. Heating for the farmhouse is supplied by solar panels and the rooms are insulated with hemp. Practise t'ai chi and chi kung, and treat yourself to a massage after a day at the beach, canoeing down the River Sella or walking in the mountains. The owners will pick you up from the railway station at Infiesto on the scenic coastal line from Santander via the portal town of Ribadesella.

From €45 B&B, plus 7 per cent VAT and 1 per cent levy donated to local ecology and human rights organisations. A day return from Infiesto to Llanes costs €7 (feve.es, +985 297 656).
terrae.net/layalga, +34 616 897 638

ECO HOTEL LA CORREA, TENERIFE
RATING:

Feast on an organic breakfast at the Eco Hotel La Correa before trying out El Medano, one of the island's top windsurfing beaches. The hotel has six rustic en-suite rooms with sea views and can arrange hiking trips to national parks and villages, mountain biking, diving and paragliding. It also runs "wellness and health weeks with nutritional advice, massage, pilates and yoga. Cleaning products are biodegradable, much of the food is organic light bulbs are low-energy and rubbish is sorted for recycling.

Doubles from €65 B&B. Week-long wellness breaks cost from €620.
ecohotelcorrea.com, +34 922 725 738

LA HUERTA YURTS, ANDALUCÍA, SPAIN
RATING:

The camp is hidden in a sprawling orchard of orange and tangerine trees and surrounded by cork and oak forest, and can only be reached via a 4km dirt track. There are just two Uzbekistani yurts, with cushions and a mattress over a wooden floor. You'll need a torch to find your way around if there's no moon, and they are fenced off from wild pigs that snuffle round at night. A log-fired sauna is yards from the solar-powered main building where you can dine on seasonal vegetables, lamb and goat's cheese on the terrace looking out towards the saddle-backed Crestillina mountain.

A yurt costs €35pp B&B (sleeps 4), dinner costs €20pp, over night trip to Chefchaouen cost €150pp.
andaluciayurts.com, +34 952 117 486

POSADA DEL VALLE, ASTURIAS
RATING:

Posada del Valle is a 19th-century stone farmhouse near Arriondas by the Picos de Europa national park. It was once the home of a parish priest, but now the English owners have turned it into a certified organic farm where rare breed sheep graze among 18 acres of wild meadow and the electricity is bought in from renewable sources. The posada is close to the sandy beaches of the Cantabrian coast, but go to the many inland rivers for canoeing and canyoning, or into the mountains for horse-riding and mountainbiking. The farmhouse is a 3km walk from Arriondas, which is four hours by bus from Bilbao, two hours from Santander.

Rooms from €58.
posadadelvalle.com, +34 985 841 157

HOOPOE YURT HOTEL, ANDALUCIA
RATING:

Yurt lovers who find the 9,000-mile round trip to outer Mongolia a little hard on the wallet can stay in a traditional Mongolian camp closer to home. The Hoopoe Yurt Hotel is in the Grazalema mountain range to the south of Ronda, in Andaluciá, southern Spain. The rustic solar-powered yurts offer a few creature comforts, including a power point, outside bamboo bathroom (including hot shower), and a private garden. Yoga, reiki, massages and aromatherapy are available in the local village and hill-walking and riding to the nearby Cuevo del Gato, where you can swim in mountain rock pools.

A yurt with one double bed costs €130 per night B&B. The camp is two hours' drive from both Málaga and Gibraltar airports, and on the train line from Ronda to Algeciras. The owners can pick you up from Cortes de la Frontera.
yurthotel.com, +34 951 168 040

Switzerland

AROLLA CAMPSITE, VALAIS
RATING: 🈂️

At 6,000ft, Arolla in the Valais region of Switzerland is one of Europe's highest campsites, reached by a one-hour bus journey from the nearest train station at Sion, or on foot along the Haute Route from Chamonix. The campsite is on a steep hillside among woods of larch and arolla pine, a 20-minute walk downhill from the village at the head of the Val d'Hérens. It is dwarfed by the enormous Pigne d'Arolla and has all the amenities you'd expect from a well-organised Swiss campsite, including hot showers, washing-up facilities and a food shop.
From 6 francs up to 12, depending on tent size.
camping-arolla.com, +41 272 832 295

WHITEPOD, AIGLE
RATING: 🈂️🈂️

A stylish camp of futuristic eco-pods offering Alpine escapism with low-impact snow sports. Choose from snow-shoeing, dog-sledging, guided back-country skiing or paragliding. Set up in the winter of 2004 with idea of offering an alternative to high-impact Alpine holidays and activities, founder Sofia de Meyer's aim was to "provoke an eco-consciousness among our guests" without sacrificing on style or comfort. Guests can soak in a wood-fuelled hot tub or use a private 600m ski run. The pods – geodesic domes like the Eden Project – have no electricity and are heated by stoves burning sustainable Swiss timber. Waste is minimised and recycled and food is local. Choose the nearby mountain refuge for a cheaper, more remote stay.
Rates start from 585CHF per pod per night.
whitepod.com; +41 24 471 38 38

AFRICA   Gambia

SANDELE ECO-RETREAT, KARTONG
RATING:

Maurice Phillips and Geri Mitchell left the UK for the Gambia in 1996 with an interest in African ways of living plus some idea of alternative technology, but with no plan to become hoteliers. Within a year they were running Safari Garden, a small urban hotel favoured by Aid workers and independent travellers. Their latest venture is a deeply green approach to an upmarket hotel. With early Islamic architecture inspiring the building design they have done away with the need for air-conditioning; construction bricks were made with an innovative soil-compacting technique, thousands of trees have been planted close by and staff are local.

Rooms start at £66 per person per night. The Gambia Experience (gambia.co.uk, 0845 330 2087) offers trips to Sandele Eco-Retreat.

Kenya

IL N'GWESI LODGE
RATING:

An eco lodge overlooking a vast forested plateau. The bandas on stilts are luxuriously simple; the pool is exquisite. Each of the 448 households of the Il N'gwesi tribe own an equal share of the lodge and make joint decisions. The lodge funds schools and mobile clinics and helps protect wildlife.

Rates are dependent on the number of guests, their country of origin and whether the lodge is booked exclusively. To book contact Let's Go Travel (+254 20 44 72 70).
laikipia.org/hotel_ilngwesi.htm

Morocco

KASBAH DU TOUBKAL, HIGH ATLAS
RATING:

A secluded and spectacular mountain retreat developed in partnership with the local Berber community, which provides all workmen, materials and staff. Water is spring-fed rather than trucked in; fruit, vegetables and meat are locally sourced. A 5% levy added to all accommodation bills has financed the valley's first ambulance and community hammam and enabled local girls to continue their education in Asni. Accommodation ranges from traditional Berber salons, which sleep groups of trekkers and extended families, to the beautiful Garden House, a self-contained, double-level sanctuary with two balconies. Its remote trekking lodge, with solar-powered under-floor heating and en suite bedrooms, allows guests to stay in comfort even higher in the Toubkal Massif.

Double rooms at Kasbah du Toubkal from €160 (£129) B&B. Minimum two-night stay.

kasbahdutoubkal.com

TOUBKAL LODGE, HIGH ATLAS
RATING:

A "sister" lodge to the Kasbah, Toubkal Lodge overlooks the Azzadene valley at the top of the Berber village of Idissa, high in the Atlas mountains. Its three double rooms are modelled on the Garden House at the Kasbah, and are designed for just a handful of guests who want to leave the comfort of the Kasbah and explore the wilds without roughing it in a tent. There's even solar powered under floor heating. The Kasbah is a joint venture between adventure tour company Discover Ltd and local Berber, Haj Omar Ait Bahmed, a partnership that has flourished since 1978.

A double room at the Toubkal Lodge costs from €200 half-board.

kasbahdutoubkal.com

RIAD EL FENN, MARRAKECH
RATING:

Vanessa Branson's stylish retreat is a favourite with Europe's jet set, but has always been run on sound principles. Natural and local materials and finishes were used in the refurbishment of the traditional riad building and staff are employed full time, all year round. Cleaning products used are 100% biodegradable and most food is grown in a 2-acre organic garden in the foothills of the Atlas mountains. Swimming pools use a saltwater cleaning system instead of chlorine and 60% of the domestic water and 30% of the swimming pool water is heated by solar panels on the terraces.

A double room costs from €270 a night to €550 for the larger suites.
riadelfenn.com, +212 2444 1210

South Africa

BULUNGULA, WILD COAST,
EASTERN CAPE
RATING:

The solar-powered lodge, certified by Fair Trade in Tourism South Africa, is a joint venture between a South African and the Xhosa-speaking Nqileni community who organise fishing, canoeing, horse-riding and guiding trips.

Double room costs R250 a night, a bed in a dorm costs R100.
bulungula.com, +2747 577 8900

HOG HOLLOW COUNTRY LODGE, WESTERN CAPE
RATING: 🏵️🏵️

One of the first places in the Western Cape to receive accreditation from The Fair Trade in Tourism South Africa scheme is Hog Hollow Country Lodge, located on a regenerated wattle plantation at the edge of the Matjies river gorge. The elegant African-style cottages have wooden bed-frames, stripy silk cushions, mosaic shower walls and private wooden decks with views of the forested hills and Tsitsikamma's blue-peaked mountains. Local produce, including the day's catch, is served outside on a wooden sundeck or around a communal candle-lit table in the main house. The staff have been recruited and trained from the nearby villages of Kurland and Kwanokathula and help organise community tours and "eco-adventures", such as canoeing and horse-riding, walks in the nearby Tsitsikamma nature reserve and whale-watching from Plettenberg Bay. There's also excellent surf at Keurbooms.

A room costs from R1,450 per person per night B&B or R1,276 in low season.
hog-hollow.com, +27 44 534 8879

BUFFALO RIDGE, NORTH-WEST PROVINCE
RATING: 🏵️🏵️🏵️

Buffalo Ridge is owned by the Balete Ba Lekgophung community and is currently applying for a Fair Trade Tourism in South Africa trademark (FTTSA), a certification system for tourism businesses that provide tangible benefits for local communities.

The tariff per person sharing is between R2,100 and R2,695 depending on the season.
buffaloridgesafari.com, +27 11 805 9995

THAKADU RIVER CAMP, GABERONE
RATING:

This community-owned safari camp lies in the malaria-free Madikwe Game Reserve along the border with Botswana and offers gourmet dining, walking and game drive safaris led by trained local rangers. The reserve is home to some of Africa's most elusive wildlife: black and white rhino, leopard and cheetah and over 340 species of birds. Rangers hail from the local Molatedi community, which wholly owns the development. It is in the process of getting FTTSA accredited.

Tariff per person sharing is between R2,100 and R2,695 depending on the time of year. Rainbow Tours (020 7226 1004, rainbowtours.co.uk) offers trips to Thakuda River Camp and Buffalo Ridge.
thakadurivercamp.com, +27 11 805 9995

DJUMA BUSH LODGE, MPUMALANGA
RATING:

Cool off in the pool while elephants do the same in a nearby watering hole. It's hard to tell where the camp ends and the game reserve begins. Part of the Sabi Sand complex, this is classic game reserve country – big, wild, uncrowded – but with a social conscience. No TV, no radios, just bags of fresh air and dining under the Milky Way.

Full-board R3,300 – R5,000 pp per night. Includes two daily safaris, guided walks & tourism levy. Self-catering R8,000 per night for the whole camp.
djuma.com, +27 13 735 5118

Tanzania

KAHAWA SHAMBA, KILIMANJARO
RATING:

Kahawa Shamba ("coffee farm" in Swahili) is a group of traditional huts run by the Chagga people in their village by the foothills of Kilimanjaro. They set up this small-scale tourism enterprise with help from the Department for International Development, development charity Twin, the fair trade coffee company Cafédirect and the fair trade travel operator Tribes Travel. Kahawa Shamba's huts are made of vines from the nearby forest and thatched with dried banana-leaf, and have twin wrought-iron beds with ensuite showers and locally made soaps. There are guided walks as well as horse-riding along the river valley.
Costs US$110 pp full-board.
tribes.co.uk, +44 (0)1728 685971

RUAHA HILLTOP LODGE
RATING:

Getting up close to Africa's finest mammals usually comes as part of a luxury package. But there are a growing number of alternatives – reasonably priced, and with a sustainable approach to tourism. Ruaha Hilltop Lodge is locally owned and managed, with access to the country's second largest national park, known for its magnificent elephant population and bird life. Perched on the slopes of Ideremle mountain, its eight cottages command an extraordinary view, while ties with local communities give visitors a look at local life that you don't see when staying in a remote lodge in the park itself.
US $80 full board, per person. Drive safaris from Hilltop Lodge: US$100 per day per vehicle, with driver/guide.
Ruahahilltoplodge.com, +255 26 270 1806/+255 784 726709

Namibia

ABA-HUAB CAMPSITE
RATING:

PIC: Fairtrade travel: Damaraland

One of several community-run campsites in the Twyfelfontein-Uibasen Conservancy in the country's north-west, from where you can go on locally guided tours of the spectacular Twyfelfontein ancient rock cavings. Desert elephants are also regular visitors to the region and you can learn about the life of the bushman.

A two-week trip including two nights at Aba-Huab and other campsites in the sand dunes of the Namib Desert, Damaraland and Etosha National park, costs from £1,275 per person, including some meals, return flights from Gatwick to Windhoek and 4x4 car hire through expertafrica.com, +44 (0)20 8232 9777

WOLWEDANS
RATING:

Among the sands of one of the largest nature conservation areas in Africa lies "Where the Wolves Dance", 80 miles from the nearest petrol station. The decks of the rustic-luxurious chalets are perfect for dune or star gazing. Down duvets, hot showers, solar lights, canvas blinds. The double tents, sitting on wooden platforms, are equally appealing. The main lodge has sepia photographs, wooden furnishings, sundowner decks.

Full-board Dunes Lodge costs from NA$3,275 pp. Park fees $135pp per day.
wolwedans.com, +264 61 230 616

ASIA India

HIMALAYAN HOMESTAYS, LADAKH
RATING:

A traditional working farm 5,000m up in the breathtaking scenery of Ladakh. The homestay accommodation is as basic but authentic as they come – a mattress on the floor and long drop for the loo. You're invited to eat meals in the kitchen with the family who make curries from local ingredients and the majestic Himalayas are on your doorstep. Ten per cent of the income is given to the Snow Leopard Conservancy and the rest is distributed among the community.

It's US $12 per person for the average homestay, $25 for the Ulley model. himalayan-homestays.com, +91 1982 250 858

APANI DHANI ECO-LODGE, RAJASTHAN
RATING:

The rooms are a cluster of traditional huts with mud-rubbed walls and thatched roofs. Wooden furniture and intriguing objets in russet-toned alcoves. Solar panels give light and hot water – and the coffee is superb – though luxuries are few. Seasonal food is dished out on leaf plates under the bougainvillea in the circular courtyard.

Rs950 – Rs1095 per room per night. apanidhani.com, +91 1594 222 239

BAREFOOT AT HAVELOCK, ANDAMAN ISLANDS
RATING: 🛇🛇

Listen to a forest-bird ballad in eight acres of gardens and mahua trees minutes from a long, white beach. These beautifully designed, conical thatched cottages are locally made from bamboo, wood and palm leaves, and draw their water from the camp's own spring. The slightly more luxurious hardwood villas have floor-to-ceiling windows on three sides and shady balconies. Relax by candlelight and listen to cool jazz in the oriental living area before dinner; the fusion food is local, organic, delicious and they cook your own catch.

The cottages vary on price from €80 to €205 per night depending on the season and whether the cottage is fan cooled or air conditioned. barefootindia.com, +91 3192 236 008

Mongolia

THREE CAMEL LODGE
RATING: 🛇🛇

In the shimmering heat, white gers rise from the wild heart of the Gobi desert in the lee of a red volcanic outcrop. Here, the traditional meets the sophisticated – with community support. The nomads' tents are hand-made from latticed Siberian larch covered with felt and contain beautifully painted beds and colourful artefacts. Sun and wind provide evening light and constant hot water; animal dung fuels stoves. Friendly staff hail largely from the local Bulgan village. Camel trek in vast dunes and sup like a Khan under a dome of stars.

A standard ger is $80 per person per night, based on double occupancy, and with three daily meals. A deluxe ger with private bathroom is $120 pppn.
threecamels.com, +976 11 313 396

Nepal

TIGER MOUNTAIN POKHARA LODGE
RATING: 📿📿

Framed at the centre of the doorway are the astonishing peaks of Annapurna, Dhaulagiri, Manaslu and Machhapuchhare. Each of the rooms have been built from hand-cut stone, floors are wooden, furnishings are simple, and there's handmade soap from Kathmandu in the bathrooms.

Full-board $200pp. Singles $300. Plus taxes.
tigermountain.com/pokhara, +977 1 436 1500

Sri Lanka

GALAPITA ECO LODGE
RATING: 📿📿

A small, authentic, locally owned solar-powered lodge in jungle bordering the Yala National Park in the south-east of the country. Getting there is best done the local way – take the bus, or drive down from Colombo, then jump in a tuk tuk at the village of Battala before crossing to the lodge over the precarious footbridge that hangs 40ft over the river Menik Ganga. There are futon-style beds in two tree houses and five mud huts on the banks of the river, from where it's a short towel-covered hop to a soak in the natural outdoor spa. Just 15 minutes away is the new entrance to the national park, where local guides run safaris to see elephants.

£85 – £100 for two people for two nights.
galapita.com, +94 11 2508 755

Malaysia

SUKAU RAINFOREST LODGE, BORNEO
RATING:

For a taste of the real rainforest, leeches and all, pack your jungle boots and head to Sabah's Kinabatangan Basin in the heart of Borneo; one of only two places on earth where there are more than 10 species of primates, including the orang-utan and proboscis monkey. Sukau Rainforest Lodge is a low-impact eco lodge designed in the style of a Malaysian longhouse with 20 comfortable but basic rooms on stilts above a silted river backed by the dense jungle. The only access to the lodge is by boat. Guided river safaris, available.

A three nights, two days honeymoon special costs RM1,831pp.
sukau.com, 0060 88 438300

CARIBBEAN   Dominica

CRESCENT MOON CABINS
RATING:

Wind and hydro generators provide the power, there's mountain spring water, and the fruit, herbs and vegetables are all home grown. The cosy wood cabins are tucked into the side of the mountain and have panoramic views of the rainforest and sea. There are locally guided trail walks, farm tours, and nearby are some of the island's stunning waterfalls, including Middleham Falls. From the cabins, stone footpaths lead into the forest or down to the river where you can have a dip; or take a midnight soak in a stone plunge pool among the mango, pawpaw and almond trees.

A cabin for two costs US$156 B&B (minimum two nights), dinner $35 per person.
crescentmooncabins.com. +1 767 449 3449

PAPILLOTE WILDERNESS RETREAT
RATING: 🌿🌿🌿

There are plenty of green options springing up on the Caribbean's "nature island", but Papillote was the first eco inn. The rooms range from simple doubles to much larger suites with private verandas overlooking the valley. There can be few better ways to relax after a gruelling day's hiking than soaking in one of Papillote's outdoor hot natural spring mineral pools surrounded by earthy moss and lichen-covered statues. And, just 15 minutes' walk away, is the towering Trafalgar Falls with its own natural rocky bathing pool. The inland retreat is surrounded by mountainous rainforest, food is local and fresh, and there is a genuinely friendly, local touch.

Rooms from US$110.

papillote.dm, +1 767 448 2287

Jamaica

HOTEL MOCKING BIRD HILL
RATING: 🌿🌿

A small, solar-powered 10-room hotel in the rainforest between the Blue Mountains and the coast, which has twice won the Caribbean Green Hotel of the Year award. The owners Barbara and Shireen have designed the hotel so that air wafts in rather than using energy-sucking air-con. Breakfast comes with homemade bread and jam and spa treatments use local products, including beeswax, papaya and coconut oil.

A room at Hotel Mocking Bird Hill costs from US$165 and includes the fee to use Frenchman's Cove.

hotelmockingbirdhill.com, +1 876 993 7134

GÎTE DU MONT-ALBERT, QUÉBEC
RATING:

Québec province is great for cross-country skiing and other low-impact outdoor activities, yet with over 2,500 miles of trails it can be hard to find a convenient place to push off from.

One of the best is the four-star Gîte du Mont-Albert in the Gaspésie national park – the highest part of the Appalachians in the province. It has 60 rooms in a huge 1950s complex as well as a dozen lodges and 25 woodstove-fired cabins dotted around the grounds. At the nearby visitor centre, you can book nature tours to see caribou, white-tailed deer and moose, and organise snowshoeing, cross-country skiing and ski-touring across the Chic Chocs mountain range.

A double room costs from C$134, a cabin (for up to four) from $244 per night including park access fee.

sepaq.com/pq/gas/en, +1 418 890 6527

AURUM LODGE, ALBERTA
RATING:

A true wilderness retreat in a natural clearing in the forest, overlooking the beautiful Abraham lake and with the Canadian Rockies looming in the distance. The emphasis is on low-impact living, no televisions or phones in the rooms, just wind whistling in the trees, water lapping at the shore and a natural adventure playground on your doorstep.

CAN$110-$220 (around £53-£106). Self-catering units $130-$240.

aurumlodge.com, +1 403 721 2117

LATIN AMERICA   Argentina

PEUMA HUE, BARILOCHE
RATING:

Gallop through forest then sit back with a cocktail as you watch the sun setting over Lake Gutiérrez and the shadows creep up the mountain. Walls are hewn from huge tree trunks, tiles inspired by cave paintings, rugs hand-woven and glass ceilings open to the peak of Cerro Catedral. Indigenous species are being reintroduced, produce is organic from the kitchen garden or locally sourced, alternative energies are on their way.

Full-board for 1, 3 or 7 days. $375-$642. Singles $284-$375. Includes activities. B&B only $103-$133pp.

peuma-hue.com, +54 9 2944 501030/504856

Bolivia

CHALALÁN ECOLODGE, MADIDI NATIONAL PARK
RATING:

Managed entirely by the indigenous Quechua-Tacana community, Chalalán is buried in the vast swathe of the wildlife-rich Madidi national park. Knowledgeable guides and themed nature trails encourage you to learn about wildlife behaviour and the medicinal qualities of the plants. The low-impact, wood and palm cabins are simple and rustic, but perfectly comfortable. Wash away the day's expedition, then soak up the sunset over Lake Chalalán from a hammock outside your cabin.

Full-board (4-days, 3 nights) $325pp Twin/triple $295pp. Singles $345. Includes transfers & activities.

chalalan.com, +591 3 892 2419

Brazil

POUSADA VIDA SOL E MAR, SANTA CATERINA
RATING:

Surfers create a buzz at weekends in season. Otherwise Rose Beach is a wild, natural place – a couple of beach shack bars on a crescent of soft sands, with dunes behind. Below the hotel are seven rustic villas – river stones, Brazilian woods, colour-washed tables, natural linen – rented whole or in part. Some have their own pool, others a close-up view of the sea. Yesterday's whale hunters are today's guides, and the whale-watching tours are the best in the area.

$72-$180. Villas $140-$180 for two.
vidasolemar.com.br, +55 48 3355 6111

Chile

PATAGONIA ECOCAMP
RATING:

One of the world's epic locations. Condors soar over the Andean mountains while herds of guanaco (wild relative of the llama) roam the foothills. The brightly painted tents are cosy inside, connected by wooden boardwalks to the friendly dining area where a huge picture window opens out to the mountains beyond.

Full-board from $823pp for 4 days. Includes activities & transfers.
ecocamp.travel, +56 2 232 9878

Costa Rica

LAPA RIOS, OSA PENINSULA
RATING:

Perched 350ft above sea level, the teak and palm lodges capture cooling breezes – no air-con required – and you peer from your terrace over rainforest and ocean. Floors are wooden, walls wide open, furniture bamboo, showers in the garden. Tropical flowers provide colour, sunshine heats the water. It's 10 minutes to the beach or the 1,000-acre nature reserve with river and waterfalls. The main lodge, with its 50ft-high platform, has sensational views.

Full-board $198-$319pp sharing. Singles $308-$463. Children up to 10 half price.

laparios.com, +506 735 5130

FINCA ROSA BLANCA, SANTA BÁRBARA DE HEREDIA
RATING:

Around 5,000 coffee trees have been planted on this inn's organic plantation, 30 minutes north of San José. Guests learn how coffee is grown and processed, and the spa does coffee body scrubs. The hotel has the maximum five green leaves from the Costa Rican Tourist Board and recycles all food and non-organic waste, while 5% of bar and restaurant profits go to local school and recycling projects.

Doubles from £290 per night.

finca-rblanca.co.cr, +11 506 2269 9392

Ecuador

NAPO ECO-LODGE
RATING:

You'll get a local's view of the Amazon rainforest at this pioneering eco lodge fully owned by the Anangua Quichua community. Local guides take you to explore jungle lakes and creeks by dug-out canoe, to see tropical birds and monkeys including monk saki, spider monkeys, and golden-mantled tamarins. You can also help the indigenous community harvest bananas and prepare chichi, a beer-like drink made from manioc.

An 11-day tour of Ecuador, including four nights at Napo costs £1,155 per person, not including flights through tribes.co.uk,
+44 (0)1728 685971

Guatemala

CHIMINOS ISLAND LODGE
RATING:

This Maya-built "island" is thick with jungle and jungle noise: howler monkeys, toucans, parrots, eagles and the odd snake. But you couldn't be safer or snugger in your reclaimed mahogany and thatch bungalow on stilts; it is open sided, deeply romantic and mosquito-protected. Solar-lit walkways weave through the jungle floor as you pick you way across raised tree roots to the lodge itself where food, drink, hammocks and floating dock await – and friendly (mostly Spanish-speaking) staff. The bungalows, all secluded with lagoon views, are warmly rustic inside: tree trunks for tables; weavings for colour; swing doors that open to big hot showers; balconies for sunsets and views.

Full-board $170. Singles $85.
chiminosisland.com, +502 2471 0855

Guyana

SURAMA VILLAGE
RATING: 🕉🕉🕉

Surama is a traditional Amerindian village in the forest-covered Pakaraima mountains 300km south of the capital Georgetown. It's the home of the Makushi tribe, and though you might come across men going out to hunt with bows and arrows, don't expect an after-dinner tribal dance. The Surama people run the show here as part of a community-based tourism initiative. There are four huts just outside the village, which are basic, but dry and cool. Guides take you on a tour of the village to watch the pounding of cassava and on dawn walks across the Rupununi savannah and up Surama mountain.

A hut costs US$110 full board including guides. Book through Last Frontiers (lastfrontiers.com, 01296 653000)

Mexico

HOTEL ECO PARAÍSO XIXIM
RATING: 🕉

Fauna, dune flora and creepy crawlies at every turn – insects are "relocated" not exterminated. Flat sands, warm sea, huge skies and organic meals (catch your own fish). On three miles of white sands, the 15 cabanas built of hi-tech adobe are simple, circular, light and cool. Ceiling fans hang from open-thatch roofs where geckos perch. No need to fight over the hammocks, each porch has two.

$144-$178. Singles $125-$152. Half-board $176-$210, singles $141-$168. ecoparaiso.com, +52 988 916 2100/2060

NA BOLOM, SAN CRISTOBAL
RATING:

Na Bolom is a unique hybrid research centre, museum and hotel in San Cristobal – a colonial town that sits at 2000m in mountainous Chiapas, Mexico's poorest and most indigenously-populated state. Set up in 1951 by Danish archeologist Frans Blom and his Swiss wife, journalist turned anthropologist Gertrude Duby, each room in the former seminary is decorated with textiles, photographs and artesania from a local village. It is a non-profit centre of excellence dedicated to the Maya and remote Lacandon people of Chiapas, with a 9,000-volume library, a garden with Maya medicinal plants and a reforestation project. The Fondo Medico Lacandon health clinic is funded by Na Bolom and tours to Maya sites and Lacandon villages can also be arranged.

Double rooms at Na Bolom from $70 – $80 depending on season.
nabolom.org; +52-967-678-1418

Nicaragua

FINCA ESPERANZA VERDE ECOLODGE
RATING:

On an organic coffee farm more than 1,200m up in the mountains of Nicaragua, this 26-bed eco lodge is situated in a nature reserve. While local people run the coffee operation, the travel side is run by volunteers from North Carolina with the aim of helping the local owners earn an alternative income to coffee. Nearby are jungle treks, waterfalls and a butterfly farm. Ten per cent of the lodge's income is invested in rural water projects and local schools.

A five-day Coffee and Campesino cultural tour costs £176 per person based on two people sharing a room, including all meals, accommodation and guided walks.
fincaesperanzaverde.org, +1505 772 5003

Peru

POSADA AMAZONAS
RATING: 🔘🔘🔘

This is one of three jungle lodges set up by a Peruvian ecotourism company in collaboration with the indigenous Ese-Eja community of Infierno in the Tambopata national reserve. The rooms are furnished with wood and cane, and dinner is served by candlelight in a lofty, palm-thatched communal dining hall where one end opens out on to the jungle. Early morning climbs up a rainforest-canopy tower are led by an ex-hunter from the village who is now the lodge's top birding guide, and there are night walks and botanical trips to Centro Nape.

Three days/two nights is US$205pp full board.
perunature.com, 0051 1 421 8347

AMAZON YARAPA RIVER LODGE
RATING: 🔘🔘🔘

Local management, local materials, local ideas, deep in the Peruvian rainforest. The focus is on research and education, and when you hold a pygmy marmoset monkey in your hand you'll know in an instant what environmental responsibility is all about. The only road is the Amazon tributary flowing alongside; the only disturbance is the occasional sound of a paddle slicing through the water, or the blast of air from a breaching pink dolphin. The roofs and walkways are thatched and provide a natural cooling system from the tropical heat.

$235 per night, $940 for 3 nights.
yarapariverlodge.com, 00011 5165 993 1172

MIDDLE EAST

DANA GUESTHOUSE, JORDAN
RATING:

50km north of the ancient city of Petra (and about a 2½-hour drive from both Amman and the seaside town of Aqaba), this guesthouse offers a closer connection to the region's wilderness. High on the cliffs overlooking the Dana nature reserve in the southern Rift Valley, the guesthouse is run by Bedouin under the direction of Jordan's Royal Society for the Conservation of Nature (RSCN), whose programme was highly commended in the 2006 *Guardian* Ethical Travel Award. The guesthouse is based on the design of local village houses and offers nine guest rooms with bare walls and camp beds – some with a private terrace.
B&B 43 dinars.
rscn.org.jo +962 6461 6523

AUSTRALASIA   Australia

KANIMBLA VIEW CLIFFTOP
RETREAT, NEW SOUTH WALES
RATING:

Eco lodges don't have to sacrifice comfort or accessibility. This one is easy to get to but feels satisfyingly remote. It's on a mountain escarpment surrounded by bush. The sunken living areas have wood-burning fires and plenty of books and information on the retreat's ecological features; kitchens are well-equipped. There's even a tennis court, while an old greenhouse has been turned into an outdoor spa.
Cottage for up to 4 A$210-$375 (around £85-£154). Bungalow $175-$225. Studio $135-$175. Entire retreat $1,100-$1,500.
kanimbla.com, +61 2 4787 8985

ROSE GUM'S TREEHOUSES, QUEENSLAND
RATING:

A secluded, luxury timber treehouse deep in the tropical rainforest, 80 minutes outside Cairns in the highlands of northern Queensland. The former dairy-farm has been restored and patiently replanted with 20,000 native trees by owners Jon and Peta Nott, resulting in a 300-tonne credit in CO_2 emissions. With that inspiring thought in mind, there's only one thing to do – tuck into your organic hamper on the deck of your cabin and enjoy the spectacular view and birdsong. In addition, the timber is sustainably sourced, showers and taps are fitted with flow-restrictors, cleaning products and practices are environmentally sensitive and much of the food is home-grown.

A three-night stay is AU$245 per night for two people, including a breakfast hamper.

rosegums.com.au; +61 7 4096 8360

PAPERBARK CAMP, NEW SOUTH WALES
RATING:

Just 15 minutes' drive away from the dazzling beaches of the White Sands walk and surrounded by a forest of enormous paperbark trees (a relative of the eucalyptus) is Paperbark Camp at Jervis Bay. Stay in one of a dozen distinctively designed tents and dine at the stilted Gunyah restaurant, named after the Aboriginal word for place of shelter. The raised safari-style tents and pathways have solar-powered night lights and you'll find plenty of creature comforts. Initiatives such as clearing the bush by hand and using the wood collected to craft furniture helped earn the camp advanced accreditation with the Ecotourism Association of Australia. A twin-share safari tent costs from

A$320.00 per night including breakfast.

paperbarkcamp.com.au; +61 (0)2 4441 6066

New Zealand

ECO INN, NORTH ISLAND
RATING:

Eco Inn is the closest hostel to the mountain and is also one of the greenest places to stay on the west coast of the North Island. The lodge is made from untreated macrocarpa wood and recycled materials, and the heating and electricity are powered entirely by solar panels, wind turbines and a water wheel. From the hot tub, you look out towards the Tasman Sea and up at Mount Taranaki before cosying up to a wood fire. The walk up the mountain is a must, but there are also mountain biking trails at the nearby Lake Mangamahoe and excellent surf along the Taranaki Surf Highway.

From NZ$160 a night
ecoinn.co.nz, +64 6752 2765

WILDERNESS LODGE, ARTHUR'S
PASS, SOUTH ISLAND
RATING:

A 6,000-acre eco-triumvirate of nature protection, sustainable merino-sheep farming and responsible tourism. Rooms keep a natural integrity of wool, lanolin and New Zealand art, even manuka shampoo. There are swathes of regenerating native forest – you may even be asked to help clear American pine seedlings or help shear sheep. The lodge works in close consultation with the local Maori tribe at the Kura Tawhiti reserve. The gourmet food provides trampers with the perfect preparation for the Southern Alps.

Half-board NZ$290-$490 (around £100-£169). Singles from NZ$380.
wildernesslodge.co.nz, +64 3318 9246

Ethical tour operators

THE LEADERS...

The following companies ensure that all their trips adhere to a strict code of ethical/responsible tourism.

Tribes, a small, niche tour operator that focuses on 'fair trade tourism' in Africa and several countries in South America and Asia. Tribes publishes an accommodation "eco-review" on its website alongside featured holidays based on their environmental performance and social responsibility. Tribes was runner up in the *Guardian* and *Observer* Ethical Travel Award, 2007.

tribes.co.uk

Discovery Initiatives 'uses tourism as a tool for conservation' by organising nature-watching holidays in partnership with conservation organisations in 35 countries. According to the company it has contributed over £750,000 to conservation projects worldwide.

discoveryinitiatives.co.uk

Saddle Skedaddle/Traidcraft a joint initiative which takes small groups to developing countries to see the 'People behind the products', including suppliers of Traidcraft's tea in India and coffee in Central and South America.

traidcraft.co.uk/get_involved/meet_the_people.htm

BEST OF THE REST...

The following companies demonstrate a tangible commitment to responsible tourism, whether that's by ensuring many of their trips use locally owned operators, hotels and local guides or through supporting charitable projects worldwide:

KE Adventure, which works closely with the Juniper Trust (junipertrust.co.uk), a charity dedicated to locating and carrying out sustainable aid projects in Peru, Ecuador, India, Tibet, Sri Lanka and other countries.

keadventure.com

Mountain Kingdoms, which specialises in treks, cultural tours and overlanding adventures across many of the world's great mountain ranges. It ensures its agents adhere to guidelines for porters' rights and conditions drawn up by Tourism Concern.

mountainkingdoms.com

Wilderness Scotland, an adventure travel company that offers low impact tours into Scotland's Highlands and Islands. It has teamed up with Trees for Life, a project working to restore 600 square miles of native Caledonian forest.

wildernessscotland.com

ATG Oxford, the walking and cycling holiday specialist, which has set up a charitable trust to support projects which conserve wildlife habitats and works of art and architecture.
atg-oxford.co.uk

Wildlife Worldwide, which has supported several wildlife conservation and community projects and charities, including The David Shepherd Wildlife Foundation (davidshepherd.org) to support long-term projects to save tigers, elephants, rhinos and other critically endangered mammals in Africa and Asia.
wildlifeworldwide.com

Geodyssey, which has formed an alliance with the Rainforest Foundation to promote sustainable tourism in the Americas.
geodyssey.co.uk

Intrepid, an Australian-based company (with a high-street office in North London), which has a long established record of working closely with local partners to hire and train local staff.
intrepidtravel.com

Rainbow Tours, which uses locally-owned accommodation, operators and local guides on many of its tailor-made holidays to Africa and the Indian Ocean. In 2004, 2005 and 2006, Rainbow was voted "Best Operator" in the *Guardian* and *Observer* Travel Awards, proving that a strong responsible tourism policy can tally with providing quality service.
rainbowtours.co.uk

The Gambia Experience, which has worked with the Eden Project to create an 85-squre kilometre conservation area, incorporating 14 villages, in The Gambia.
gambia.co.uk

Dragoman, the overland specialist in Africa, Asia and South America, which trains its crew in responsible tourism issues and funds several community projects, such as the Inca Trail & Quechua Community Project in Peru and the Kariandusi School Trust in Kenya.
dragoman.com

Explore Worldwide, which works with many of its ground operators, hoteliers and other suppliers to implement responsible tourism policies.
explore.co.uk

Exodus, which organises several funds for guests to donate to community projects in Africa and Asia.
exodus.co.uk

Expert Africa, whose wide-ranging portfolio of holidays in sub-Saharan Africa includes organising sensitively managed trips to meet the Bushmen of the Kalahari and to see traditional life in Zambia.
expertafrica.com

Last Frontiers, which uses local guides on all its tailor-made trips in Latin America and was a founder donor to the LATA Foundation (set up by the Latin American Travel Association: latafoundation.org), which aims to develop responsible tourism to Latin America.
lastfrontiers.com

Journey Latin America, whose suite of holidays includes community-run Amazon lodges and local family homestays in Central and South America.
journeylatinamerica.co.uk

InnTravel, whose walking and cycling holidays in Europe focus on locally run guesthouses and small hotels.
inntravel.co.uk

Wild Frontiers, which pledges a percentage of its trip's costs to local charities and NGOs in each destination, such as Adopt-a-Minefield in Afghanistan, Children of the Caucasus in Georgia, The Hope Foundation in Calcutta.
wildfrontiers.co.uk

Andante Travels, a specialist in archaeology tours, which provides a grant to the winner of its annual Archaeological Award, for use in projects that conserve and educate about archaeology.
andantetravels.co.uk

Symbiosis Travel, which organises tours and expeditions in South East Asia, with a focus on generating income for local destination economies.
symbiosis-travel.com

The following companies are members of Tourism Concern's Ethical Tour Operator Group, which meets four times a year to work towards better practice in ethical tourism among operators:

Adventure Alternative, Baobab Travel, Cazenove & Lloyd, Different Travel Company, Dragoman, Expert Africa, Exodus, Explore Worldwide, Gane & Marshall, Hands Up Holidays, Into Africa, Livingstone Tanzania Trust, Nepal Trekking, Oasis Overland, Rainbow Tours, Saddle Skedaddle Simply Tanzania, Tribes Travel, Wilderness Journeys.

Hiking the Peak District, Stanage
Edge, Hathersage, Derbyshire
photo: britainonview/McCormick-McAdam

The approach to Glamis Castle,
Tayside, Scotland
photo: britainonview/Rod Edward

EXCESS BAGGAGE

The way you travel to your holiday destination and your choice of accommodation are the most important factors in lowering the environmental impact of your holiday. However there are plenty of smaller actions you can take to help reduce your overall footprint and raise awareness about responsible travel practices. Using degradable toiletries, for instance, can have an important impact on sensitive habitats. Leaving unnecessary packaging and gadgets at home can help reduce waste and energy use. Some small steps taken this year will hopefully lead to larger ones in the future – by travellers and the tourism industry alike.

What to pack

The long-term impact of many of the chemicals contained in beauty products and toiletries is unknown. They travel down the drain and into the rivers, lakes and coastal waters and many are persistent and bioaccumaltive – in other words they take a very long time to break down in the environment and can build up in living tissue. So for both the sake of the local ecosystem and your own health, the greener traveller may well want to limit their exposure as a precautionary measure.

Many of the new range of organic and eco-friendly products perform just as well, if not better, than their chemical-laden forebears, and increasingly come in far more environmentally-friendly packaging – important when visiting destinations with limited waste disposal and recycling facilities. There is also now a broad range in price to suit all budgets.

SUN PROTECTION

The best advice for avoiding sunburn is simple – stay covered up. However the reality is that regardless of the longterm consequences, getting a tan is still important to a lot of people.

There are two basic kinds of sun protection – those that provide a physical barrier, and those that create a chemical one. The former prevent the sun's rays actually reaching your skin, reflecting them like a mirror. The latter actually absorb the light particles (photons). For the green traveller, the former are certainly the best option. There is some evidence that chemical sunscreens actually generate the same kind of free radicals that direct exposure to sunlight does. The chemicals are also more likely to cause skin irritation, particularly in very young or sensitive skins.

Physical blocks used to be unpopular because they tended to leave a rather obvious tidemark in their wake, but a new generation of products has conquered this problem. Of these, the best is Dr Hauschka's range. It is easily absorbed, has a pleasant smell and comes in varying sprays and factors as well as soothing after-sun. The excellent Lavera brand also has a very reasonably priced range – cheaper, indeed, than many sold in the high street. At the other end of the scale, The Organic Pharmacy have a beautiful-smelling but rather expensive sun-care range.

Aloe vera or lavender oil also take the sting out of the worst sunburn. Just don't go back into the sun covered in oil …

HAIR CARE

Shampoos and conditioners often contain an astonishing cocktail of chemicals on their ingredients lists, and given the frequency with which you might be washing your hair in a hot climate or after chlorine or sea-water dips, a more natural option might be best for both you and the environment.

John Masters Organics do a small travel set in recyclable bottles. Because they contain no sodium lauryl sulphate the shampoo doesn't foam up but this does not stop it working just as well and a little goes a very long way. Lavera is once again an excellent budget buy. Aesop products from Australia are also of superb quality.

NB Hair care is one of the main areas where you will find the words "natural" and "organic" casually applied. Look at the ingredients, not the label.

INSECT PROTECTION

Nobody likes mosquito bites, but if the alterative is a DEET spray, you might just want to put up with the itch. If you've ever spilt some, you'll know just how powerful this stuff is – anything that can melt printed plastic is something you might hestitate to plaster yourself in. It's also been found to

be toxic to certain marine species. Of course you need to be careful to avoid excessive exposure to bites, particularly if you are in an area prone to malaria, but there are plenty of less invasive options if you have the choice.

The Natural Collection sell a chemical-free insect repellent while So Organic sell Mosimix, a certified organic oil containing lavender and thyme. Citronella is the popular natural choice, but be aware that some citronella products on the market are mixed in with rather more harmful chemicals. The pure oil can be used if diluted in a carrier oil.

SKIN CARE AND MAKE-UP

If you want to avoid unnecessary chemicals you will be spoilt for choice for skin care and make-up, from moisturisters to anti-ageing creams to mascara. Lavera and Weleda both have large ranges of both skin care and make-up, Burt's Bees ditto, Skin Boutique is a new range specifically designed for teenage skin while at the mid to upper range, Dr Hauskcka, Jurlique, Aesop and Organic Pharamacy are all of superb quality. A new French range, Doux Me, also comes in compostable bottles. The range that regularly wins the highest plaudits, though, is the wonderful REN.

TOOTHPASTE

Many toothpastes – particularly the "whitening" kind – contain harsh abrasives that literally scrub away the stains. They also contain chemicals like sodium lauryl suphate and triclosan. Overuse of the fluoride commonly found in toothpastes can also be harmful, particularly for very young children. There are plenty of alternatives now readily available in health food shops – high recommended is AloeDent's excellent range.

OTHER PRODUCTS

Most antiperspirant deodorants contain alumunium salts. Aluminium is a proven neurotoxin. Many also contain parabens and triclosans. Opt instead for an aluminium-free version that you will find even in a high street chemist.

And finally, if you're about to pack a bag of Bics – consider that 2bn disposable razors end up in US landfills alone every year. Instead, use reusable fabric strips for waxing, or a non-disposable razor.

Power up

Portable solar chargers have come on in recent years, but still require strong, direct sunlight: not ideal for our patchy weather. Solio is one of the biggest names and its three-panel designs, such as the Solio Classic (around £50), are well-regarded. The Freeloader may be cheaper (£25-£30), but many users say it doesn't give enough consistency to go permanently off the grid. Both gizmos will generally need between four and six hours of strong sunlight to charge the average mobile phone.

For better performance, try the Voltaic backpack (£190) or Reware Juice Bag (around £200). Both have built-in solar panels, which are useful if you're out walking, and offer higher output. Another alternative is the Soldius 1, a little book-like charger that doesn't have a built-in battery, which means it can't store energy to dish out at a later point, but it does result in a lower

environmental footprint. It seems to have faster charging times (two to three hours for a mobile phone, for example). There is no supplier in the UK, but you can pick one up on eBay for around £40 plus postage.

Travel insurance

Travel insurance policies are designed to cover your trip against unexpected emergencies, and generally offer a pay out if you have your journey delayed, have an accident or illness while overseas, or any of your personal possessions are lost or stolen. Because it's intangible, it's pretty difficult to make the cover itself green. You can buy online to reduce paperwork, but even then you would be well advised to print off the policy details to take with you in your suitcase. Some insurers offer carbon offsets with their policies, designed to counter emissions from the trip being covered, but the best way to green up your travel insurance is to buy it from a company that takes care to keep its own environmental footprint as small as possible.

CLIMATESURE

Every travel insurance policy bought from Climatesure comes with built-in carbon offsets to cover your journey, up to a maximum of 40 hours' flying. You can choose from single-trip, multi-trip or backpacker policies, and get up to £7.5m cover for medical expenses, up to £3,000 for a cancelled trip and up to £2,000 for lost or stolen baggage. Carbon offsets are provided by Climatesure's sister company Climate Care and policies are backed by insurance company Axa. Climatesure says its policies don't cost more than standard travel cover, because green travellers are considered a lower risk. It quotes £43.05 for

Bobbie Johnson

an annual multi-trip policy for Europe for a single adult aged up to 65.

climatesure.co.uk

CO-OPERATIVE INSURANCE SERVICES (CIS)

The Co-operative Bank has had an ethical investment policy since 1992, but its insurance arm only followed suit in 2005. However, it was still the first insurance firm in the world to adopt such a policy and has a rigorous set of criteria that companies must meet before it will invest in them. If you buy a travel insurance policy from CIS, you are dealing with a company that supports awareness of climate change and uses its influence as an investor to make companies cleaner and greener. CIS offers only an annual travel policy, which covers policyholders for an unlimited number of trips of up to 42 days each. Up to £5m cover is available for medical expenses, and up to £3,000 for cancellations. Prices are based on a number of factors, including the policyholder's age and sex. A 30-year-old female travelling in Europe will pay £49.00. For travellers taking their accommodation with them, CIS also offers caravan insurance.

co-operativeinsurance.co.uk

NATURESAVE

Buy a travel insurance policy through Naturesave and 10% of your premium will go to the Naturesave Trust, which backs projects run by environmental and conservation organisations. The annual policy, which is available to travellers aged up to 70, was last year recommended as a best buy by Ethical Consumer magazine. It covers trips of up to 60 days at a time, and includes winter sports cover for up to 17 days. Unfortunately, applying for a policy is fiddly – you either have to fill in a paper proposal and send it off or, if it's a last minute purchase, call

the company (01803 864 390) – and cover is expensive. Travellers aged up to 65 pay £108 a year, while those aged 66-70 are charged £139.50.

naturesave.co.uk

ECCLESIASTICAL

Like Naturesave, Ecclesiastical has been recommended by Ethical Consumer magazine. Set up in 1887 to provide services for the Anglican church, the insurer, which is owned by a charity, uses green energy providers to power its offices and focuses on helping individuals and has a mentoring group looking at other ways it can cut its environmental footprint. Two types of travel cover are available – a policy for single trips and an annual multi-trip policy. The annual policy covers trips of up to 31 days at a time, subject to a maximum of 90 days over the year, and costs a fairly substantial £122.79, or £87.89 if personal possessions are not covered. To apply, you need to fill in a form and post it off, or telephone 0845 777 3322.

ecclesiastical.com

ENVIRONMENTAL TRANSPORT ASSOCIATION

Buy a travel insurance policy from the ETA and you will be helping to fund its research into sustainable transport. You will also get an eco discount if you trip does not include any air travel. Policies are available on an annual or single-trip basis and there are three levels of cover: gold, silver and bronze. The main differences between these are the level of excess you have to take on and the length of journey you can take. An annual gold policy for Europe, excluding winter sports cover, costs £70, or £63 with the eco discount; a bronze policy for a green traveller costs £38.25.

eta.co.uk

Breakdown cover

If you're planning to make your journey by car, you will also need to consider breakdown cover.

ENVIRONMENTAL TRANSPORT ASSOCIATION

ETA describes itself as an "ethical alternative motoring organisation". As well as commissioning research on the environmental impact of car use, it produces the green car buyers' guide to help motorists make an informed choice about what they drive, and offers a green route planner on its website. It offers three levels of breakdown cover: gold, silver and bronze, costing from £23 a year. ETA members who buy a policy get a free carbon offset to cover some of their journeys during the year. You can cover travel in the UK and the EU. There are discounts if you apply online – either direct, or through a partnership charity, such as the RSPB.

ETA also offers a cycle rescue service for those travelling on two wheels. For £60, you can be rescued and taken to a station or cycle shop if something goes wrong with your bike in the UK or mainland Europe.

eta.co.uk

....

Car insurance

CO-OPERATIVE INSURANCE SERVICES (CIS)

Buy your car insurance from CIS and it will offset 20% of a car's CO_2 emissions, based on the average mileage done by an average family car over a year. Its network of repairers are all required to reuse and recycle used car parts whenever possible, reducing the environmental impact of any accident or breakdown. Policies include 30 days' cover in Europe as standard and a free accident recovery service.

co-operativeinsurance.co.uk

IBUYECO

Insurance policies bought from Ibuyeco come with carbon offsets for 100% of your journeys, based on the details of your driving habits you give when buying the cover. The insurer uses the Carbon Neutral Company for its offsets, which were included free of charge in 2008. The insurer's website features guides to greener driving and caravanning.

ibuyeco.co.uk

THE GREEN INSURANCE COMPANY

An insurer that's green by name and green by nature: every employee at the Green Insurance Company drives a hybrid Toyota Prius, and 100% of the company's business travel is offset. Just 1% of recyclable waste gets thrown away, and all of the paper used is recycled. Customers who buy a car insurance policy get 100% of their journeys offset free of charge, while those who drive a green car and/or do low mileage get up to 5% off the cost of their policy.

greeninsurancecompany.co.uk

Hilary Osborne

A view of the Matterhorn,
Zermatt, Switzerland
photo: shutterstock/Lazar Mihai-Bogdan

INDEX

Z

The bridleway at the top of
Whinstone Lee Tor, Peak District,
Derbyshire

Acknowledgements

I am indebted to the many people who gave up their time to speak to me in the course of researching this book. In particular, I would like to thank Richard Hammond for his inspirational commitment to green travel issues, encyclopaedic knowledge and generosity with his time. My gratitude also flows to Lisa Darnell at Guardian Books for her patience and enthusiasm for this project, Polly Pattullo for her expertise and transatlantic editing skills, Cameron Fitch at Two Associates for a beautiful design and the travel teams of the *Guardian*, *Observer* and guardian.co.uk for their ideas, contributions and support. A big thank you too to Louis Wise for his dedicated multilingual factchecking and the guardian.co.uk production team for coping without him. Even more thanks to Leo Hickman, Alastair Sawday, Tom Hall, Hilary Bradt, Ed Gillespie, Mark Smith, Kevin Rushby, Catherine Mack, Carolyn Fry, Sarah Siese, Michael Fordham, David Adam, Alok Jha, Deborah Summers, Hilary Osborne, Kate Carter, Gwyn Topham, Gwladys Fouché and Susan Greenwood, for their contributions; and to Harold Goodwin at Leeds Metropolitan University, Tricia Barnett at Tourism Concern, Sue Hurdle at The Travel Foundation, Michael Buick at Climate Care, Rupert Fawcett at Forum for the Future, Roger Diski at Rainbow Tours, Alex Randall at the Centre for Alternative Technology and Charlie Kronick at Greenpeace for their time and information. Last but certainly not least, my husband Alex for unfailing support and listening power.

Published by Guardian Books 2009

2 4 6 8 10 9 7 5 3 1

First published in Great Britain in 2009 by
Guardian Books
Kings Place
90 York Way
London
N1 9GU

www.guardianbooks.co.uk

A CIP catalogue for this book is available from the British Library

ISBN: 978-0852651162

Designed and typeset by Two Associates
Printed and bound in Germany by Firmengruppe APPL

FSC
Mixed Sources
Product group from well-managed
forests and other controlled sources
Cert no. SGS-COC-004238
www.fsc.org
© 1996 Forest Stewardship Council